INTERPERSONAL SKILLS
FOR LEADERSHIP

INTERPERSONAL SKILLS FOR LEADERSHIP

Susan Fritz
*Assistant Professor, Department of Agricultural Leadership
Education and Communication
Director, Nebraska Human Resources Institute
University of Nebraska-Lincoln*

F. William Brown
*Associate Professor, College of Business
Montana State University-Bozeman*

Joyce Povlacs Lunde
*Professor, Department of Agricultural Leadership
Education and Communication
Consultant, Office of Professional and Organizational Development
University of Nebraska-Lincoln*

Elizabeth A. Banset
*Instructional Consultant
Teaching and Learning Center
University of Nebraska-Lincoln*

Prentice Hall
Upper Saddle River, NJ 07458

Library of Congress Cataloging-in-Publication Data
Interpersonal skills for leadership / Susan Fritz ... [et al.].
    p. cm.
  Includes index.
  ISBN 0-13-244773-8
  1. Leadership. 2. Interpersonal communication.
HD57.7.I58   1999
650.1'3—dc21   98-16748
                                                   CIP

Acquisitions Editor: Elizabeth Sugg
Director of Production and Manufacturing: Bruce Johnson
Managing Editor: Mary Carnis
Editorial/Production Supervision and Interior Design:
Inkwell Publishing Services
Cover Design: Miguel Ortiz
Manufacturing Buyer: Edward O' Dougherty

 © 1999 by Prentice Hall, Inc.
Simon & Schuster / A Viacom Company
Upper Saddle River, New Jersey 07458

Printed in the United States of America

10 9 8 7 6 5 4 3

ISBN 0-13-244773-8

Prentice-Hall International (UK) Limited, *London*
Prentice-Hall of Australia Pty. Limited, *Sydney*
Prentice-Hall Canada Inc., *Toronto*
Prentice-Hall Hispanoamericana, S.A., *Mexico*
Prentice-Hall of India Private Limited, *New Delhi*
Prentice-Hall of Japan, Inc., *Tokyo*
Prentice-Hall of Southeast Asia Pte. Ltd., *Singapore*
Editora Prentice-Hall do Brasil, Ltda., *Rio de Janeiro*

CONTENTS

CONTRIBUTORS

Lloyd Bell is an Associate Professor in the Department of Agricultural Leadership, Education and Communication at the University of Nebraska-Lincoln.

Laura E. Casari is an Associate Professor Emerita in the Department of Agricultural Leadership, Education and Communication at the University of Nebraska-Lincoln.

Marta M. Hartmann is the Assistant Director of Academic Support Programs at the University of Florida.

Tracey Hoover is an Assistant Professor in the Department of Agricultural Education and Communication at the University of Florida.

Dann Husmann is an Assistant Professor in the Department of Vocational-Technical Education at South Dakota State University.

Sheila Kepler is an Instructor in the Department of Agricultural Leadership, Education and Communication at the University of Nebraska-Lincoln.

Valerie J. Konecky is a Case Manager with the Big Brothers/Big Sisters program in Lincoln, Nebraska.

James Legacy is a Professor in the Department of Agricultural Education at Southern Illinois University.

Elmer H. Miller is an Associate Professor in the Department of Agricultural Leadership, Education and Communication and an Associate Director of the Center for Leadership Development at the University of Nebraska-Lincoln.

Jerry Parsons is an Associate Professor in the Department of Agricultural Leadership, Education and Communication at the University of Nebraska-Lincoln.

C. Van Shelhamer is a Professor in the Department of Agricultural Education at Montana State University-Bozeman.

Michael K. Swan is an Assistant Professor in the Department of Biological Systems Engineering at Washington State University.

M. Susie Whittington is an Assistant Professor in the Department of Agricultural and Extension Education at Pennsylvania State University.

PREFACE

Effective skills in interpersonal communication are essential for successful leaders. This book is designed as a practical resource providing an introduction to interpersonal skills theories that are reinforced through experiential activities. Previous versions of this book have been field-tested nationally by well over 30 faculty and over 1500 students. Their feedback has allowed us to refine the text into what we believe to be one of the most practical, useful interpersonal skills texts available.

The ability to be in command of one's own life, to relate well to other people, and to lead others in positive directions is a valuable commodity in the exciting and changing time in which we live. Our futures are more than ever bound to those of other people, both the neighbor next door and the business colleague around the world. The pace of living is fast, and huge quantities of information are available to us in the blink of an eye (or a tap on the computer keyboard). Still, the measure of one's success depends, as it always has, on our dealings with the people beside whom we walk on the fast track and whom we engage in information exchange.

For all its burgeoning possibility, or perhaps because of it, the world must still deal with incivility, violence, discord, and distress. Even the seemingly minor stresses of daily life—a malfunctioning teller machine, traffic jams, long lines at the food market—are not easily resolved with superficial solutions. Both leaders and followers can make their lives and the lives of those with whom they live and work less stressful and much richer through the exercise of good personal skills. Time devoted to learning to listen well, to act with commitment and vision, to value yourself and your capabilities, to handle stress and conflict, to communicate with trust and empathy, to lead wisely, and to truly value others is indeed time well-spent.

For these reasons, we offer this book as a guide to developing interpersonal skills that will serve you well in all aspects of your life—on campus, at home, in the community, and in the workplace.

We acknowledge colleagues across the country who provided invaluable scholarly contributions to this text and extend to them our sincerest thanks.

And we welcome you to these pages, in which we hope you find a true reflection of yourself. Practice what you find here in whatever ways best suit your needs; we wish you every success as you test your leadership wings. May you fly high and happily.

We encourage you to use this text as a workbook, selecting and augmenting to fit the particular needs of teachers and students in leadership education. We hope this book meets your needs and we welcome your feedback.

Acknowledgments

Without the contributions and feedback of colleagues across the country this text would not be a reality. We acknowledge their invaluable scholarly contributions and offer them our sincerest thanks. We also thank the publishers at Simon and Schuster Custom Publishing for their support and encouragement in our earlier publishing endeavors.

SUSAN FRITZ

F. WILLIAM BROWN

JOYCE POVLACS LUNDE

ELIZABETH A. BANSET

INTERPERSONAL SKILLS FOR LEADERSHIP

Chapter 1

INTRODUCTION

*. . . in order to be masterful in the outside world, it is necessary to start
the practice of mastery deeply within oneself.*
—Charlotte Roberts, *The Fifth Discipline Fieldbook* (1994)

ADVANCE PLANNER: INTERPERSONAL SKILLS FOR LEADERSHIP

When you complete this chapter, you will be able to:

✓ Explain the importance of interpersonal skills for leadership as they apply in professional settings.

✓ Describe the course purpose, contents, and processes.

✓ Set forth your expectations for the course.

✓ Identify something you have in common with another person in the class.

✓ Memorize names of new people you meet outside class and find out something about them.

To accomplish these objectives, you will complete some or all of these activities:

1. Take an inventory of interpersonal skills, personality type, or interpersonal actions you engage in.

2. Discuss the importance of interpersonal skills in present and future relationships (home, family, friends, school, work, community).

3. Review the processes we will use to learn and apply interpersonal skills.

4. Participate in one or more exercises in which you:

   ✓ Learn the names of your classmates.

   ✓ List expectations you have for the course.

   ✓ Discover something important about another person in class.

   ✓ Discover what members of a small group have in common.

5. Write a memo to the dean of your college about how to prepare for communicating on the job.

A CASE STUDY IN INTERPERSONAL SKILLS FOR LEADERSHIP

Who Needs This Class?

It was the first day of classes on the campus of a large university. In an interpersonal skills course, Professor Young had begun with an icebreaker activity, asking students to form groups of four and discover five things they had in common. "Be sure you introduce yourselves," the professor added. Maya, Rod, Alicia, and Travis—four complete strangers—found themselves in one group.

Maya, a single parent, had managed to provide for her two children over the years by working in a large greenhouse and retail florist business. Now that her children were older, and with the encouragement of her employers, she decided to return to school and pursue a degree in horticulture. She had taken this course in interpersonal skills because she thought it might help her to be more outgoing with customers in the florist shop. Looking at the others in the group, she wondered what their thoughts were. "These kids are young enough to be my children!" she thought. "They probably think I'm just another boring adult."

Rod was usually a cheerful person who combined talent in the graphic arts with a talent for speaking and writing. One of the teachers in his Chicago high school introduced him to the idea of majoring in journalism. He enrolled in the interpersonal skills course not only because it was required in his major, but also because he had confidence in his ability to get along with people. Now, looking around at the members of this group, he wasn't so sure. "I bet they will ask me if I play football just because I'm black and come from Chicago. Will I ever find anything in common with these people?" he thought.

Alicia was from a small town and small high school (graduating class of 55 students) in the far western part of the state. Coming to the university was an adventure for her. Her activities in high school included being a class officer, basketball player, and soloist in the chorus. She looked forward to an exciting social life in college, although she wasn't sure what her major would be. She was taking interpersonal skills because a new friend had told her she'd meet a lot of interesting people—maybe even some great guys—in this class. She looked around this group, however, and her heart sank. "These people do not look very exciting to me at all. What on earth am I supposed to ask them?" she worried.

Travis graduated from a large suburban high school. His parents worked in banking. After visiting several private college campuses in other states, Travis and his parents had decided that he would major in marketing at the university. Travis, whose small, close-knit circle of friends were all planning to attend the university, was satisfied with the decision. On campus, an advisor in the marketing program gave him a list of courses for the fall semester. Somewhat surprised when he found himself in an interpersonal skills class, he was dismayed that he was expected to strike up a conversation with the strangers in this group. "What's the purpose of this?" he asked himself. "It's not as though I'm going to associate with these people outside of class."

After a few moments of silence in the group, one of the four looked at the others and said with a sigh, "Well, I guess we better get started. If you really want to know, my name is. . . ."

Discussion Questions

1. Can you think of some reasons the professor gave this assignment at the beginning of the interpersonal skills class?

2. Describe some of the feelings the four persons are experiencing. Do they have any feelings in common?

3. Would you predict that these four students could find five things in common? Why or why not?

4. If you were one of the group members, how would you act and what would you say? What would you do both to fulfill the assignment and to have a positive experience?

STUDYING INTERPERSONAL SKILLS FOR LEADERSHIP

Beginnings—how important they are in life! Our parents tell us about the day we were born. We remember the first day of kindergarten or first grade. Frightened, excited, perhaps with some turmoil in the stomach, we entered a room of strangers our age and met the teacher, a new and perhaps formidable authority figure. We continued to make new beginnings each school year. Perhaps we began anew when our family moved across town or across the country. We entered college where we begin a new academic year and new courses over and over again. All through our lives, we begin new relationships. Some are destined never to grow, while others become central to our happiness. Throughout our lives we begin jobs and careers or start off in new directions. In all of these beginnings, meeting new people, getting along with others in the workplace, and maintaining positive personal relationships are essential to our own success, as well as to the influence we have on others.

This class provides an opportunity for a beginning for you and offers a special kind of instruction in improving your understanding of yourself and others. This is a different kind of class, one in which the stuff of everyday experience provides the material for discussion, and life outside the classroom serves as a laboratory. The book you are holding in your hands is a different kind of text. It is a resource book in learning and practicing interpersonal skills for leadership.

The underlying purpose of this text and the course you are taking is twofold: to help you 1) become competent in conducting interpersonal relationships in your daily life, and 2) acquire skills basic to becoming a leader in your professional life.

Leadership in Professional Careers

When we think about leadership, we often make the mistake of assuming that it might be the exclusive province of generals, politicians, and corporate executives. This book is based on the premise that leadership is a much more diverse concept that affects us all in every aspect of our lives. Persons with some sort of title or position may, in fact, be leaders, but are not necessarily so. Leadership is that unique form of interpersonal influence that causes us to voluntarily and enthusiastically respond. We respond to the leader because we want to, not because we have to. We experience the effect of leadership when someone influences us to accompany him or her to lunch after class, to decide what sort of clothing to wear, or to shape our attitudes toward the rules of the university. In short, most of the important and not so important aspects of our lives are in some way driven by leadership.

Another overarching principle of this book is that leadership capacity is something everyone can learn and improve upon. Undoubtedly each of us is born with certain characteristics that both enhance and impede our ability to exert leadership; however, there is overwhelming evidence and good reason to believe that each of us has **lots** of room to improve our abilities in this area. The philosophy of this book is that enhanced leadership capacity arises from our ability to add skills to our behavioral repertoire, to learn from our experiences, and to build a positive and accurate self-concept. The readings, exercises, and activities in this text and the courses it supports are intentionally designed to assist students in developing all those abilities.

Importance of Interpersonal Skills

Whether your major is in a college of agriculture, education, social sciences, engineering, arts and humanities, or business administration, employers are telling colleges and universities the graduates they employ have adequate technical preparation but lack sufficient interpersonal skills. Often this deficit in interpersonal skills gets in the way of success in the workplace (Phillippi & Banta, 1992, cited in Bosshamer, 1996). Learning, developing, expanding, and improving interpersonal skills and competencies is essential for future success.

Interpersonal skill development is really about discovering who you are. Self-discovery and, eventually, self-confidence are "really awareness of and faith in your own powers. These powers become clear and strong only as you work to identify and develop them" (Kouzes & Posner, 1990, p. 298). You will discover that a course in interpersonal skills, therefore, not only prepares you for the future—it also helps you improve relationships with family members, friends, classmates, roommates, co-workers in current jobs, and even people who may be perceived as difficult (these often overlap with any of the above!).

Television newscasts and headlines in newspapers paint for us a picture of a world that is harsh, uncaring, cruel, and filled with violence. Civility and respect for human beings disappear, in situations ranging from abuse in the home to atrocities of war. The ugly side of human behavior and the disasters it causes have no simple explanations or cures and none are offered here, but at least this course and resource text offer a place to start. A good way to learn interpersonal skills and to serve others is to volunteer in a service agency or public school in your community. You may be asked to undertake a formal project in this course, or you may work on your own. The basic assumption is that the study and practice of interpersonal skills, joined with a deliberate attempt to understand and appreciate others, can go a long way not only to make our lives more rewarding, but also to smooth the way for others.

Conceptual and Experiential Learning

Learning in interpersonal skills moves between concept and concrete experience—between theory and application. Each chapter in the resource text focuses on one or more concepts related to interpersonal skill development. In addition to providing you with current thinking about each concept, we also include a number of experiential activities that help you practice a particular set of skills. In addition, Further Activity assignments encourage you to take these skills beyond the classroom to practice in your everyday life. Often you will be asked to observe what happens, reflect on your experiences, analyze them, and record what you learned.

The proof of your learning will be found not only in remembering concepts, but also in what you do and the attitudes you express. Even if we think we are very good at interpersonal communication, just as accomplished musicians and athletes continue to hone their skills, so too can we constantly work to polish and improve our skills in communicating with others.

Interpersonal Skills for Leadership is designed to be used in a highly participatory classroom. A classroom that provides opportunities for students to engage in active learning usually creates a good environment for learning. In the last dozen years, classrooms in higher education have begun moving away from the strict lecture format, to a format whereby students are engaged in discussion, in small group work, and other forms of overt active behavior (Bonwell & Eison, 1991). Our classroom falls into this category. Our goal is to build a community for learning and practicing interpersonal skills. In order for this learning to take place in a positive climate, we propose the following ground rules for our community:

1. *Active participation:* Everyone—students, teachers, and teaching assistants—will be actively involved in the class. This involvement will range from note taking and discussion to participation in peer teaching, team learning, role play, and a variety of small group activities. Often you will have choices in activities, so if you wish, you may move gradually to more active modes of participation. Small groups may be formed for short durations or for longer projects. You also may be assigned to a permanent small group with a designated group leader.

2. *Self-disclosure:* Successful interpersonal relationships rely on sharing something about yourself with others, as well as on listening to what others say. In this class, be prepared to talk about yourself in your interactions with your classmates. You might talk about your hometown, family, career goals, opinions, and feelings. What you choose to tell and how much you say about yourself is up to you. You should not feel pressured into telling what you prefer not to reveal. Whatever you tell others should be authentic—an honest representation of your experiences and feelings. Using self-disclosure as described here will enhance your understanding of yourself and others.

3. *Confidentiality:* If we practice self-disclosure in this class, we also will observe confidentiality. All of us—students, teachers, and teaching assistants—should agree not to talk about each other or an individual's experiences outside the classroom community.

4. *Listening:* A major underlying principle we follow in this class is listening to others. Two chapters are devoted to the skills needed to listen actively and with empathy. In addition to telling something about yourself, you will need to become a good listener for someone else. You will engage in turn-taking as you listen to others and offer your own opinions.

5. *Mutual respect:* Together we appreciate that each of us brings to the class a unique set of experiences, attitudes, and values. We may come from many backgrounds and from a diversity of races and cultures. The more diverse our group, in fact, the better our community for learning will become.

The Assignments

Specific assignments and schedules for topics will be given to you by your instructor. Major assignments may include journaling and a service learning project.

Journal Writing

Journals are tools for expanding interpersonal awareness and growth. An essay on journal writing is presented in the Appendix, and each chapter contains some suggestions for journal writing that focus on course concepts and their practice in your life. Journals are kept in a small notebook, with each entry at least a page in length. Each entry should be dated and titled and recount in specific language the interpersonal skill you practiced, what happened, and what conclusions you can draw. Entries also may reflect on your growing abilities in interpersonal skills or the frustrations you may feel in putting concepts into action.

Service Projects

You also may be required to complete a service project to which you devote about 20 hours throughout the semester or term. This project, which will be based in an agency in your community, will give you the opportunity to practice interpersonal skills with individuals who may be total strangers to you but very much need your help. Sites for service projects include community centers, public schools, special federal programs such as Head Start, family service agencies, retirement and nursing homes, and correctional institutions. If you are required to complete a service project, you will have some choice in your placement. Often you will be working with children and will have an opportunity to make a difference in their lives. At the end of your service project, you will be asked to write a report about persons with whom you worked, what you did, and what you gained from the experience. Although the service project may seem scary at first, the vast majority of students report having a positive learning experience and gaining a sense of satisfaction from helping someone else to learn and grow.

Contents of the Text

The chapters in *Interpersonal Skills for Leadership* are arranged in three main groups, followed by an appendix on journal writing. These groups, described below, contain chapters on the basics of interpersonal communication, understanding yourself, and understanding and helping others. Each chapter guides you from concept to application and practice of important interpersonal competencies.

The Basics of Interpersonal Communication

The three chapters that follow this one introduce you to some basic topics in interpersonal skills. In Active Listening you will learn how important listening is to effective communication and have an opportunity to practice it. Another basic chapter, Nonverbal Communication, builds awareness of what meaning our behavior apart from our words might convey. The chapter on Perception shows you the impact your view of reality has on your understanding of the world and the people in it.

Understanding Yourself

Effective leaders know their strengths and capabilities. Knowing something about yourself will give you a base for writing a plan for self-improvement. Chapters in this section focus on how you view yourself, form values, give direction to your life, and cope with the competing demands of daily life. The chapters are titled Self-Concept and Self-Esteem, Values, Creating the Vision and Establishing Goals, Time Management, and Handling Stress.

Understanding and Helping Others

This section builds on your knowledge of yourself and the support you give others. In it we examine types of relationships, suggest some ways of dealing with conflict that inevitably arises on the job or in day-to-day life, describe how to use leadership skills in influencing others, explain how to develop a deeper understanding of and caring for others, and build awareness of issues related to gender and other perceived differences. Chapter titles are Levels of Communication; Trust: The Foundation Element in Leadership; Resolving Conflict; The Nature of Power, Influence, and Leadership; Responding with Empathy; Cross-Cultural Communication; and Gender Issues. The last chapter, Servant Leadership, illustrates how you can integrate your learning as you continue to employ interpersonal skills and help others throughout your college career. This chapter ends with a look into the future—how you can become a leader in your community.

Setting Expectations

It is important that all of us take time to set expectations at the beginning of the course. Both teachers and students need to ask: What are the goals of this course? What do I expect to gain? What interpersonal skills do I need to develop? Perhaps you will be asked to fill out a questionnaire about yourself, your skills, or your activities and relationships. In Exercise 2 at the end of this chapter, for example, you will discover expectations the members of the class have in common. Some other ways of guiding your learning include goal setting for improving interpersonal skills and understanding the responsibility you assume for learning.

Practicing interpersonal skills can be both hard work and a great deal of fun. If we enter into this classroom with the intention of building a learning community, we will lay the foundations not only for success in this particular course, but also for developing leadership skills that can last a lifetime.

EXERCISE
The Name Game

Purpose To learn the names of others in the class and to remember as many names as possible.

Activity As directed, take seats in a circle. The first person will introduce himself or herself to the next person, using a mnemonic device, such as the name of a food, to make his or her name easier to remember. Throughout the activity everyone concentrates to meet the challenge of remembering names, encouraging others and attaching names to faces. You may not take notes.

In your turn, say your first name along with a food that starts with the first letter of your name. Example: "My name is Jane and I like jam." The second person introduces Jane to the person next to him and then adds his name and food. Example: "This is Jane and she likes jam. My name is Harry and I like hamburgers." The next person introduces Jane who likes jam and Harry who likes hamburgers and adds her name and food, and so on around the circle. (You do not actually have to like the food you name.) Once a food has been taken, it cannot be repeated. Herman, for example, may not choose hamburgers (perhaps horseradish?). The last person has the biggest job, but after the circle is completed, Jane, Harry, and the others who were first may be asked to repeat all the names and foods.

It is all right to help others out, but everyone should try to name as many people as possible without help. Everyone should make a point to address one or two persons by name at the end of class.

EXERCISE
Two by Fours

Purpose   To set expectations and responsibilities for individuals as well as the class as a whole.

Activity   1. List three expectations about what you would like to experience and learn in this class.

1. _____

2. _____

3. _____

2. Pair up with someone you don't already know, introduce yourself, and compare your lists. Together decide on the top four expectations from both your lists.

1. _____

2. _____

3. _____

4. _____

3. Now find another pair and compare your answers (completing the two by four), and together decide on the top five expectations of the four of you.

1. _____

2. _____

3. _____

4. _____

5. _____

4. One of your group of four should write your top five on the chalkboard or on an overhead transparency to share with others.

5. With your instructor and the rest of the class, identify top expectations for the class.

Discussion Questions

1. Is there a strong consensus in the class for these expectations? Do any need adjusting?

2. How closely do your individual expectations agree with the top ones determined by the class? What can individual students do to get their needs fulfilled?

3. Determine who in the class, including the instructor, will be responsible for seeing that expectations are met. (You may refer to the ground rules listed in the chapter to guide your discussion.)

Hot Buttons

Adapted from Dodge, 1988.

Purpose To become acquainted with a stranger and be able to introduce that person to others by telling about some important things—*hot buttons*—in his or her life.

Hot buttons are topics, ideas, interests, or activities that are especially meaningful to you. If this topic is mentioned in conversation, you will become much more involved in the dialogue and motivated to share details about the topic. Some examples are: your high school sport; members of your family; favorite pastimes; your love of jazz; your travels to Alaska; and many other such topics. Although the phrase *hot button* is commonly used to refer to a topic that elicits your anger, in this case you want to look for a positive special interest of the other person.

Activity Your instructor will help you form a pair with someone you do not know (or do not know very well). You will have about 20 minutes to get to know the other person's hot buttons. Take turns interviewing each other. Listen carefully, ask follow-up questions, and encourage your partner to give details. Without taking written notes, try to remember the person's name, hometown, and at least one hot button. If you discovered anything in common, one of you may wish to mention that, too. When you are asked to return to class, be prepared to introduce your partner to the class as a whole, along with his or her hometown and one hot button.

EXERCISE
Finding Things in Common in Small Groups

Adapted from Panitz, 1995.

Purpose The hot buttons exercise probably led you to discover both commonalities and differences with another person. The purpose of this exercise is to extend your acquaintanceship in a small group and, by finding things in common, begin to establish a relationship with the members of your group who will be working together for an extended time.

Activity Your small group should have a private and comfortable place to work. You will have about 30 minutes to complete this exercise.

1. Form groups of four (or five, if necessary). In your group be sure everyone knows first names.

2. By conversation or dialogue, discover at least five things (for groups of four) or six things (for groups of five) that all of you have in common. Excluded are the obvious: taking this class, attending the university, etc. A recorder should write down your list to share with others.

3. After time is called, post your list to share with the other group(s).

Discussion Questions

1. Was it difficult to find similarities in the smaller group?

2. Compare the group lists to discover if there is an overlap of things in common.

3. Can you find other commonalities among members of the larger group?

4. What does the total group need in order to work together?

EXERCISE
Memo to the Dean

Purpose To describe the importance of interpersonal skills on the job and link them to your academic preparation and field of study.

Activity This activity combines a role play and a case. Your group (large or small) assumes the role of members of the student advisory council. Together, read the case presented in the situation below and follow the instructions at its end.

A Case: An Invitation from the Dean

As a member of the student advisory council in your college, you and your group have been invited by Dean Helen Martinez to attend a meeting in her conference room. When you and the other council members are seated, Dean Martinez recounts the following story to you. She asks you to listen carefully because she wants your opinion on what she should do.

I [Dean Martinez begins] *wanted to find out how our graduates were doing in business and industry. So I invited several corporate recruiters to provide feedback regarding graduates they had hired. The meeting yesterday opened with introductions and pleasantries about the educational and professional backgrounds of the recruiters.*

Then we got down to the matter at hand. I posed the question of the day. "How well are our graduates meeting your company's expectations?"

Well, to put it mildly, the responses were not quite what I had hoped to hear. The first recruiter, Ann Post, represented a pharmaceutical company, and she spoke candidly about some areas of concern her company had noted in new hires. "The company has divided the country up into regional divisions and the divisions are expected to function as a team," Ann explained. She went on to say that most of the new hires were company representatives and, therefore, were the newest members of the team. Unfortunately, some of them were not working out. Although incredibly knowledgeable about the science side of the product, the new hires were not able to communicate effectively and efficiently with their team members and customers. "What's worse," Ann added, "they don't even seem to recognize the importance of good communication skills or even what these might be!"

The next recruiter stepped in where Ann left off. Ted Knight represented a multi-site cooperative in the state. Most of the recent hires had been placed as customer representatives in either the wholesale division or retail division. He agreed with Ann, remarking, "The graduates certainly know the technical material related to their fields, but interpreting the data for the customer is another matter." He continued to explain that the graduates had fallen short in their ability to listen to the customers' concerns and relate information in a manner the customers could understand. Several valuable customers had actually been lost, Ted said with dismay, because the customers believed the representatives were talking down to them. When the representatives were confronted with this concern, they responded that they never intended to insult customers, but they could not say how they were putting the customers' needs first. Ted wondered out loud, "Where on earth in the curriculum are students being taught to listen effectively, to consider the needs and desires of others, and to understand that building relationships with others is the means to success for all involved?"

I'm afraid that the other recruiters echoed the opinions expressed by Ann and Ted. At the conclusion of the meeting, I thanked the recruiters for their helpful opinions, but after they left, I was very troubled about what had been said. I will share the comments with the college's curriculum committee, but maybe you can help me out.

After Dean Martinez finishes speaking, your group remains silent, looking a little puzzled. Then Dean Martinez reveals the following questions she had written on the conference room chalkboard:

1. What kinds of skills do you think the graduates are lacking?

2. Why would these skills be important in career areas, yours included, that are associated with majors in the college?

3. As a customer, what experience have you had relating to company representatives or salespersons? If possible, give an example of someone who did not relate to you effectively. What impact did that have on your perception of that company? How many friends and family members did you tell about your experience?

Dean Martinez then explains that in addition to discussion, she wants the group to write a memo that she can share with the faculty on the curriculum committee (the faculty committee that sets the policy for what is studied in the core requirements and courses in the college). The discussion begins.

Instructions

1. Discuss your answers to the dean's questions. Your discussion may be in a small group or in the class as a whole. Your instructor or group leader will write your answers on an overhead transparency or chalkboard. Take notes on the points raised.

2. After the discussion, assume that you as an individual have been asked to write the memo to Dean Martinez for the group. The group wants you to incorporate their ideas into your work, but they agree that you may give your own views too. Cover these points:

   ✓ Indicate what skills are missing and should be included in courses in the college.

   ✓ Tell how the college might help you avoid some of the problems described by the representatives.

3. Hand in your memo to your small group leader or instructor at the assigned time.

FURTHER ACTIVITY

Journal Writing

1. Write your observations and reflections on the contents and the process in the course. What do you like about the course? What are some of your concerns?

2. Write a contract with yourself in which you identify major areas in which you wish to make improvement. Include something about potential career goals and how work in interpersonal skills for leadership relates to your career choice.

3. Analyze a conversation you recently had with an acquaintance and evaluate the interpersonal skills you used. Did you detect any areas that need improvement?

Independent Practice

1. Practice learning the names of those you meet this week—in classes, socially, and at work.

2. In a class or at a social event, introduce yourself to someone you do not know. Choose someone who appears very different from you. In your conversation, find out that person's hot buttons. How well did you get to know this person?

3. Interview a businessperson in a field of your career interest about skills expected in the professional persons he or she hires. Ask a general question about expectations. Make a list of skills mentioned.

LEARNING POINTS

- ✓ Improving interpersonal skills has benefits in one's daily and professional life.

- ✓ Interpersonal skills are basic to leadership in a variety of professions.

- ✓ Preparation for leadership is important for anyone entering a professional career.

- ✓ Leadership skills can be learned.

- ✓ Interpersonal skills are important in being successful in employment, having satisfying personal relationships, and contributing to the improvement of the quality of life for all.

- ✓ The basic learning pattern in interpersonal skills is to learn concepts and apply them in class, in further activities outside class, and in special service projects. Interpersonal skills are mastered most successfully in interaction with others.

- ✓ A goal for the class is to build a learning community where students can actively learn and practice the skills being taught.

- ✓ Ground rules for the community include: participating actively, using appropriate self-disclosure, maintaining confidentiality, practicing active listening, and respecting others.

REFERENCES

Bonwell, C. C., and Eison, J. A. (1991). *Active learning: Creating excitement in the college classroom.* ASHE-ERIC Higher Education Research Reports. Washington, D.C.: Georgetown University.

Bosshamer, B. K. (1996). *An assessment of employers and faculty of the College of Agricultural Sciences and Natural Resources: Adequacy of student preparation and future curriculum needs.* Unpublished master's thesis, University of Nebraska-Lincoln, Lincoln, NE.

Dodge, G. W. (1988). *Handbook for teaching assistants.* Lincoln, NE: Department of Agricultural Education, University of Nebraska-Lincoln.

Kouzes, J. M., and Posner, B. Z. (1990). *The leadership challenge.* San Francisco: Jossey-Bass.

Panitz, T. (April 25, 1995). Finding things in common. [Discussion], [Online]. Available e-mail: LISTSERV: <pod@lists.acs.ohio-state.edu>.

Phillippi, R. H., and Banta, T. W. (1992). Critique of a method for surveying employers: A look at the Tennessee experience. Paper presented at the Annual Forum of the Association for Institutional Research, Atlanta, GA.

Chapter 2

ACTIVE LISTENING

Know how to listen and you will profit even from those who talk badly.
—Plutarch

ADVANCE PLANNER: ACTIVE LISTENING

When you complete this chapter, you will be able to:

✓ Distinguish between hearing and listening.

✓ Explain the crucial role listening plays in the communication process.

✓ Identify and practice the stages of the active listening process.

✓ Analyze both effective and ineffective listening habits.

✓ Practice active listening techniques and demonstrate skills in active listening.

✓ Create and evaluate your own personal plan for improving listening skills.

To accomplish these objectives, you will complete some or all of these activities:

1. Take a preliminary listening inventory to help you evaluate your present listening skills.

2. Discuss a case study to help illustrate some key points of active listening.

3. Read and discuss a brief summary of some theories of active listening.

4. Complete an exercise designed to illustrate the limitations of learning by hearing alone.

5. Complete several exercises to help you identify and practice positive active listening behaviors.

6. Role play an activity in which you both practice and evaluate active listening strategies.

7. Create a self-improvement contract in which you target specific listening skills you want to improve.

8. Write in your journal to describe and explain the outcome of day-to-day listening situations in which you try out some active listening strategies.

A CASE STUDY IN ACTIVE LISTENING

"Everybody's Talking at Me, but I Can't Hear a Word They're Saying"

Marvin plunks his lunch tray down on an empty table and says to his friend Carmen as he swings into a chair, "Hoo, boy, has it been a long day, and it's not even noon yet!"

"Tell me about it," Carmen replies, dumping her book bag on a chair and rummaging inside it (the bag, not the chair) to extract a well-rumpled paper. "I got my latest history test back today. That jerk Coburn gave me a *D*. Can you believe it—a *D*! Academic probation, here I come. Boy, am I mad!"

"You think that's bad," Marvin says as he maneuvers a french fry into his mouth. "I just got assigned to a small work group in my chemistry class and you'll never guess who's in my group—Barb Johanssen. Boy, out of the hundreds of people in that class I could have been teamed with, I get stuck in a group with my old girlfriend. And not an ancient history old girlfriend, but the one I just broke up with last week. I already feel really guilty about the way everything ended. I don't think I can stand to work with her that closely once a week for the next eight weeks. I'll be a basket case."

"Oh, come on, Marv. You can't avoid her for the rest of your life. Here's a great chance for you to show her there are no hard feelings. I wish my problem was as simple as an old flame showing up in a small group. If I fail this course, my parents will kill me."

"I never worry about you, Carm. You always get yourself into corners, but you always figure a way to get out. I need a plan to get myself moved to another chemistry group. Otherwise, just to avoid Barb I'm gonna start missing recitation and that means I'll end up with a *D,* too."

"But you don't have one yet. I'll have a lot more sympathy for you when I see a big red *D* scrawled across the top of your next chemistry exam."

"Yeah, well. Good luck with history. I have to run. It was great talking to you, Carmen."

Discussion Questions

1. Marvin and Carmen are talking at each other, but do they really hear each other?

2. Are these people listening to each other?

3. If you were either Carmen or Marvin, what would you do to listen more attentively and more actively?

4. How do you think the conversation would go if Marvin and Carmen were better listeners?

INTRODUCTION TO THEORIES OF ACTIVE LISTENING

Why should a textbook on interpersonal skills include a lesson on listening? People who study the way humans communicate have found that most people spend 70 percent of their waking day engaged in some form of communication; college students may spend as much as three-fifths of that time listening. That means if you are awake for 16 hours, you're communicating in some way during 11 of those hours, and you spend between six and seven hours listening (Osborn & Osborn, 1994). Studies of student listening habits have shown that good listeners earn better grades. Still, many college students are remarkably inefficient listeners. At any given time, only 20 percent of the students present at a college lecture are paying attention, and only 12 percent are actively listening (Carosso, 1986).

On the job, many employers have discovered that balanced listening skills result in fewer misunderstandings, more innovation, improved morale, and a more pleasant and productive work environment (Hanna, 1995; Yukl, 1994). The national Agribusiness Management Aptitude and Skill Survey (AGRI-MASS), conducted by researchers at Texas A&M University (Litzenberg & Schneider, 1988), asked 543 agribusiness managers to rate the relative importance of 74 personal and professional skills and characteristics required for successful agribusiness careers. The general categories of Interpersonal Characteristics and Communication Skills proved to be the highest rated areas. In the Communication Skills category, the ability to "listen and carry out instructions" was rated highest; furthermore, out of all 74 characteristics (including business skills, computer skills, and technical skills), listening ranked fifth.

In spite of the importance of listening in school and in the workplace, "most people make numerous listening mistakes [in family communication, business, government, and international affairs] every week but the costs—financial and otherwise—of poor listening are seldom analyzed. Because of listening mistakes, appointments have to be rescheduled, letters retyped and shipments rerouted. . . . At the least, productivity is affected and profits suffer. . . . Many of the divorces granted annually in the United States are related to the inability or unwillingness of one or both partners to listen to the other" (Nixon & West, 1989, p. 28).

Listening is a crucial element of the communication process that also includes speaking, writing, and reading. Yet very little time (if any) is devoted to teaching people the skills they need to become better listeners. We learn in elementary school how to write, read, and speak, but virtually no class time is spent teaching techniques to make listening more effective. While the other three modes of communication are important, listening deserves at least as much attention in the skill-building process. The table below (Nixon & West, 1989) ranks the four basic communication skills in the order in

Basic Communication Skills Profile

Communication Skill	Order Learned	Extent Used	Extent Taught
Listening	First	First	Fourth
Speaking	Second	Second	Third
Reading	Third	Third	Second
Writing	Fourth	Fourth	First

which they are learned, used, and taught. It's clear that listening, our most called-upon communication faculty, receives the least attention.

In the next few pages, we'll look at some of the theories communication specialists have developed to help them understand how people listen. We'll first look at the general nature of listening, then analyze the listening process. Next, we'll consider some common barriers to active listening and present several suggestions for improving listening skills.

What Is Listening?

Just as reading is not merely the sensory perception of words on a page but the act of interpreting those words and making meaning from them, listening is much more than the sensory perception of sounds. It is the act of interpreting those sounds and making meaning from them. Both the speaker and the listener share the responsibility for making meaning—a process Osborn and Osborn (1994) call participative communication.

Think about the way in which you learn best. Do you prefer to listen to information or to read it? Which is easier for you—that is, which requires the least amount of effort? Which is most effective—that is, which mode of taking in data helps you remember the most information? Do you see the difference between ease and effectiveness? Most people say listening is easier than reading, despite the fact that reading is a more effective way for most people to learn.

Readers have more control than listeners do over the process by which information is delivered. They can control the pace of its delivery; they can return to previous information or skip ahead, bypassing information they don't need or rereading information they want to focus on. Listeners, on the other hand, are subject to the whims of the speaker, receiving information at the speaker's own pace, limited to the information they are receiving at the moment, without the freedom to move backward or forward in the message to refresh memory or anticipate later ideas. But to many people, the control that comes with reading requires a significant expenditure of energy to extract the message the words convey. They believe listening is less strenuous, requiring only that they be there for the message to hit its mark. However, most people remember only half of what they hear immediately after listening to someone talk, no matter how carefully they thought they were listening. Two months later, they can remember only 25 percent of what they heard.

Listening may seem to be a passive activity: Just sit there and take in what you hear. But active listening requires the expenditure of much more energy than many people are willing to give. Not only do good listeners help themselves, they also help the person to whom they are listening. It may seem that listening doesn't communicate much to the speaker, but the listener's attitude and responsiveness can say a great deal (Rogers & Farson, 1992).

Think about a time when you tried to have a conversation with someone who was reading a newspaper or watching TV while you were talking. You may have offered to continue the conversation later, but the other person replied, "No, it's okay. I can hear what you're saying." But their attitude—their unwillingness to give you their full attention—probably conveyed the message, "I don't think what you have to say is very important. I'm not all that interested in you or your ideas." Good listening conveys another message altogether. The listener who looks at you, who gives you his or her undivided attention, says, "I'm interested in you as a person. I think what you have to say is important. I think you are worth listening to." The mere behavior of listening conveys the listener's message without the listener having to say a word.

Stages of the Listening Process

✓ Hearing
✓ Focusing on the Message
✓ Comprehending and Interpreting
✓ Analyzing and Evaluating
✓ Responding
✓ Remembering

It's much harder to convince someone that you respect her and her ideas by telling her you do—but attentive, active listening convinces rather easily.

The Listening Process

Active listening is a process that passes through several stages: hearing, focusing on the message, comprehending and interpreting, analyzing and evaluating, responding, and remembering (Osborn & Osborn, 1994). We don't always move consciously through these stages in a linear sequence, and sometimes we spend more time in one stage than another. Still, if you are a good listener, you'll recognize all these stages. If any seem to be missing from your listening repertoire, something crucial may be missing in your interpersonal communication.

Hear the Message

Hearing is the physiological process in which sound waves stimulate nerve impulses that the brain interprets as sound. Sound travels in waves, which are captured by the outer ear and directed into the ear canal. There they strike the ear drum, which begins to vibrate at the same frequency as the sound waves. The vibrations of the ear drum pass to the small bones (ossicles) in the middle ear, which themselves start to vibrate. The ossicles transfer the vibrations to the fluid within the cochlea, a seashell-shaped, fluid-filled structure lined with many specialized hair cells. The hairs move in response to the waves the sound vibrations create in the cochlear fluid. Movements of the hair cells stimulate fibers in the eighth cranial nerve to send signals to the brain, which reads those signals and interprets them as distinct sounds (Auditory Pathway, 1994).

You may hear many things, but you don't listen to everything you hear. Listening is a voluntary process that goes beyond mere reaction to sounds.

Focus on the Sounds of the Message

Focusing requires that you block out other distractions that may compete for your attention. Most listening problems occur because we fail to focus adequately. We let other stimuli interfere with our ability to hear the words the other person is saying. Some common listening problems may stem from environmental, physiological, or psychological factors, all of which may impede our ability to listen carefully. You'll find a description of common impediments to listening and how to deal with them in a later section of this chapter.

Comprehend and Interpret What You Hear

Comprehension requires you to attach meaning to combinations of sounds—you must understand both the language and the point of view of the speaker—as well as process visual and tonal cues in combination with the sound cues. Remember that in your attempt to discern the speaker's intention, you sometimes need to look beyond the words. Often you must hear things that aren't said, but are evident in body language, inflection, and tone (Rogers & Farson, 1992; Minninger, 1984). For example, you may hear someone say, "Oh, I couldn't possibly eat dessert. I'm on a diet," or "I'm sure you have better things to do than waste your time playing checkers with your old Grandpa." But in each case, the speaker's intention may not be consistent with the words. As a listener, you must discern the intent before you can respond appropriately.

Analyze and Evaluate What You Hear

A crucial part of the listening process that leads to understanding is to examine the message—not to just accept it at face value. That doesn't mean you should judge whether the message is right or wrong, good or bad. Instead, try to see beneath the message to the speaker's attitudes and emotions. If you disagree with what the speaker says, try to explore the reasons for the person's conclusions or assertions, without challenging his or her honesty or intelligence (Yukl, 1994). Sometimes it's more important to respond to the emotion underlying the speaker's message. If a colleague says, "I'd like to melt this copy machine down and make paper clips out of it," you can't really respond to the content of the message. Instead, you need to respond to the anger or disgust the colleague feels about the machine. You need to be sensitive to the total meaning of the message (Rogers & Farson, 1992).

Offer Feedback (Respond)

Your movements and facial expressions, as well as questions or vocal comments, let the speaker know how you are responding. There are a number of ways a listener can provide feedback—both positive and negative. A good listener responds in ways that signal acceptance and positive regard (Yukl, 1994). Good feedback should be immediate, honest, and supportive. Sources of feedback include (Hanna, 1995):

✓ *Eye contact.* Have you ever tried to carry on a conversation with someone who doesn't look at you? Or who makes eye contact with the top of your head, your left ear, your feet, but never your eyes? This doesn't mean you have to look the speaker squarely in the eye the entire time she is talking. Eye contact is almost never a direct meeting of the eyes. If you focus anywhere on the speaker's face, you'll achieve the positive effects of good eye contact. As a rule of thumb, look at the speaker's face about 75 percent of the time, in glances lasting from one to seven seconds. (A speaker will look at a listener for less than half that time, and in glances that last no more than a second or two.)

✓ *Facial expression.* Save the poker face for card games—good listeners let their faces register their responses: they smile, frown, express bewilderment, show surprise.

✓ *Head movements.* An affirmative nod of the head signals not only understanding, but agreement. Even a negative shake of the head sends a useful signal to the speaker.

✓ *Touching.* Sometimes, if your relationship with the speaker warrants it, a gentle touch on the arm can be reassuring and signal understanding. The arm is generally considered a non-vulnerable or neutral area, but avoid touching if it seems at all inappropriate. While touching can provide positive feedback, appropriateness is more important.

✓ *Verbal responses.* Even though you can't listen well when you are talking, some verbal responses can make listening more effective. Simple *words of affirmation* or encouragement ("I see," "That's interesting," "Go on") tell the speaker you continue to be attentive. *Questions* that encourage the speaker to continue also provide good feedback ("How does that make you feel?" "What is it that seems to be frustrating you?"). *Paraphrasing,* or restating in your own words what you think the speaker has said, offers several benefits. It shows the speaker you received the message and it lets you test your understanding (Yukl, 1994). Some effective lead-ins to a paraphrase include: "Let me make sure I understand what you mean," "What I hear you saying is," and "In other words." Here is an example of paraphrasing:

> Speaker: *"I can't get this assignment done by Monday. Don't teachers know that we take more than one class in a semester? I've got two other projects due next week, too."*
> Listener: *"It sounds like you have more work than you can manage."*

Remember

The last stage of the listening process helps you build a storehouse of information you can use in a variety of ways, including future listening tasks. Store what you have heard for future reference. Good listeners may use several devices to help them remember key information—from something as simple as a person's name to a complex process introduced in a college lecture. *Repetition* helps anchor information. When someone tells you his name for the first time, make a point of repeating it or using it again in the conversation. *Mnemonics* (any artificial technique used as a memory aid) let you put information in a form that's easier for you to recognize. At some point in an elementary school geography class, for example, you probably used the acronym HOMES as a mnemonic device to remember the names of the Great Lakes (Huron, Ontario, Michigan, Erie, Superior).

Note-taking, while inappropriate in casual conversations, can be a powerful tool for increasing recall when used in connection with phone calls, briefings, interviews, classes, and business meetings. Notes provide a written record of key ideas. More importantly, some research shows that the act of writing notes is more helpful than the notes themselves—that is, by taking notes, we play a more active role in the listening process (Verderber & Verderber, 1995).

Barriers to Active Listening and How to Overcome Them

To become more active listeners, we need to acknowledge listening problems that could become barriers to good communication. Most problems are one of three types: environmental, physiological, or psychological. You will soon see, however, that most listening problems are psychological in nature.

Environmental Barriers

Many distractions that keep us from listening actively are physical, coming from outside us or from within. External noises (traffic, a radio playing in another room, other conversations) compete with the speaker for our attention. Not only do we have to listen over other sounds, we often have to repress other sensory stimuli that may interfere with our ability to listen attentively. It's harder to give your full attention to the act of listening if you're too hot or too cold, tired, hungry, sitting in an uncomfortable chair, wearing tight-fitting shoes, or suffering from a headache or upset stomach or other physical ailment.

To overcome environmental barriers, you need to do everything you can to minimize physical distractions when it is important for you to listen carefully. Turn off the TV or radio. Consciously screen out other noises you can't so easily control, or move to a quiet place. Get comfortable. Turn your back to visual distractions. Prepare to listen by directing your attention to the speaker. Adjust your physical posture to enable you to listen. Make eye contact.

Physiological Barriers

Another barrier to active listening is caused by the different rates at which we think and speak. A person is capable of thinking at a rate about five times faster than he or she can speak. While the average rate of speech is 125 to 150 words per minute, the brain can think at a rate between 500 and 1000 words per minute (Hanna, 1995). That difference can cause a listener's mind to wander, leading to daydreaming and unconscious self-talk. The speaker's message may have to compete with random, unrelated snippets of thought: "I like her shoes," "I need to remember to turn in that history paper before four o'clock," etc.

It's not easy to eliminate this physiological hurdle altogether, but you can try to reduce it. As you listen, try to keep pace with the speaker. Use your mental energy to think about what the speaker is saying and to analyze and interpret his or her words. Paraphrase silently if you don't have an immediate opportunity to paraphrase aloud. Try to be aware of intrusive mental noise and block it out. If you find your mind shifting to an unrelated subject, deliberately bring it back to the message.

Mishearing also accounts for some errors in listening (Minninger, 1984). One obvious physiological barrier to active listening arises whenever a physical condition affects the organs of hearing. A cold, an ear infection, or other conditions that prevent the eardrum, ossicles, and cochlea from functioning normally will certainly interfere with your ability to simply hear sounds. At other times we may hear incorrectly because the speaker has used a word that is hard to interpret: homonyms (plain/plane, tied/tide) can cause confusion, as can words that mean more than one thing (bill, check, let). Another source of erroneous interpretation is the speaker's use of slang expressions or incorrect pronunciation (youse/use; grammar/grandma).

If you hear something that seems to make no sense or leads you to an apparently incongruous interpretation of the speaker's message, try to correct what may be a mishearing. (Could Eliza Doolittle possibly have meant the rain in Spain stays mainly in the *plane*? Probably not—she must have meant *plain*.)

Psychological Barriers

Almost everyone comes equipped with a set of psychological filters through which any spoken message must pass. Psychological factors that influence listening include "preconceived ideas, moods, assumptions, labels, stereotypes, past experiences, emotions, hopes, memories, and even degree of self-esteem" (Hanna, 1995, p. 185). We form fast impressions of both speaker and message, and our filters strongly influence those impressions. As a result, we may erect these psychological barriers to active listening: selective listening, negative listening attitudes, personal reactions to words, and poor motivation to listen well.

Selective listening. Selective listening is the process of choosing to hear only what we consider important and disregarding the rest. For example, if you go into your annual review with your supervisor, and, among other things, she tells you that some clients say they think your telephone manner is somewhat stiff and formal, your self-esteem filter may catch only that criticism and you won't hear your supervisor praise your record-keeping skills, your diligence, and your dependability. The only thing that sticks with you is the critical remark—psychological noise has made it impossible for you to hear the positive things that were said.

Be on your guard for selective listening. Practice listening for the whole message, not just those parts that get caught in your psychological filters.

Negative listening attitudes. Attitudes, too, shape our ability to listen. Negative listening attitudes interfere with reception of the entire message and lead to selective listening. In addition, those attitudes go hand in hand with behaviors that are counterproductive to good communication. Your attitude sends both verbal and nonverbal signals to the speaker; negative attitudes may make the speaker feel nervous, uncomfortable, and unappreciated. Your feedback clearly tells the speaker, "I'm bored," "I don't care about what you're saying," "I'm anxious to get out of here," "I don't respect your views," or "My ideas are more valuable than yours." The speaker may decide to stop talking and the communication fails.

Hold your reactions and attitudes in check. If you begin to feel a negative listening attitude creep up on you, force yourself to practice behaviors of the positive opposite. For example, if you feel yourself growing bored, sit up straight, look at the speaker, and analyze what she is saying in terms of its relevance to you. Some people say that "attitude follows behavior"—if you *act* interested, you may soon find that you *are* interested.

Personal reactions to words. We respond to words at two levels of meaning: the denotative and the connotative. Denotative meanings are those literal meanings assigned to words to which we all subscribe. But connotative meanings develop when certain words are used in certain contexts and come to be associated with words beyond the denotative level (Verderber & Verderber, 1995; Osborn & Osborn, 1994). Everyone has a red flag filter that catches words that may cause strong reactions—like *liberal, feminist, income tax,* or *communist.* For example, if you hear a speaker use *girls* in reference to adult females, the rest of the message may get lost in your reaction to the connotation you associate with the term *girls* and the related assumptions you make about persons who would refer to women as *girls*.

When a speaker uses a word that waves a red flag at you, look past it. Instead of giving in to the emotional deafness such a word is likely to inspire, focus on the entire message and try to see where the word fits in the overall context.

In other cases, connotative meanings may smudge the message with inadvertent humor or ambiguity. Consider this situation: When Marge visited California for the first time several years ago, she rolled up the legs of her jeans and waded into the Pacific Ocean. Unfortunately, she didn't roll them up far enough, and one of the waves she hadn't anticipated doused her to mid-thigh. She called her children that evening to describe her experience and told them, "I wet my pants in the Pacific Ocean." They laughed because the connotation of the phrase "wet my pants" was stronger than the literal meaning Marge had intended.

We also need to beware of chance associations a speaker's words may trigger in us as we listen. The speaker may be telling you about a problem she is trying to resolve with the instructor of her art history class, but the word *art* makes you think of painting and painting makes you think about the garage you are building but haven't been able to finish because it has been too rainy to paint it, and suddenly you are focusing not on your friend's problem, but your own. The message has fallen by the wayside along the path of your free association.

It's important to focus on the denotative meanings of words. Use non-verbal cues to help you determine what the speaker meant. If the connotation was unintended, let it go. If other cues tell you the connotative mix-up was intended, enjoy the resultant humor. If a speaker's word triggers an unrelated association, you may need to make a conscious effort to suppress it. Just attend to the speaker's words extra carefully and intently for a couple of minutes to force the intrusive association away.

Poor motivation. Another psychological impediment to active listening is lack of preparation. You can listen most actively if you know your listening goals. Without goals, you have no point on which to focus, and, consequently, no motivation to stay attuned to the speaker's message. So, while the other person is speaking, you may be thinking your own thoughts or preparing your rebuttal, without giving the speaker's ideas the attention they deserve.

Listening Goals Ladder

Response/Action
Analysis
Retention
Understanding
Enjoyment

To deal with motivational problems, you must clearly define your reasons for listening. The ladder shown in the box suggests the increasing level of complexity of listening goals. The higher the goal on the ladder, the more intense your listening needs to be. When you know what your goal is, you can identify and practice listening behaviors that will help you achieve your objective.

To Be a Good Listener

Good listening behaviors can be learned, but like any skill, they require practice to be perfected. Here are ten guidelines for good listening that you can practice right away (Sayre, 1989). They work in any listening situation and can lead to more sophisticated and refined listening habits.

1. Stop talking. Listen quietly until the speaker's message is complete.
2. Avoid, reduce, or eliminate distractions.
3. Expend the energy needed to give the speaker the benefit of your attention.
4. Use pauses to reflect on what the speaker is saying.
5. Identify the speaker's main ideas and central themes.
6. Judge the content of the message, not the speaker's delivery style.
7. Use paraphrasing, note-taking, and questions when appropriate to ensure understanding.
8. Interpret loaded emotional words appropriately; don't overreact.
9. Give useful feedback.
10. Listen between the lines and beyond the words: Listen for the speaker's feelings as well as facts.

EXERCISE
Listening Profile

Adapted from Brownell, 1989.

The self-rating questionnaire on the next page is designed to give you some descriptive feedback about your own listening behaviors. You can use your listening profile to help you target specific listening components for improvement. The results also can be the basis for small group discussions on differences in listening behavior that may result from variables like gender, age, profession, academic major, etc.

Each question on the following page addresses one of these five stages of the listening process:

1. focusing attention
2. comprehending and interpreting
3. analyzing and evaluating
4. responding
5. remembering

Before you go any further, make a guess about how you will do:

I think I will score the highest on _____.

I think I will score the lowest on _____.

Listening Profile Questionnaire

Respond to these questions by assessing your perceptions of your listening behavior. Use the following key:

5—always   4—usually   3—sometimes   2—infrequently   1—never

_____ 1. I weigh all evidence before making a decision.

_____ 2. I am sensitive to the speaker's feelings in communication situations.

_____ 3. I approach tasks creatively.

_____ 4. I concentrate on what the speaker is saying.

_____ 5. I encourage others to express their opinions.

_____ 6. I am able to see how different pieces of information or ideas relate to each other.

_____ 7. I listen to the entire message when someone speaks, whether I agree with what the speaker says or not.

_____ 8. I let the speaker know immediately that he or she has been understood.

_____ 9. I remember what I am told, even in stressful situations.

_____ 10. I recognize the main points in a presentation and am not distracted by supporting details.

_____ 11. I notice the speaker's facial expressions, body posture, and other nonverbal behaviors.

_____ 12. I hear what is said when someone speaks to me.

_____ 13. I give an individual my complete attention when he or she is speaking to me.

_____ 14. I can recall several days later the specific information someone gave me.

_____ 15. I respond in an appropriate and timely manner to information and requests.

_____ 16. I am ready to listen when approached by a speaker.

_____ 17. I wait until all information is presented before drawing conclusions.

_____ 18. I allow for the fact that people and circumstances change over time.

_____ 19. I overcome distractions, such as the conversations of others, background noises, and telephones, when someone is speaking to me.

_____ 20. I seek information for better understanding of a situation.

_____ 21. I communicate clearly and directly.

_____ 22. I focus on the main point of a message rather than reacting to details.

_____ 23. I am receptive to points of view that are different from my own.

_____ 24. I remember the details of things that happened weeks or months ago.

_____ 25. I let the speaker complete his or her message without interrupting.

How to Arrive at Your Self-Rating

The specific questions that correspond to each of the five listening components are listed here. Begin with Component 1. Find the numbered questions for that component on your completed questionnaire. Write in the number (1–5) of your response to each question. When you have finished entering your scores for Component 1, add them up and enter the total on the Total line. Continue in the same manner with the remaining components.

Component 1: Focusing
Question 4_____ 12_____ 13_____ 16_____ 19_____ = Total_____
Component 2: Comprehending and Interpreting
Question 2_____ 10_____ 11_____ 22_____ 25_____ = Total_____
Component 3: Analyzing and Evaluating
Question 1_____ 7_____ 17_____ 18_____ 23_____ = Total_____
Component 4: Responding
Question 5_____ 8_____ 15_____ 20_____ 21_____ = Total_____
Component 5: Remembering
Question 3_____ 6_____ 9_____ 14_____ 24_____ = Total_____

Use this chart as a guide to assessing each skill area:

20–25 points	You see yourself as an excellent listener.
15–20 points	You consider your listening skills adequate.
10–15 points	You perceive some problems in your listening behavior.

1. Based on your totals, in which skills do you rate yourself highest? Which ones do you see as potential problems? How did your actual ranking compare to your earlier guess?

2. How close are the totals in all areas? Is there one component with a score considerably higher or lower than any of the others?

3. How do you think others would rank your listening behaviors? Take the perspective of an important person in your life (parent, significant other, supervisor, teacher) and answer the questions as if that person were rating *your* listening skills. Are the scores different from your original ranking? If so, why do you think they are different?

EXERCISE
Driven to Distraction

Purpose To help you become more aware of the screening processes that affect listening behavior, by identifying external and internal noises that interfere with active listening.

You Will Need Pencil and paper

Activity Sit comfortably and stop all talking. When your leader gives you the signal to begin, close your eyes, and for the next 30 seconds focus on as many sensory distractions as possible. Don't focus on sounds alone, but any other sensory noises of which you might be aware.

When your leader tells you time is up, write down all distractions you were aware of.

When your leader asks, tell how many distractions you identified. Discuss your observations about the kinds of distractions you noted and their potential effect on good listening.

EXERCISE
Information Overload

Purpose   To identify and apply techniques to help you remember what you hear. In everyday conversations, we often have to sort through a lot of extra information to find the message. Listening can be hard work—if you want to really remember what you hear.

Activity   Working in pairs or groups of three, consider the following cases and discuss the questions that follow. If you wish, you may role play one or both of the cases to demonstrate how you would apply strategies for active listening. One person should play the speaker and another the listener (the listener, of course, should not follow along as the speaker reads the statement). Listeners should practice any active listening strategies they think are useful. Listeners then should repeat the message, focusing on the specific actions they think the speakers want them to take.

Mini Case #1: The Party

In this case, you and your roommate are getting ready for a birthday party that you're throwing for another friend. Your roommate says:

"We have a lot to do before the party. I don't know if we have enough glasses. Could you call your sister Angela and ask her to bring ice when she comes, if she's coming before seven o'clock? If she won't get here until later, ask Tim to pick it up on his way home from work. The tablecloths are in the bottom of that box of stuff I got from my mom and the folding chairs need to be brought in from my car. I guess Angela can help with those if she comes early. I don't know if we have enough glasses. I better get the tablecloths out of that box before they get too wrinkled. Do you think your sister and Tim will hit it off?"

Discussion

1. Can you sort out the essential information from the extraneous information you just heard?

2. What are you being asked to do?

3. What do you have to do in order to accomplish the tasks your roommate has asked you to do?

4. What could you do as you listen to help you understand what your roommate is asking?

Mini Case #2: Summer Job

Here's another situation that may be more typical of business life. You have a summer job as a messenger for your state soil conservation service. You're responsible for running errands and doing odd jobs for several people in the agency. Mr. Fickle, the agency accountant, tends to think out loud, so whenever he asks you to do something, you have to listen double-time.

"I need a new desk calendar from the Personnel Office in the basement. Try to get Jesse to take care of it for you; Charlie Conrad will just give you a hard time about it. Before you go down, take this report to Mrs. Nguyen— you know where her office is? Over in the annex? You get there through the atrium on the third floor. Give it to her secretary. If she isn't there, get somebody to sign for it. Last month someone lost the report and I got in trouble. Make two photocopies of it just to be safe. One copy should go to national headquarters today, so drop it off at shipping, but tell them to send it book rate. It may take longer to get there, but Mrs. Nguyen says we're spending too much on postage, so I guess the delay is her problem, right? Leave that calendar on the file cabinet if I'm not here when you get back."

Discussion

1. Most of what Mr. Fickle said was instructions, some expressed and some implied. Your listening challenge is to figure out what he wants you to do and in what order.

2. What could you do while listening to Mr. Fickle to make it easier to do what he asks?

EXERCISE
Attitude Adjustment

Adapted from Coakley, 1989.

Purpose To sensitize you to positive and negative listening attitudes and to the ways in which listeners convey those attitudes, both verbally and nonverbally.

You Will Need A moderator for your small group

One of the cards your instructor will distribute

Paper and pencil

Activity Within your group, carry on an 8–10 minute discussion of the topic your instructor assigns. The moderator you have selected is responsible for keeping the discussion moving and trying to get all group members involved. As you participate in the discussion, you are to convey the listening attitude described on the card you received. Use both verbal and nonverbal behaviors associated with the attitude. The entire group should stop the conversation when your instructor gives the signal.

On a piece of paper, write the names of everyone in your group. Next to each name, write the listening attitude you think that person was trying to convey. Also note some verbal and nonverbal cues you noticed and associated with the attitude.

Discussion

1. What listening attitudes did you identify during the conversation? What verbal and nonverbal clues led you to recognize each specific attitude? Did you identify the attitudes correctly?

2. How did you feel when faced with various listening attitudes when you were speaking? How much of the conversation are you able to recall (who said what)? To what extent did your own listening attitude interfere with your ability to remember what was said?

EXERCISE
Irritating Listening Habits

Adapted from Dodge, 1988.

Purpose   To demonstrate poor listening habits prevalent in everyday communication and to call attention to your own poor listening habits.

Activity   Your leader will ask for three volunteers to role play a communication situation in which effective listening is important. One person has a serious problem he or she is trying to confide to another. The problem should be realistic and relevant to the people who will be observing the role play. The person confiding the problem should act sincere and genuine.

The listener should dramatize many poor listening habits (fidgeting, yawning, interrupting, looking at the time, etc.), yet should still act interested in the other person's problem.

The third person should enter the conversation appearing to be eavesdropping. He or she can interject irrelevant information, offer advice, change the subject, or simply interrupt with a question or comment. This person may be reading a magazine, fiddling with something, or daydreaming.

The skit should take five to seven minutes, and should be creative and imaginative. It should be true to life and the bad habits portrayed should be overemphasized and recognizable.

Discussion

When the role play is over, identify the habits you saw that inhibit effective listening. Why are these habits irritating?

Activity   Complete the Irritating Listening Habits Checklist. Put a check mark in the space before the ten listening habits that you find most irritating.

Discussion

1. Which three habits did the largest number of people check?
2. What do these irritating habits have in common? Why are they irritating? Can you think of some examples?
3. How do you feel when someone exhibits these habits in conversation?
4. Do you have any of these habits yourself? What can you or someone else do to shake irritating listening habits?

Irritating Listening Habits

Check the ten habits on this list that you find most irritating.

_____ 1. Doesn't give me a chance to talk. I present a problem and I never get a chance to talk about it.

_____ 2. Interrupts me when I try to talk.

_____ 3. Never looks at me when I talk.

_____ 4. Continually fidgets with a pencil or paper or something, and looks at it and not me.

_____ 5. Treats me like an inferior.

_____ 6. Never smiles.

_____ 7. Asks questions that seem to doubt everything I say.

_____ 8. Whenever I make a suggestion, throws cold water on it.

_____ 9. Is always trying to get ahead of my story and guess what my point is, sometimes even finishing my sentences for me.

_____ 10. Argues with everything I say even before I have a chance to finish stating my case.

_____ 11. Frequently answers a question with another question, usually one I can't answer.

_____ 12. Continually interrupts to tell me about a personal experience that my story brings to mind.

_____ 13. Picks hangnails, clips fingernails, or cleans glasses while I'm talking.

_____ 14. Just seems to be waiting for me to get through talking.

_____ 15. Says something like, "Oh, yes, I've been thinking about that, too," whenever I have good ideas.

_____ 16. Stares at me while I'm talking and looks me in the eyes too intensely.

_____ 17. Inserts humorous remarks when I'm trying to be serious.

_____ 18. Overdoes the attention—too many heads nods or _uh huhs_.

_____ 19. Acts as if it is a hardship to see me and often looks at the clock while I am talking.

_____ 20. Passes the buck about problems I raise.

_____ 21. Asks questions that demand agreement, such as "Don't you think so?" or "Don't you agree?"

EXERCISE
The Listening Circle

Adapted from Smith, 1989.

Purpose To practice strategies for listening actively to the opinions of others, responding appropriately, and conducting an orderly discussion. In this activity, you can select topics about which you have definite opinions, express your opinions, and agree or disagree with others' opinions. The stipulation that you speak one at a time in a predetermined order forces you to listen to each speaker's complete message and to evaluate the message before responding.

You Will Need Pencil and paper

Activity Arrange chairs in a circle so each person is sitting between two others. Your leader has written some discussion topics on the board, all of which are somewhat controversial. As you scan the list of topics, select one about which you have an opinion. Take a few minutes to jot some notes to yourself to help you formulate a couple of thoughts about the subject.

Round 1 Your leader will call on someone to begin the exercise. That person is designated Person A. Person A expresses an opinion on her or his selected topic. (e.g., "I'm in favor of raising the driving age to 18 because then high school students would not be interested in buying cars. Without cars, they would have more time to spend studying.")

The person to the right of Person A (Person B) must respond to Person A, either by agreeing with the stated opinion and adding more information to it, or disagreeing and giving reasons why.

Person B then becomes Person A and expresses her or his opinion on the topic she or he previously selected. The process is repeated around the circle until the original Person A has had a chance to be Person B. (You don't have to change topics if someone before you has selected the same topic.)

You should take notes as opinions are expressed so you can remember later who said what. However, you are not permitted to say anything during round one, except when you are either Person A or Person B, and then you may speak only in your turn. No one is allowed to interrupt or contradict.

Round 2 Any topic is acceptable for discussion. If you want to respond to something that was said during round one, raise your hand. The last person who spoke in round one may call on any other person who has raised a hand to speak. If you are called upon, identify whose comment you are responding to and whether you agree or disagree. (e.g., "I'd like to comment on something Mary said earlier. I disagree that high school students would study more if they didn't have cars because . . . .") You may speak as long as you like, and then you may call on someone else to speak, who may speak as long as he or she desires. You may speak only when someone else recognizes you—you may not interrupt or speak out of turn. This process continues until your leader tells you time is up.

Note: Be sure to address your comments either to the entire group or to the person whose views you are responding to. The instructor is only one equal person in the group; don't let him or her be the focal point of this activity.

EXERCISE
Try to Remember

Purpose   To demonstrate the limitations of listening and to demonstrate that even though most of us think we are good listeners, we forget much of what we hear right after we hear it.

Activity   Four volunteer listeners will leave the classroom so they can't hear what is being said while they are gone. When the volunteers have left, your instructor will read a short passage or incident report to the fifth volunteer listener, who will then go to the hall and call just one of the listeners back. When they have returned to the classroom, the first listener will relate the tale she or he has just heard. The person who came in from the hall then will select another listener to return to the classroom and will, in turn, relate the report he or she has just heard. This process continues until all volunteers have returned to the classroom. The last person to hear the report will write it on the chalkboard.

Other nonparticipating members of the class will be divided into observer groups and assigned to specific listener volunteers. As an observer, you should note any active listening skills you see the listener practicing, as well as the changes that occur in the story when your assigned volunteer retells it.

When the last volunteer has written his or her version on the chalkboard, observers should report the changes they noted as the story passed from listener to listener.

Discussion

1. Which details seemed the most difficult to recall correctly?

2. What type of details did listeners seem to assume or invent to make the account seem valid?

3. What listening behaviors did you observe that seemed to help volunteers remember what they were hearing?

4. Why do you think there were so many changes in the account? What does this suggest you might do when you are trying to clearly and accurately convey a message to an audience?

5. What other listening strategies might have helped increase listening accuracy?

FURTHER ACTIVITY

Journal Writing

1. Think about at least five occasions in the past 24 hours when you were cast in the role of listener. Describe each situation in your journal and characterize the effectiveness of your listening. Was your listening behavior the same or different in each of the five situations? In which situation do you think you were the best listener? The worst? What behaviors distinguished your effective listening from ineffective listening?

2. Over the next few days, choose a communication situation that you participate in regularly (in the classroom, on the job, in a personal relationship, etc.). Make a concentrated effort to practice all the active listening behaviors you've learned about in this chapter (but don't let the other person know what you are doing). Do you think your listening in that situation has improved? Describe in your journal what you did to listen better, and reflect on the effects of better listening.

3. Watch at least 15 minutes of your favorite talk show program (or set your VCR to tape the program if you can't watch when it regularly airs). In your journal, briefly describe the conversation you were watching and identify the listening techniques you observed in the talk show host. Do you think he or she exhibited the qualities of an active listener? Did anyone on the program demonstrate inappropriate listening? If so, describe what you saw and heard.

Self-Improvement Contract: Toward More Active Listening

A contract form is provided that allows you to commit in writing to specific goals for improving your listening behavior. The written contract, as opposed to a mental resolution, may strengthen your commitment to improve. Before you write your contract, you need to evaluate your present listening skills. You can use the self-rating you computed when you filled out the listening inventory earlier to help you identify specific listening behaviors that may need improvement.

Read the following description of the parts of the contract before you proceed.

Listening Goal: A specific statement that targets a particular listening behavior you want to improve. For example, "To listen better when teachers give me instructions for assignments."

Listening Problem to Be Solved: Describe the specific situation in which you want to apply your improved listening skills. For example, "When my composition instructor gives assignments for essays, I find myself daydreaming or thinking about a possible topic. As a result, I miss important points of the assignment or I misinterpret what I am supposed to do. Then I do the assignment wrong and get a low grade because I haven't followed instructions. I want to improve my ability to listen attentively to what my composition teacher is telling me."

Procedure for Reaching the Goal: State specific behaviors you can modify to reach your listening goal. For example, "I need to practice strategies of questioning and silent paraphrasing to help me understand and remember what my composition instructor tells me. I will listen carefully to the message, think about what it means to me, and repeat to myself in my own words what I think the message means. If I am not sure my mental paraphrase is correct, I will ask the teacher to explain further."

Method for Determining When the Goal Has Been Achieved: Write the minimum requirements for knowing you have accomplished your goal. For example, "I will know I have improved my listening in composition class when I can ask questions and paraphrase instructions and complete assignments the way the teacher has requested."

Now complete the contract and ask a friend to witness your signature. If you act as a witness for someone else, follow up in about six weeks by calling and asking if your friend has met the listening goal.

Self-Improvement Contract: Toward More Active Listening

My Listening Goal:

Listening Problem I Want to Solve:

Procedure for Reaching My Listening Goal:

Method for Determining When I Have Reached My Listening Goal:

Signed: _____

Date: _____

Witness: _____

LEARNING POINTS

✓ Listening is the most often used mode of communication, but for most people it is the least efficient and the least developed.

✓ Although we may think we are good listeners, most of us cannot remember half of what we hear immediately after hearing it.

✓ Active listening is a six-stage process that moves from the reflexive, physiological function of hearing to the higher order intellectual function of remembering. In between are the stages of focusing, comprehension/interpretation, analysis/evaluation, and response.

✓ Common barriers to effective listening may be environmental, physiological, or psychological in nature.

✓ Overcoming barriers requires concentration, deliberate reduction of distractions, and development of positive listening attitudes.

✓ Good listening skills can be learned and can improve, with practice, over time.

REFERENCES

The auditory pathway. (1994). In *3-D body adventure* [CD-ROM]. Knowledge Adventure, Inc.

Brownell, J. (1989). Listening questionnaire. In Coakley, C. G., and Wolvin, A. D. (Eds.). *Experiential listening: Tools for teachers and trainers.* New Orleans: Spectra, Inc.

Carosso, R. B. (1986). *Technical communication.* Belmont, CA: Wadsworth.

Coakley, C. G. (1989). What a difference an attitude makes. In Coakley, C. G., and Wolvin, A. D. (Eds.). *Experiential listening: Tools for teachers and trainers.* New Orleans: Spectra, Inc.

Dodge, G. W. (1988). *Handbook for teaching assistants.* Lincoln, NE: Department of Agricultural Education; University of Nebraska-Lincoln.

Hanna, S. L. (1995). *Person to person: Positive relationships don't just happen* (2nd ed.). Englewood Cliffs, NJ: Prentice Hall.

Litzenberg, K. K., and Schneider, V. E. (1988). Educational priorities for tomorrow's agribusiness leaders. *Agribusiness, 4* (2), 187–195.

Minninger, J. (1984). *Total recall: How to boost your memory power.* Emmaus, PA: Rodale Press.

Nixon, J. C., and West, J. F. (1989). Listening: The new competency. *The Balance Sheet,* 27–29.

Osborn, M., and Osborn, S. (1994). *Public speaking* (3rd ed.). Boston: Houghton Mifflin.

Rogers, C. R., and Farson, R. E. (1992). Active listening. In Haney, W. V. *Communication and interpersonal relations: Text and cases* (pp. 158–171). Homewood, IL: Irwin.

Sayre, J. M. (1989). Focus. In Coakley, C. G., and Wolvin, A. D. (Eds.). *Experiential listening: Tools for teachers and trainers.* New Orleans: Spectra, Inc.

Smith, I. H. (1989). The listening circle. In Coakley, C. G., and Wolvin, A. D. (Eds.). *Experiential listening: Tools for teachers and trainers.* New Orleans: Spectra, Inc.

Verderber, R. F., and Verderber, K. S. (1995). *Inter-act: Using interpersonal communication skills* (7th ed.). Belmont, CA: Wadsworth.

Yukl, G. (1994). *Leadership in organizations* (3rd ed.). Englewood Cliffs, NJ: Prentice Hall.

Chapter 3

NONVERBAL COMMUNICATION

If you say something to me
An' you mean, you mean what you say
An' you're wanting my attention
There's a game you must play . . .
Use your eyes and your face
Words have no place
Move your body in a way
That I will know what you say
Body language . . .
Body Language Yo O O O O O
—INXS, "Body Language"

ADVANCE PLANNER: NONVERBAL COMMUNICATION

When you complete this chapter, you will be able to:

✓ Explain the impact of nonverbal communication on the communication process.

✓ List and define the channels of nonverbal communication.

✓ Identify and interpret nonverbal behaviors in others.

✓ Explain how space or proxemics communicates meaning.

✓ Improve your communication skills by monitoring your nonverbal behaviors.

To accomplish these objectives, you will complete some or all of these activities:

1. Discuss a case study to test your ability to identify and interpret nonverbal behaviors and their effect on the communication process.

2. Read and discuss a brief summary of some theories about nonverbal communication.

3. Complete exercises that will help you see the impact of nonverbal signals on the communication process.

4. Write in your journal about nonverbal communication you see in others and yourself.

A CASE STUDY IN NONVERBAL COMMUNICATION

The Meeting

Vanessa has worked as a market analyst for Widgets Inc. for six months; this morning she's scheduled to present a proposal for a new marketing strategy to her supervisor, Rod Zoeller. Although the work atmosphere at Widgets Inc. is fairly informal, today Vanessa has replaced her usual office attire of slacks, casual jacket, and penny loafers with a navy pinstripe suit, crisp white blouse, and moderately high-heeled shoes.

As Vanessa waits outside Mr. Zoeller's office, she clutches her briefcase in her lap, her hands gripping the handle tightly. She takes several deep breaths as she mentally rehearses the points she plans to make in her meeting. Rod opens his office door and sticks his head out. "Vanessa, you can come on in now." Vanessa stands quickly, nearly dropping her briefcase, and teeters for just a second as she adjusts her balance. She swallows, takes a deep breath, and walks purposefully to Rod's office. Rod extends his hand and says, "Hope you haven't been waiting too long out there. I had a couple of fires to put out, but I think things are okay now." Vanessa grips his hand loosely in hers, conscious that her palms are perspiring.

Rod puts his arm around Vanessa's back and guides her by the waist to a chair opposite his desk. Vanessa involuntarily shrinks away from his touch and he drops his arm. He says, "Have a seat, Vanessa." Vanessa sits and places her briefcase on the floor beside the chair. Rod remains standing only a foot away from Vanessa, directly in front of her. He crosses his arms. Vanessa shifts in the chair, crosses her legs, uncrosses them, tugs at the collar of her blouse to pull it away from her neck, looks up at Rod, then looks down at the edge of the desk.

"You said you had an idea you wanted to run by me?" Rod inclines his head forward slightly.

"I think I've come up with a new strategy that will really boost Widget sales, Mr. Zoeller." She looks him in the eye now. "That's what I want to talk to you about." Vanessa picks up the briefcase, places it flat on the desk in front of her and snaps open the latch. She pulls out a folder and a ballpoint pen. "The figures bear me out and I've researched other companies like ours and discovered that what I have in mind has worked well for many of our competitors." She hands a bound report to Rod, who takes it, gives it a cursory glance, then sets it on the desk.

Rod leans back and sits on the edge of the desk, stretching his legs out in front of him. He checks his watch, then directs his gaze out the window behind Vanessa. His foot is raised slightly off the floor and he jiggles it back and forth as he says, "Uh huh, well, I'll be happy to read your proposal. Sounds interesting."

Vanessa clears her throat and when she speaks this time, her voice goes up slightly in pitch. "Well, yeah, I mean, I've put a lot of time into the proposal. I think you'll like the bottom line." As she speaks, she unconsciously clicks the button on the ballpoint pen rapidly back and forth.

Rod walks around the desk and sits in his chair. "I appreciate your coming to see me with this, Vanessa." He picks up the bound report from the desktop and tosses it casually in a basket on the bookcase behind him. "I'll give it some thought and get back to you later, okay?" He then opens his calendar, looks across the desk at Vanessa, smiles briefly, and says "Thank you."

Rod picks up his telephone and dials, waving impatiently at Vanessa with the back of his hand. She slams her briefcase shut, turns sharply and strides quickly out of the office without a word.

Discussion Questions

1. How seriously does Vanessa take her meeting with Mr. Zoeller? How do you know?

2. What do Rod's nonverbal cues say about his attitudes about the meeting? His power relationship to Vanessa? His interest in her proposal?

3. What do Vanessa's nonverbal signals tell us about her perception of the power relationship between Mr. Zoeller and her?

4. What unintended messages might Vanessa be sending to Rod? Are her nonverbal messages consistent with what she says? What unintended nonverbal messages might Rod be sending to Vanessa?

5. What advice would you give to Vanessa and to Rod about monitoring nonverbal signals to improve the quality of their next meeting?

INTRODUCTION TO NONVERBAL COMMUNICATION

Although we may assume that the words we speak carry significant weight when we communicate with someone else, the fact is the true nature of our communication with other people has little to do with words. We depend instead on a language without words referred to collectively as nonverbal communication.

Various experts in communication estimate that between 75 percent and 90 percent of the information we gather from others is nonverbal in nature. In some cases nonverbal communication is used to either affirm or contradict a verbal message. At other times the nonverbal channel carries the primary message. Audience members listening to a public speaker, for example, communicate their responses, attitudes, and questions almost exclusively through nonverbal signals, without saying a single word. Active listeners look at the speaker and respond honestly with smiles, nods or other forms of body language, which can improve the quality of communication and keep the dynamic circle intact (Osborn & Osborn, 1994).

It is important to remember that we send nonverbal signals all the time, whether we are listening or speaking. The most profound impact of nonverbal communication is the degree to which it reinforces or contradicts other communication channels. The presidential debate between Richard Nixon and John Kennedy in 1960—the first ever televised—is often cited as an example of how nonverbal channels can be more powerful than the verbal message.

After the debate there was considerable disagreement as to which candidate won the contest. Television viewers generally believed that Kennedy had carried the day, while those who listened to the debate on the radio felt Nixon had prevailed. The difference in the perceptions of these groups had to do with the nonverbal messages that were visually apparent on television, but not discernible on radio. Nixon's nonverbal signals made him appear ill at ease and nervous. His stance was closed, his shoulders slightly turned away from the camera. He was a man with heavy facial hair and his five o'clock shadow was not well concealed by his stage makeup, making him look a little "shady." Kennedy, on the other hand, looked relaxed and vibrant. He used open gestures and faced the camera directly. His hands were often open as if ready to embrace. He was clean-cut and he smiled.

The difference in appearances strongly influenced the television viewers, to the point that their impression of the event was significantly different from the impression of radio listeners. Television viewers felt more comfortable with Kennedy because the nonverbal portions of his presentation were complementary to his verbal message. Nixon was the favorite going in to the debate, but Kennedy was in the White House soon afterward.

What are you communicating to others through the signals you send by your movements and gestures? How do you interpret or read the same nonverbal cues from others? Are you communicating honesty, competence, and positive assurance? Are your nonverbal messages consistent with the message contained in the words you say?

Channels of Nonverbal Communication

Nonverbal communication channels play incredibly important roles in communication. The way these channels affect and influence the communication process may vary from culture to culture, but in virtually every situation they carry a significant portion of the communication load, and in many cases the message is dominated by nonverbal symbols. Nonverbal communication channels can include, but are not limited to:

- ✓ physical appearance.
- ✓ facial expressions.
- ✓ eye contact.
- ✓ body language (including gestures, posture, and body orientation).
- ✓ proxemics (relating to the distance between two communicators) (Marsh, 1988).

Appearance

Appearance is an important channel of nonverbal communication. Most of us, whether we admit it or not, do pick up signals from a person's physical appearance. Within the first two minutes of seeing someone, we make some kind of judgment about them, and appearance is the largest single factor guiding that judgment. Overall appearance is one nonverbal channel over which we have considerable conscious control and it tells others a good deal about how we feel and how we wish to be viewed.

We respond differently, for example, to a young man with neatly combed hair dressed in a business suit and wire-rimmed glasses than we do to the same young man with day-glo orange and green spiked hair, wearing cut-off jeans, tank top, and chrome-plated sunglasses. Our responses are governed by our expectations and the communication context. In a job interview situation, we would respond more positively to the appearance of the young man in a business suit; but at a rock concert we might consider the same young man (dressed in professional attire) extremely out of place. The choices you make about your appearance clearly signal your attitudes and expectations about the communication context you have entered. Personal grooming (cleanliness, hairstyle, use of makeup) also conveys unspoken information to complement verbal messages.

Facial Expressions

Our language is full of expressions reflecting the powerful influence of facial signals. When we say that someone is shifty-eyed, is tight-lipped, has a furrowed brow, flashes bedroom eyes, stares into space, or grins like a Cheshire cat, we are speaking in a kind of shorthand and using a set of stereotypes that enables us to make judgments—consciously or unconsciously—about a person's abilities and qualities. Those judgments may not be accurate, but they are usually difficult to reverse.

It is possible to read emotion and attitude from people's faces. Smiles and frowns are often spontaneous expressions of happiness and anger. Yet we use smiles-and frowns for other purposes—to greet someone or to show doubt. Using facial expressions this way does not necessarily mean we have strong feelings, but that we are simply following conventional rules for using the face as a vehicle for expressions.

Researchers have demonstrated that certain clearly distinguishable facial expressions communicate the same emotions in every human culture studied. The six basic emotions (happiness, sadness, anger, surprise, fear, and disgust) are expressed and recognized in pretty much the same way in all parts of the world, using three independently expressive regions of the face—eyebrows, eyes, and lower face (Marsh, 1988).

Emotion	Brows	Eyes	Lower face
Happiness		Wrinkles around the eyes	Smiling mouth
Sadness	Raised	Lowered upper eyelids	Down-turned mouth
Anger	Lowered or drawn together	Penetrating stare or tensed eyelids	Lips pressed together or opened and pushed forward
Surprise	Raised	Open wide	Dropped jaw, open mouth
Fear	Raised and drawn together	Open and tense, lower lid raised	Mouth open, lips drawn back tightly
Disgust	Lowered	Lower eyelid pushed up	Wrinkled nose, raised upper lip

Humans are capable of blending facial expressions, which explains why it is sometimes difficult to say what emotion someone's face may reveal. For instance, there may be anger or fear in the brows but a smile on the lips. We may be aware of the mixture of feelings we see on the face, but unable to see immediately what the feelings truly are.

The ability to control facial muscles voluntarily means that some people can display as much or as little emotion as they wish. It takes considerable effort to suppress spontaneous facial expressions, and those who can do so have learned the skill because they were taught self-control. Voluntary control of the face allows us to suppress emotional displays and to mask negative feelings with imitations of happiness. It also allows for many other social uses of the face.

The nonverbal signals sent by facial expressions are a constant source of information in a conversation. Many expressions used in conversation are not emotional. For instance, raising the eyebrows may not signal surprise, but instead serves as a question mark or a sign of emphasis. Listeners, too, nod and smile, frown in puzzlement, or widen eyes and raise eyebrows to encourage speakers and show they have understood and are impressed or dismayed at what they heard. People also may yawn deliberately as a signal that they do not want the speaker to go on.

Eye Contact

The eyes are the most important feature of facial expressiveness. Looking at the eyes of another person is such a powerful act of communication that we must control it carefully. We rarely maintain long stretches of eye contact (unless we are gazing lovingly at someone close or fixing someone we dislike with a hostile stare). Instead, we restrict eye contact to brief glances and it is the nature of these glances that determines the impression we make on others. When people are forced into close physical contact, as in subways and elevators, eye contact decreases considerably.

Eye contact helps us know when it is our turn to speak in conversation (through a characteristic pattern of looking, making eye contact, and looking away). Listeners use more eye contact than speakers, looking at the other person's face for three-fourths of the time in glances lasting from one to seven seconds. Speakers look at their listeners for less than half the time and maintain eye contact through intermittent glances that last no more than a second each (Marsh, 1988). We generally maintain eye contact better when we are talking about topics with which we are comfortable and with people in whose ideas we are genuinely interested. Conversely, we avoid eye contact when discussing topics that make us uncomfortable or when we have little interest in the person to whom we are talking.

It should be noted, too, that eye contact behavior differs between sexes and among cultures. Women hold eye contact longer than do men, regardless of the sex of the person with whom they are interacting. Amount of eye contact varies from culture to culture, too, with the highest levels shown in Arab and Latin American cultures and lowest in Indian and northern European cultures (Verderber & Verderber, 1995). In American culture, frequent and sustained eye contact suggests honesty, openness, and respect. People who use eye contact are viewed as confident, credible, and having nothing to hide.

If eyes are windows into the self, then lack of eye contact is like drawing the shades on the windows of communication. It suggests you don't care about the person you are talking to, or that you're afraid of them, or that you're trying to put something over on them. Little eye contact can communicate a desire to hide something (Osborn & Osborn, 1994). In fact, studies have shown quite clearly that when people are required to lie, or have been encouraged to cheat, their deception is accompanied by an averted gaze (Marsh, 1988). Some people, however, have learned to hide their emotions to manipulate others. They are practiced at lying while maintaining eye contact. So the mere fact that someone looks you in the eye is not an unquestioned indicator of honesty or trustworthiness. (Likewise, failure to look you in the eye isn't necessarily a sign of dishonesty, either.)

Body Language

Our bodies say a lot about us in many ways as we communicate. Studies have demonstrated the significance of body language to the communication of attitudes. Words are a minor contributor (only about 10%) to one's perception of attitudes. Vocal qualities reveal much more (30%) of what we think and feel. But body language (a combination of gestures, posture, facial expressions, patterns of eye contact, and touch) conveys attitudes more readily (60%) than words and vocal qualities combined (Covey, 1989).

Body language is often called *kinesic code,* a package of behaviors that are classified as emblems, illustrators, regulators, affect displays, and adaptors. They may be displayed through movement of the head, the arms and hands, the torso, or the legs and feet, and serve important communication functions.

Types of Body Movements

Posture. The first important kinesic behavior is posture, which involves positioning and movement of the body. Posture communicates interest, respect, and openness to ideas, and it can change from moment to moment in a social encounter. Changes in posture can send nonverbal messages. For example, if someone stands up suddenly, that movement may signal "I'm done now," while turning one's back says, "I'm no longer interested."

The most common messages conveyed by posture indicate levels of interest or agreement. When we disagree with what is being said, we use

Common Postural Cues and Their Interpretation

Slumped posture	Low spirits
Erect posture	High spirits, energy, and confidence
Lean forward	Open and interested
Lean away	Defensive or disinterested
Crossed arms	Defensive
Uncrossed arms	Willingness to listen

closed postures: holding trunk and head straight and folding the arms, or, if sitting, crossing the legs above the knee. A more neutral posture is conveyed by hands folded in the lap and legs crossed at the knee. When we agree, we are more likely to have open postures: leaning head and trunk to one side and leaving the legs uncrossed.

An interested listener typically leans forward (if seated, he or she also will draw his or her legs back). When interest fades, the head begins to turn while the trunk and legs straighten. When a listener is bored, the head may begin to lean and require support from a hand. Complete boredom is signaled by letting the head drop and leaning the body backward with legs outstretched.

Transition from one body position to another carries the most significant meaning. If a person spends the entire conversation leaning forward, that may be just a matter of comfort. But if the same person starts out leaning back and then gradually leans forward as the conversation progresses, that's nonverbal communication.

Most people can more easily read postural cues than they can consciously produce them. Being aware of them can help overcome the gap between reactions you *want* to communicate and those you *can* communicate on the occasions you need them (as in a job interview, for example, or trying to give encouragement to a respected but boring speaker).

Hand Gestures. Gestures, or movements of hands, arms, and fingers, are used to describe or emphasize. One type of hand movement, called the baton gesture, actually beats time to what you or someone else is saying. Baton gestures put emphasis on what is being said, add punctuation to verbal communication, and remove ambiguities. Some people use gestures, or talk with their hands, much more freely than others, but speech and gesture are closely bound together for almost everyone. One way to see the strong connection between the two is to watch someone speaking on the telephone. Even though the person on the other end of the line cannot see body movements and gestures, it is almost impossible to talk without them (Marsh, 1988).

Some gestures, however, can be an obstacle to successful interaction. Watch out for hands and fingers that take on a life of their own, fidgeting with themselves or other objects such as pens, paper, or your hair. Pen tapping is interpreted as the action of an impatient person. Rubbing the palms together or clasping hands are signs of nervousness or anxiety.

Body Gestures. Nonverbal signals communicated by moving your body are called body gestures. We may move the entire body to change the mood or pace of a conversation, to draw attention, or to reinforce an idea. Here are some examples of body gestures:

Rapidly nodding your head can leave the impression that you are impatient and eager to add something to the conversation. Slower nodding emphasizes interest, shows that you are validating the comments of your conversation partner, and subtly encourages him or her to continue. Tilting the head slightly, when combined with eye contact and a natural smile, demonstrates friendliness and approachability.

Smiling is one of the most powerful positive body signals in your arsenal. Offer an unforced, confident smile as frequently as opportunity and circumstances dictate. But avoid grinning idiotically; this will only communicate that you are either insincere or not quite on the right track.

It's worth noting that the mouth provides a seemingly limitless supply of opportunities to convey weakness. This may be done by touching the mouth frequently and unconsciously; faking a cough when confused with a difficult question; or gnawing on the lips absentmindedly. Employing any of these insincerity signs will confirm or instill suspicions about your honesty and effectiveness.

Some foot signals can have negative connotations. Women and men wearing slip-on shoes should beware of dangling the loose shoe from the toes; this can be quite distracting and, as it is a gesture often used to signal physical attraction, has no place in most communication situations. Likewise, avoid compulsive jabbing of the floor, desk, or chair with your foot; this can be perceived as a hostile and angry motion, and is likely to annoy your conversation partner. Rapid tapping of the foot may signal impatience.

Uses of Body Language

Although movements of the body may seem random and not clearly connected to a verbal message, they do serve important communication functions that can be classified as emblems, illustrators, affect displays, regulators, and adaptors (Verderber & Verderber, 1994).

Emblems are body motions that supplement or replace words. Some emblems we know and use daily; others we may not use ourselves but can recognize if others use them; still others require us to discover their meaning. For example, almost all Americans use a nod of the head to signify "yes," or a shrug of the shoulders to signify "I don't care." Some people recognize or understand certain obscene gestures but wouldn't use them themselves. Finally, we may encounter emblems we don't understand because they are gestures that have meaning only for members of a specific group.

Illustrators are movements or gestures that accent or emphasize what is being said. We may emphasize by pounding the table to make a point. We may show the path or direction of thought by moving our hands from one point to another to show the range of ideas we are discussing, We may indicate position by pointing. We may describe by using hands to imitate shape or size ("The fish that got away was this big."). We may use gesture to mimic (waving as we say, "Did you see how she waved at me?").

Affect Displays are movements (usually facial expressions or body responses) that display the nature of a pronounced physical sensation. For instance, when you stub your toe, you not only say "Ouch!", you also make a face that displays the pain you feel. Affect displays are generally unconscious and will take place whether you are with someone else or alone.

Different people have adapted different patterns of affect display (just as some people have mastered control of facial expressions). They may be able to deintensify the display (attempt to look less afraid, less happy, less hurt than they actually are); over-intensify or amplify the display; take neutral positions (or display a poker face—that is, whether they are experiencing joy, fear, or sadness, their displays tend not to vary); and mask displays by showing a reaction that is the opposite of what would be expected (smiling, for example, when one is hurt).

Regulators are nonverbal communication cues that regulate the flow of conversation. They include such movements as shifting eye contact, changes in posture, raised eyebrows, and slight head motions. (Try holding your hand up in a stop gesture the next time someone starts to interrupt you and you'll easily see the regulating effect of body language.) Some nonverbal cues serve more than one function. For example, nodding the head can be an emblem for "yes," but also can be a regulator that means "go on, continue."

Most people are aware of regulators only on the periphery of consciousness—unless they become exaggerated to the point of rudeness. Someone who puts on a coat, picks up things, and heads toward the door is regulating the conversation, but in a fairly noticeable and emphatic way. Usually regulators are not so obvious; we do not know we are using them and don't necessarily notice when others do so.

Adaptors are nonverbal efforts to satisfy personal needs that arise as people relate to each other. They are difficult to define because they change from person to person and situation to situation. We employ adaptors based on previous experience with someone, by changing body posture, gestures, facial expression, and amount of eye contact to suit our perception of the other's degree of comfort. Some researchers believe that we are attracted or repelled by others based on their adaptive behaviors.

Proxemics

Proxemics is the study of informal space—the amount of space around or between us and others. How closely people position themselves to each other during a discussion communicates the type of relationship that exists be-

Distance	Type of Space	Uses
0–18 inches	intimate space	interactions with family and close friends
18 inches to 4 feet	personal space	most interpersonal interactions
4–12 feet	social-consultative space	more formal interactions
more than 12 feet	public space	large audience interactions

tween the two people. This space and meaning differ from culture to culture, but in American culture the following standards generally apply:

Intimate distance is the one that should be of greatest concern. People become uncomfortable if an outsider violates the 18-inch circle reserved for family or intimate friends.

A number of factors influence the way people use space, as well as the ways they defend it. Here are some examples of the effect of power, gender, and culture on space:

✓ In almost all cultures, high-status people are given more space than low-status people.

✓ Aggressive people tend to take up—and are granted—more space than less dominant people.

✓ Men generally occupy more personal space than women.

✓ A woman's intimate space tends to be violated more frequently than a man's.

✓ Extroverts take up more space than introverts.

As these examples suggest, not only do more powerful people take up more space and freely invade the intimate space of others, but less powerful people actually yield space to them. You can give an impression of personal power if you simple occupy more space than someone else when you sit or stand and if you do not move out of the way or allow someone else to enter your personal space. You also are more likely to sit or stand closer to someone you feel positive about (Elsea, 1984).

Touching, too, can be a very powerful communicator, especially for establishing a link to a receiver or conveying emotion. A strong handshake may acknowledge equality, while a limp handshake may signal lack of interest or timidity. One of the dangers of communicating via touch, however, is the fact that it invades a person's intimate space and may be perceived as an unwanted intrusion. Because power, gender, and status play such significant roles in the use and perception of tactile communication, it is important to pay attention to the other person's nonverbal cues before deciding to initiate a touch. In most cases, it is best to limit tactile communication to a firm handshake when meeting someone you have not met before or do not know well.

Using Nonverbal Communication to Your Advantage

Body language is more meaningful when several expressions take place at the same time. For example, the combination of leaning forward, nodding, and smiling is a strong indication of agreement and openness. Most meaningful is a matched set of gestures that also agree with what the person is saying.

The main problem with interpreting nonverbal language, however, is that it is dangerous to draw conclusions from single actions. For example, crossed arms are said to indicate distance or defensiveness, but they could also mean that the person is chilly or just striking a comfortable pose. Interpreting an isolated action is a little like taking a word or sentence out of context; it changes the meaning. In order to read body language accurately, it is necessary to consider all of the evidence: eye contact, body positioning, facial expression, and appearance.

Here are some things to keep in mind as you pay greater attention to nonverbal signals—both those you receive from others and those you convey yourself. Also see the chapters on active listening and cross-cultural communication for more information on how to monitor and interpret nonverbal communication behaviors.

1. Become aware. Pay attention to what others communicate nonverbally. Examine what you convey with your own facial expressions, posture, and gestures. Note when someone misinterprets what you have said and look for ways in which nonverbal communication might have affected your message (Carter & Kravitz, 1996).

2. Don't contradict your words with body language. Watch out for saying things with your body that run counter to what you speak. The mixed message can confuse your listener and may make you appear to be dishonest (Carter & Kravitz, 1996).

3. Know what your face says. Facial expression may be the most controllable nonverbal cue, but it is also the one others use to gauge your attitude, feelings and emotional state. You may be able to fool yourself into feeling better than you do simply by smiling (Elsea, 1984).

4. Smiling and head nodding are the most powerful nonverbal cues in social attraction. A blank expression ranks lowest in terms of attractiveness, power, and credibility.

5. Direct eye contact is more powerful than averting the eyes. If you're uncomfortable about making direct eye contact, look at the other person's forehead or hairline.

6. Gesture with purpose.

7. Establish your intimate space and deal assertively with those who violate it.

8. Touch appropriately and deal assertively with those who touch you inappropriately.

9. Note cultural differences. Certain aspects of body language are interpreted differently from culture to culture. In some cultures, casual acquaintances stand very close to each other when speaking; in others only intimate, personal relationships would allow such closeness. American culture encourages eye contact as a sign of honesty and openness; other cultures may interpret too much eye contact as a sign of dominance or disrespect. Let the context of the conversation help you determine what type and degree of body language is appropriate. Take your cues from the person you are talking to (Carter & Kravitz, 1996).

10. Occasionally monitor your nonverbal cues. Look at yourself in a mirror, on videotape, or in photographs to examine your body language. Or ask a close friend to give you feedback about the nonverbal signals you send.

The Vocabulary of Body Language

This list provides you with some common body language terms and their generally accepted meanings:

Nonverbal Behavior	Interpretation
Brisk, erect walk	Confidence
Standing with hands on hips	Readiness, aggression
Sitting with legs crossed, foot kicking slightly	Boredom
Arms crossed on chest	Defensiveness
Walking with hands in pockets, shoulders hunched	Dejection
Hand to cheek	Evaluation, thinking
Touching, slightly rubbing nose	Rejection, doubt, lying
Rubbing the eye	Doubt, disbelief
Hands clasped behind back	Anger, frustration, apprehension
Locked ankles	Apprehension
Head resting in hand, eyes downcast	Boredom
Rubbing hands	Anticipation
Sitting with hands clasped behind head, legs crossed	Confidence, superiority
Open palm	Sincerity, openness, innocence
Pinching bridge of nose, eyes closed	Negative evaluation
Tapping or drumming fingers	Impatience
Steepling fingers	Authoritative
Patting or fondling hair	Lack of self-confidence; insecurity
Tilted head, lean forward	Interest
Stroking chin	Trying to make a decision
Looking down, face turned away	Disbelief
Biting nails	Insecurity, nervousness
Pulling or tugging at ear	Indecision

(Seitz, 1996)

Face Off

Purpose To illustrate the effect of facial expression on the ability to communicate accurately.

Activity Work in a small group. Each person say one of these phrases in turn, keeping your face as expressionless as possible.

I am absolutely delighted by your gift.

I don't know when I've been this excited.

We don't need to beg for change—we need to demand change.

All this puts me in a very bad mood.

Discussion

What effect does lack of facial expression have on the message to be delivered?

Repeat your phrase, this time exaggerating facial expression.

Now what effects do you notice? On vocal quality? On other body language?

EXERCISE
No Body Talking

Purpose To demonstrate the effect on listeners when speakers do not pay attention to body language.

Activity Form pairs, designating one of you as the speaker and the other as the listener. If you are the speaker, tell your partner about your family (talk for two minutes) without changing your expression, with no direct eye contact and no gestures. If you are the listener, try to actively listen—that is, use eye contact, body position, facial expression, etc., as you listen to your partner.

Discussion

Now join two other dyads to form a group of six. Discuss how it felt (if you were the speaker) to talk without using body language. If you were the listener, how did the lack of body language affect you? What signals did you perceive the speaker to be sending? Can it truly be said that in this situation there was *no* body language at all?

EXERCISE
Hand Gestures

Adapted from Suler, 1996.

Purpose To illustrate the range of hand gestures that are part of our common non-verbal vocabulary.

Activity In five minutes, make a list of as many hand gestures as you can think of. Also describe their meaning.

Discussion

How do facial expressions and other body movements influence the meaning of a hand gesture? What do hand gestures mean in different cultures?

EXERCISE
Party Body Behavior

Adapted from Suler, 1996.

Purpose To illustrate the effect of context on body language.

Activity As a group, create and perform a mini role play of various people at a typical college party.

Discussion

What personality types can you detect just by how people use their bodies? What are the obvious and subtle behaviors of the braggart, the flirt, the wallflower, the drunk, etc.? Consider such factors as personal space, posture, eye contact, speed, and angle of movement.

EXERCISE
Mirroring

Adapted from Suler, 1996.

Purpose   To sensitize you to the details of body movement and expression and to see the influence of interpersonal styles on body language and nonverbal communication.

Activity   Work with a partner. Complete this exercise without talking.

Step 1: Either sitting or standing, Person A should take the lead and begin to move in any way you wish. Use both obvious and subtle behaviors. Person B should follow or mimic everything the leader does.

Step 2: After a minute, switch roles.

Step 3: Do the exercise one last time except that *no one* is the leader or the follower. Both of you should try to move in unison, as if you are mirroring each other simultaneously in a body language "dance." This is somewhat hard to do and takes a bit of practice before you get the hang of it, if you can do it at all. If you are successful, what usually happens is that there are rapid, minute shifts between leading and following.

Note: Mirroring can be done with body language alone, facial expressions alone, or body language with facial expressions. This last one is considerably more difficult to do than the first two.

Discussion

What did you notice about the intricacies of movement and facial expression? Did you prefer to lead or to follow? Were you comfortable or did you find it hard to focus? Did you find moving in unison easy or not? What did the exercise tell you about the ability to work in sync with someone?

EXERCISE
Improvised Role Plays

Adapted from Suler, 1996.

Purpose To demonstrate the power of nonverbal language as a medium for communication.

Activity Divide into small groups.

Step 1: As a group, create a role play that involves only body language and no talking. You can pick any scene and characters you want (or use a situation your instructor provides). Do not over-plan the role play. Instead, pick a scene, define the characters in the scene, and think of a few possibilities for events that might occur in the scene. Then improvise within that general structure.

Step 2: Each group takes a turn at improvising a scene in front of the whole class. You set up the role play by telling the class where the scene is taking place and who is in the scene. Another interesting and fun alternative is to provide no introduction to the role play and let the class guess what is happening in the scene.

Discussion

After each role play, discuss what you believe was happening in the scene based on what you saw in the body language. What are the personalities of the people, their relationships with each other, the issues affecting them, etc.?

EXERCISE
The Interview

Purpose To help you recognize your own nonverbal behaviors in order to determine which are effective and ineffective.

Activity You will role play a job interview. The open position is shift manager for Burger Dream, a fast-food restaurant. Duties include scheduling workers, supervising the shift, accounting for and depositing receipts at the end of the shift, periodically evaluating employees, and writing daily reports and employee evaluation reports.

Divide into groups of four or five. Within each group, assign these roles: interviewer, applicant, and observers (two or three). Be sure the person assigned the applicant role has some real-life experience that can qualify him or her for the shift manager position.

Step 1: 10-minute planning. All interviewers get together and decide on a scenario for a hypothetical job interview. Make a list of questions to ask and important things to tell the applicants. All applicants get together and discuss specific skills and relevant experience you have that qualify you for the position. All observers take a 10-minute break.

Step 2: Return to your groups and conduct the role play. Observers should take careful notes during the course of the interview, paying close attention to nonverbal behaviors of both the interviewer and the applicant. Take no more than 10 minutes for the role play.

Discussion

1. *Applicant:* Analyze the way you presented yourself in the interview. How do you believe you were perceived? What nonverbal behaviors were you aware of that you think helped make a positive impression? Any that made a negative impression?

2. *Interviewer:* How were you impressed with the nonverbal behaviors of the applicant? Did your perceptions match the impressions of the applicant?

3. *Observers:* Did you notice the same nonverbal cues (positive and negative) that the applicants and interviewers mentioned? Did you see any others?

4. *All:* Generate a list of tips (Dos and Don'ts) for nonverbal communication in a job interview.

FURTHER ACTIVITY

Journal Writing

1. How do you dress for different occasions (class, home, job, social events, professional meetings, etc.)? What nonverbal messages do your clothes convey?

2. Reflect back on a time when someone told you something you believed to be untrue. What nonverbal cues reinforced your perception? In what nonverbal ways did you react?

3. Analyze a sequence from a favorite movie, paying close attention to the body language of the characters. Classify the body movements as emblems, illustrators, regulators, affect displays, and adaptors. Were the cues consistent with the emotions the characters were feeling?

4. Do one of the mirror exercises with a close friend and describe how you felt and what you learned about the role nonverbal communication plays in your relationship.

5. Interview a student from another culture. Talk about differences in nonverbal communication between his or her culture and yours. What are the implications of these differences in trying to develop a relationship with a person from that culture?

6. Do some people-watching. Select a category of persons (teachers, supermarket clerks, fellow students, fans at a sporting event) and within that group notice similarities and differences in nonverbal behavior. What do you discern about thoughts, feelings, and attitudes based on nonverbal cues?

7. Observe several pairs of persons together (walking on campus, sitting in a restaurant, etc.). Using the distances of proxemics, can you guess the nature of their relationship by how close they are to each other?

LEARNING POINTS

✓ Nonverbal communication carries significant weight in our communication with others—sometimes much more weight than our words.

✓ 75 to 90 percent of the information we gather from others is nonverbal in nature.

✓ Nonverbal channels include (but are not limited to) physical appearance, facial expressions, eye contact, body language, and proxemics.

✓ We have the most control over our appearance, and people respond to appearance almost immediately, in terms of its appropriateness for the communication context.

✓ Facial expressions convey six basic emotions: happiness, anger, sadness, disgust, surprise, and fear.

✓ Some people can control facial expressions voluntarily, allowing them to suppress emotional displays or mask negative feelings.

✓ The nature and degree of eye contact sends a number of messages. We avoid eye contact when the subject of a discussion makes us uncomfortable. In American culture, eye contact denotes honesty and credibility.

✓ Body language is called kinesic code, a package of behaviors classified as emblems, illustrators, regulators, affect displays, and adaptors.

✓ Primary types of body movements are posture, hand gestures, and body gestures.

✓ Posture is the position of one's body that communicates degrees of respect, interest, and openness.

✓ Transition from one body position to another often carries more meaning than the position itself.

✓ Baton gestures are hand gestures that keep time with what someone is saying, punctuate conversations, and remove ambiguity.

✓ Body gestures like head nodding, smiling, and foot tapping can be used to change the mood or pace of a conversation, draw attention, or reinforce ideas.

✓ Emblems are body motions that supplement or replace words.

✓ Illustrators are movements that accent or emphasize what is being said.

✓ Affect displays are movements that display the nature of a pronounced physical sensation.

✓ Regulators are nonverbal cues that regulate the flow of conversations.

✓ Adaptors are nonverbal efforts to adapt to the particular needs of people in particular communication situations.

✓ Proxemics is the study of the amount of space around or between people.

✓ The way people use space is affected by a number of factors, including culture, status, gender, and personality type.

✓ Touching can be a powerful communication tool, but generally should be limited to a handshake if you do not know the other person well.

✓ It is dangerous to draw conclusions from single nonverbal cues; body language is more meaningful when several expressions take place at the same time.

REFERENCES

Carter, C., and Kravitz, S. L. (1996). *Keys to success: How to achieve your goals.* Upper Saddle River, NJ: Prentice Hall.

Covey, S. R. (1989). *The seven habits of highly effective people.* New York: Simon & Schuster.

Elsea, J. G. (1984). *The four-minute sell.* New York: Simon & Schuster.

Marsh, P. (Ed.) (1988). *Eye to eye: How people interact.* Boston: Salem House Publishers.

Osborn, M., and Osborn, S. (1994). *Public speaking* (3rd ed.). Boston: Houghton Mifflin.

Seitz, V. A. (1996). Your executive image. [Online] Available: http://www.careercity.com/edge/getjob/prep/dress/dress4.htm. Adams Media Corporation.

Suler, J. (1996). Body language. *Teaching Clinical Psychology.* [Online] Available: http://www1.rider.edu/~suler/bodylang.html. Lawrenceville, NJ: Rider University.

Verderber, R. F., and Verderber, K. S. (1995). *Inter-Act: Using interpersonal skills* (7th ed.) Belmont, CA: Wadsworth.

Chapter 4

PERCEPTION

People only see what they are prepared to see.
—Ralph Waldo Emerson

ADVANCE PLANNER: PERCEPTION

When you complete this chapter, you will be able to:

✓ Evaluate the accuracy of your perceptions.

✓ Compare your perceptions of behavioral traits with the perceptions of your peers.

✓ Describe how people form perceptions.

✓ Identify where perceptions originate.

✓ Debate the role of culture and gender in forming perceptions.

✓ Distinguish between self-perceptions and metaperceptions.

To accomplish these objectives, you will complete some or all of these activities:

1. Discuss a case study to examine the accuracy of your perceptions regarding culture, behavioral traits, and gender.

2. Complete an exercise designed to help you determine which behavioral traits you most value and compare your perceptions with those of your peers.

3. Complete an exercise to describe your self-perceptions (beliefs) and meta-perceptions about leadership.

4. Write in your journal about your perceptions of a newly acquired friend, or explain how an event caused you to perceive someone in one way, only later to discover that your perception was inaccurate.

5. Interview an elected state or county official to determine his or her perceptions about leadership.

A CASE STUDY IN ACCURACY OF PERCEPTION

The Job Interview Workshop

As a service to the students in your college, the Student Advisory Board is sponsoring a workshop on resume development and job interviews. You made all the arrangements and organized a 30-minute session on interviewing for 10 a.m. Ms. Black Wolf, your favorite professor, is making the presentation to 30 students. During her presentation the following events occur:

✓ Two unshaven, poorly dressed students arrive five minutes late. They walk to the front of the room, talking audibly and making noise as they take their places. Ms. Black Wolf raises her voice in an effort to be heard and regain the audience's attention.

✓ A male and a female student sitting next to each other frequently whisper to one another.

✓ Two students of Asian heritage are constantly raising their hands and trying to ask questions. After several interruptions, Ms. Black Wolf walks over and whispers something to the students.

✓ When Ms. Black Wolf's presentation is finished, the audience responds with 15 seconds of loud applause.

Discussion Questions

1. As a member of the Student Advisory Council and the organizer of this event, how would you perceive the success of the presentation?

2. What do you think of the two students who arrived late? What might be their excuse?

3. What is going on with the whispering students? What are they discussing?

4. What do you think Ms. Black Wolf said to the two students who were constantly asking questions?

5. What role do you think culture plays in your perceptions about the participants?

6. Do your answers to these questions differ from those of your classmates? Discuss your differences and why they occurred.

INTRODUCTION TO THEORIES OF PERCEPTION

George Gissing writes in *The Private Papers of Henry Ryecroft* (1927): "It is the mind which creates the world about us, and even though we stand side by side in the same meadow, my eye will never see what is beheld by yours, my heart will never stir to emotions with which yours is touched."

Perception is the mental process of observing the outer physical world and processing that information into patterns meaningful to the brain, to fit the environment of our inner world. The brain is a pattern-making organism that is always processing information the conscious mind receives from the physical world, in order to make sense of it. The brain associates unfamiliar information with what it already knows in an attempt to understand or to create new personal knowledge (Caine & Caine, 1991). Thus, the brain is engaged in the process of assigning meaning to sensory input. The process represents a comparison between reality and one's *perception* of reality, or one's truths about reality.

Consider the experiences of the speaker and his stepmother in the following story and think about what the story says about different realities.

One day my newly acquired stepmother, who had not spent a great deal of time in the country, came running into the hay field where I was swathing hay. In a state of excitement she shouted "Did you see the flying saucer?" "What flying saucer, and where?" I asked. "Up on the hill by the dump," she replied. "I saw it three different times, about two minutes apart." Not knowing what to think, I suggested she wait by the pickup at the edge of the field and I would watch for something as I moved closer to the area with the swather. Reluctantly she agreed and I continued swathing hay, envisioning all kinds of strange things as I approached the area my stepmother had indicated. However, I saw nothing unusual until I turned the corner at the end of the field, and out of the corner of my eye, I saw a flash of something on the hill. I immediately stopped and watched the area for about five minutes. I saw nothing more until the next time I turned the corner and the flash of light was there again. Now I was really concerned, yet afraid to go to where the flash of light had occurred. I continued to watch the area as I moved around the field, observing nothing until I began to turn the corner again. Once more the flash of light appeared. I stopped the swather immediately; the light also stopped and remained in the same spot. As I climbed down from the swather, I noticed the sun reflecting off a large piece of shiny metal near the rear of the machine. As I moved the shiny metal, the bright spot on the hill also moved. The cause of the flying saucer had been discovered.

In this story, two people formed the same perception of a visual image, leading them to believe one thing when another was true. Perceptions are fundamental to our forming opinions about ourselves, others, and reality. What factors determine our understanding of reality? To answer this question, we must look at the process by which perceptions are created. Because perception is a mental process, it is difficult to describe exactly; but we can examine its elements and come to a closer understanding of how perception develops and the role it plays in our lives.

A Model of Perception

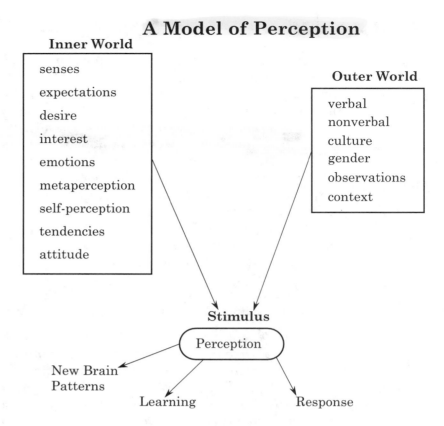

Inner World

- senses
- expectations
- desire
- interest
- emotions
- metaperception
- self-perception
- tendencies
- attitude

Outer World

- verbal
- nonverbal
- culture
- gender
- observations
- context

Stimulus

Perception

New Brain Patterns

Learning

Response

Elements of Perception

Perception involves the interaction of the outer world with our inner world. Kenny (1981) suggests perception depends on three components: the effect on the person observing the behavior, the effect on the person acting, and the observer's unique reaction to the behavior. Research in the area of perception suggests that many factors—stemming from both the inner and outer worlds—play roles in forming perceptions (see A Model of Perception, above). The inner world factors are: metaperception (an individual's awareness of others' judgment of him or her), self-perception, the five senses, expectations, desire, interest, emotions, attitude, readiness, and tendencies. The outer world factors most frequently mentioned as influencing perceptions are: observable traits, verbal and nonverbal communication, context or situation, culture, and gender (Verderber & Verderber, 1992; Haney, 1979).

Inner World

We gather information about the physical world through our five senses. Our expectations about an event influence the sensory input, as do our degree of desire to know about it and interest in it. The context in which the event is occurring, our emotions and attitudes, as well as the ambiguity of certain kinds of input, all influence what bits of sensory data we respond to.

The ability of our sensory system to take in information is unique to each of us. Some people may be hearing- or vision-impaired. Their perceptions, then, may not accurately represent reality because of different or inaccurate sensory input. Some people like the taste of spinach and others dislike it. Is this due to differences in sensory information—taste of spinach—or expectations of the taster? If the spinach came from the same plant and was prepared in the same pan, we can eliminate the flavor as the deciding factor.

If we were to give the spinach to two people who had never tasted spinach before, we could eliminate the expectation factor. Given these conditions, if the two people described different flavors, we would conclude that their ability to taste was different due to sensory input. If you dislike spinach, is there anything anyone can do to make you eat spinach? Probably not, because you perceive what you expect to perceive: Spinach does not taste good. Yet other people love the taste of spinach.

The desire to be loved leads us to ask another for a date, based on our perceived interest in and desire to get to know the other person. Frequently, we discover that our perceptions are incorrect and the other person is not as interesting or as desirable as we had originally thought. Factors that may influence our perception of the other person as desirable are our emotions and attitude at the time of perception formation and the context in which the observation occurs. After breaking up with someone, we may consciously try to avoid a similar person because we perceive that someone who looks and acts like the person we broke up with will be like that person. We perceive that someone different would be better for us and set out to find that type of person. We may find that again our perception has not accurately reflected reality.

Our tendencies and past experience influence our perceptions by causing us to associate ideas with sensory data in the same ways we associated them in the past. Some of us tend to give more credence to an idea if it comes from a person of status rather than from a peer, yet both people may have expressed exactly the same idea. We may see a tall, muscular high school student and assume he is a football or basketball player because we associate the young man's physical characteristics with those sports. We may view a new employee as incompetent and lacking knowledge because we assume that someone new to an organization knows very little about the workplace.

Context

Perception is influenced by our association of characteristics with groups in a given context. For instance, a theory of perception in the area of leadership suggests that it is the result of an interaction of three elements: the leadership characteristics, the follower's perception, and the characteristics of the situation (Hollander & Julian, 1969). This suggests that an individual can display or express certain characteristics in a given context. If the characteristics fit an existing contextual brain pattern of the observer, the person is viewed as a leader in that context. However, if the situation is different from the one in which the perceiver formed the original pattern, the observer may not perceive the person as a leader in the new situation.

Metaperception

Metaperception is the ability to look beyond our immediate perceptions of ourselves to what others think of us. If I think that you think I am a good person, then I am generally accurate in that metaperception. However, if I think that you do not view me as a good person, then I must try to modify the behavior that led you to this conclusion.

Metaperception appears to serve a regulator role in our social interaction (Laing et al., 1966). Thus, it represents our attitudes, habits, and comfort zones. It forms our truths. Some individuals know how others generally perceive them, but do not know how other specific individuals perceive them. At times our metaperceptions may be unrealistic and based on inferences rather than fact. However, some researchers believe that our metaperceptions are generally correct.

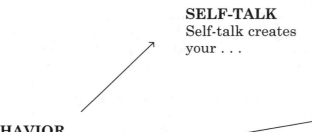

SELF-TALK
Self-talk creates
your . . .

SELF-PERCEPTION
Subconscious data
determines your . . .

BEHAVIOR
Experiences, successes,
and failures produce your . . .

Initially, at basic levels of perception, we focus on traits and behaviors we perceive as appropriate to a role in a particular context. As we age and have more experiences, we begin to look for different information in forming perceptions and are able to use available cues more fully and efficiently.

Self-Perception

The terms *self-perception* and *metaperception* may be confusing, but they are different. Self-perception focuses on how we view ourselves and does not involve what others think of us. How do we develop a perception of self? Self-perception develops as we participate in activities and then evaluate our own performance. Based on our one-sided analysis and impression of ourselves, we form a self-perception. Self-talk is critical in helping us form a self-perception. Self-talk not only helps develop self-perceptions, but also contributes to the development of the belief that in turn influences how we perform. (See Chapter 5, Self-Concept and Self-Esteem.)

Feedback from others seems like a logical building block of self-perception. Yet Kenny and DePaulo (1993) suggest that our self-perception is based primarily on how we perceive ourselves, independent of what others think. Nonverbal communication may play a role in providing information to help us make decisions. On the other hand, the brain does not always take in all information available to it. Even if someone were to tell us about our performance, we likely have already formed a perception about our performance. Hence we do not need others to tell us how we have done.

Expectation

A number of years ago, research by Rosenthal (1993) connected expected behavior with performance. Rosenthal used a story from classical mythology to explain how our perceptions of others can influence their behavior. In the myth, Pygmalion, a sculptor, created a statue of a beautiful woman, Galatea, and then fell in love with her. He wished so fervently that she were real that eventually Galatea became a real person. Rosenthal called the influence of perception on behavior the *Pygmalion effect*. The Pygmalion effect is the same as self-fulfilling prophecy—that is, a person will perform at a given level of expectation. In other words, if you raise your expected level of performance, you will generally perform at the new level (Eden, 1993). Likewise, if expectation is low, then you may very well not reach a higher level. For example, if your teacher thinks you are hopeless at math, he or she may not offer you much assistance, and thus your self-perception will reinforce your lack of confidence in your ability to do mathematics. Therefore, how others treat you can have impact on your expectations for yourself and your subsequent behavior. If you are the teacher or leader, your behavior toward others, based on the expectation you have for them, can influence your students' or followers' perceptions of themselves and their behaviors.

What is more important in forming a perception—the perceiver or the one perceived? Markus and Zajonc (1985) suggest that the feeling or attitude of the perceiver (affect) plays a significant, if not major, role in determining judgments about others. This is supported by Kenny and LaVoie (1984) when they conclude that the perceiver contributes almost as much to the perception as the person being observed.

If you and I were to observe a person working in a certain situation, we may not reach the same conclusion about the person's ability. Thus, if two people observe the same behavior and do not reach the same conclusions about the performance, it follows that perceptions are determined by the observed behavior.

For example, your boss may observe you with your head on your desk. You may be solving a complex mathematical equation, but your boss may conclude you are sleeping and perhaps label you as lazy. The observer is influenced by generalizations about workers who rest their heads on desks (sleeping, not thinking). To reverse such a perception may be very difficult, even if you can provide proof that you were indeed solving an equation. Likewise, making first impressions in job interviews, introducing new co-workers, or meeting strangers at social events can be governed more by the observer's perceptions than by the behavior of those in the spotlight.

If much of the decision is made by the perceiver, how can a person influence the perceptions of others? We are currently unsure what makes a better perception receiver. Experience in observing others is usually helpful but may not be accurate in certain situations. If we cannot say for sure how to influence the way others perceive our own behavior, we can at least heed advice about making good first impressions in job interviews, at work, or in meeting new people.

Perception of Others

Self-fulfilling prophecy may be one way we influence our own self-perception and consequent behavior. How we perceive others is equally important, but most of us are limited information processors. We take many shortcuts in forming expectations about other peoples' traits and behaviors. We develop bias because we do not take in all the information available to us or we do an incomplete analysis to build our perception. Hastie and Park (1986) assert that most judgments about someone's characteristics or traits are made spontaneously (without intention) during social interactions using information readily available from stimuli or working memory. Perceptions can be formed when our attention and motivation are focused on task activities. Thus, we build perceptions automatically with very little cognitive thought, based on traits and behaviors in a given context.

Our ability to think about or discuss a topic also involves controlled processes—processes that require awareness, intent, and effort and do not interfere with other activities (Hasler & Zacks, 1979). Lord (1985) suggests that we can make perceptions based on qualities and behaviors revealed through normal day-to-day interaction with others, or from inferences we draw from the outcomes of significant events. The inferential perception is based on events and appears to be a logical cause-and-effect analysis. In addition, Lord and Maher (1991) suggest that event-based perceptions arise from the successful completion of some task. For example, the financial turnaround of the Chrysler Company caused most of us to perceive Lee Iacocca as a leader, even though we had no personal knowledge of him as an individual.

Just as the inner world influences perception, observations from the outer world also cause us to form certain perceptions. These outer world influences include perceptions others have of us, the verbal and nonverbal behavior we observe in others, gender roles, and culture.

Observable Traits

Our belief system determines the traits we exhibit to others, upon which they base their perceptions about us. For example, if I believe I am an excellent country western dancer, my actions on the dance floor will help others form a perception about my ability as a dancer. Factors that affect the influence of the trait are a set of shared or overlapping experiences, the perceiver's level of acquaintance with the person, and a shared meaning system (Malloy & Janowski, 1992).

Verbal Behavior

The effect of verbal communication on perception is evident. For example, most of us believe a person must be an effective communicator to be a leader. If leadership is inferred from perceived quality of speaking and sociability, judgment on these variables should predict leadership ability. In a study by Sorrentino and Boutillier (1975), the group member who talked the most was perceived as a leader. Malloy and Janowski (1992) found that perceived quality of speech and quality of ideas were significantly associated with leadership. As a result it appears that ability to speak up and share ideas influences the perception of others.

Nonverbal Communication

By a smile or the touch of a hand, people communicate to others their perception of behavior. Our interpretation of those gestures can contribute to self- or metaperceptions. However, we may not correctly interpret the communications. Generally we can understand nonverbal cues under given circumstances. Different contexts, however, may affect the impact of nonverbal communication: multichannel communications (tone, smile, etc.), presence of verbal and nonverbal cues, prior experience with the person, a continuous stream of gestures, length of time the cue is observed, context in which the communication takes place, and recognition versus interpretation (Archer et al., 1993). Because many cues more obvious than the nonverbal are usually present, we may pay more attention to them and ignore nonverbal cues. Hence, the effect of nonverbal communication on our perceptions depends on whether we observe the cues and how we interpret them.

Gender Roles

Gender by itself does not appear to influence self-perception. However, gender and context interact in the formation of perceptions. In Western societies, certain psychological characteristics have traditionally been perceived as either feminine or masculine. Malloy and Janowski (1992) found that men were perceived as showing more leadership than women. The women in that study also believed that they would be judged lower than men on leadership. If a person viewed himself as masculine, others perceived him as masculine and high on the leadership scale. The opposite was found for perceptions of femininity. Wildman and Clementz (1986) found that when males and females observed assertive models on video tape, males would characterize assertiveness as either male or female. Females, however, tended to classify assertive models as masculine. In a study involving 44 male and 46 female university students, females were more likely to select women as leaders than were men (Major et al., 1994). Unfortunately, it appears that gender and traits that imply gender enter the perception-forming process.

Culture

We can expect perceptions to reflect prevailing cultural stereotyping. This notion is supported by the belief that the brain is always trying to make sense of our experiences (Caine & Caine, 1991). Thus, as we live and observe the world around us, we are influenced by the culture. Types of information processed in a certain cultural context can affect perceptions and outcomes. For example, the traits used to identify perceived leaders in the military are different from those in business, national politics, religion, or education. No one set of traits will create perceived leadership ability in all of the professions. Perceived leadership is context-specific. One study revealed that leaders in 11 different contexts or situations did not share the same set of traits (Lord & Maher 1991).

Belief Systems

What happens to all of our perceptions? Perceptions combine with experiences to build a belief system that defines each individual's map of reality, connects feelings to behaviors, and links behaviors to emotions (Levine & Lightburn, 1989). Beliefs may exist separately and independently from each other, but when beliefs share an attribute or a relationship, a system exists. From birth to death we build and change our belief systems based on perceptions or facts. However, belief systems are not easily changed and require a conscious awareness of a specific problem before they can be changed. As mentioned earlier, the brain does not always take in and process all available information. Thus, meta- and self-perceptions can sometimes be inaccurate. Using leadership as an example, an illustration of a leadership belief system is shown below.

Self-Perceptions of Leadership Abilities

LEADERSHIP BELIEF SYSTEM

I can lead	I can conduct a meeting
I am a leader	People look to me for leadership
People respect my opinion	People will follow my leadership

SUPPORTED BY

ATTITUDES	HABITS	COMFORT ZONE
I like helping people	I always go to meetings	I sit at the front of the room
Helping others is fun	I volunteer for committees	I'm comfortable in new situations
Leading is fun	I speak up in meetings	I like being in front of people
People are eager to change	I read to stay informed	I enjoy meetings
I want to improve my club	I arrive early for meetings	

Suppose for a moment that you are about to attend a meeting with a group of strangers. As you enter the cool, smoke-free room, several people gather at the front of the room. You become aware that other people are seated in small groups of two or three around the room. The mind, in trying to make sense out of this information, will go through a five-step process. The steps of the conscious mind process are:

✓ *Perception:* Reception of millions of bits of sensory stimuli information about the environment through the five senses.

✓ *Organization:* Search for patterns, for good form, or for something that looks similar.

✓ *Association:* Comparison of this information with the information or brain pattern that has developed from experiences and been stored in the subconscious.

✓ *Evaluation:* Weighing of the value of the new information.

✓ *Decision:* Determination of whether to take action or to ignore the information.

Several conclusions are likely after following this process. Perceptions stored as patterns in the subconscious would indicate that meetings are conducted from the front of the room; therefore the group in the front of the room must be in charge of the meeting and most likely are the leaders. The other small groups of people must know one another or they arrived at the meeting together.

The decision the mind must make is where the comfort zone of the room is for you. The decision will be based on the belief system that has resulted from your personal experiences. If the belief system places value on sitting close to those conducting the meeting, the conscious mind will decide you should sit toward the front of the room. If your belief system, however, has been shaped by unpleasant experiences associated with sitting at the front of the room, your conscious decision will be to sit toward the back. Thus, perceptions formed in the past serve to control your behavior in the present.

Errors in Perception

Your perceptions of others and the situation around you are basic to your acquiring effective interpersonal skills. If you are aware of how you form perceptions, you can avoid forming hasty opinions of yourself and of others. These are some errors in perception to avoid:

1. *Stereotyping* is a hasty or faulty generalization you form about someone else based on a category or class. It may be based on limited experience or be culturally determined. It is at the heart of prejudice and bias. Some stereotyping may have only prejudice at its heart. When you meet someone from a different cultural background, instead of thinking he or she is "one of those," try to get acquainted through self-disclosure and turn talking.

2. *Halo effect* is a complex picture you form about someone else based on very limited information (Verderber & Verderber, 1992). The halo may be positive or negative. For example, if you meet Jenny and she smiles brightly at you, you may conclude that she is an outgoing, friendly person and someone you would like to know better. Jenny, however, has many more personality traits that may include being timid and grumpy at times. If you meet

Jenny on a bad day, you might decide that she is a rude person. Rather than leaping to conclusions about someone you meet for the first time, let the acquaintanceship move along and unfold as you learn about the other person.

3. *Attribution* is assigning a reason or motive to someone's behavior without further evidence (Verderber & Verderber, 1992). Bill, the boss, notices that Ray, his employee, has come to work late the last three days. Bill confronts Ray on the third day, asking him why he is not more responsible. Bill *attributes* the reason for Ray's lateness to irresponsibility. In such situations, it is better to ask why the behavior is occurring rather than assigning meaning to it. For example, Ray may be late because he is having a sudden child care crisis at home. When the behavior of another is annoying or puzzling, asking that person to clarify the behavior is better than leaping to conclusions about him or her.

Faulty perceptions of ourselves and others can be avoided by practicing good interpersonal skills. These skills, as we have already examined in Chapter 2, Active Listening, provide the foundation upon which to build leadership competencies.

EXERCISE
How I Lead

Purpose   Self-perception and metaperceptions play a large role in perceiving others. The purpose of this activity is for you to examine your self-perception and metaperception and to determine their accuracy.

You Will Need   The activity sheets on the next two pages

Pen or pencil

Activity   Spend 10 minutes completing the self-perception activity sheet. Try to list at least 15 things in each area that you can say about yourself that fit your perceptions of a leader.

After completing the self-perception sheet, turn your attention to the metaperception sheet. Metaperceptions are what you think others think of your leadership traits. Describe or list those things that you think others would say about your leadership.

Select someone you know fairly well and ask him or her to mark those statements that describe your leadership ability and add other descriptors that describe your leadership ability.

Self-Perception of Leadership

(Beliefs about myself as a leader)

	Supported By	
My Attitudes	My Habits	My Comfort Zones

Metaperception of Leadership

(Beliefs about how others see me as a leader)

	Supported By	
My Attitudes	My Habits	My Comfort Zones

FURTHER ACTIVITY

Journal Writing

1. Perceptions develop without our consciously being aware of the process. Make a list of traits you perceive in a new friend. Using this list, describe how you became aware of the traits and the role they had in forming the friendship.

2. What *expectations* did your parents or teachers have for you? How did these expectations serve as a self-fulfilling prophecy for you?

3. Select an event that has happened in your community as a result of strong leadership. Write about what caused you to perceive the individual involved as a leader.

Independent Practice

The purpose of this activity is to explore the behavioral traits that elected public officials perceive as being important in those elected to a public office. You should discover that the traits in this context are different from those in a different context.

Conduct an interview of an elected public official about the traits that are needed to gain public support. To accomplish this you should:

✓ Develop a list of questions to ask.

✓ Make an appointment at least two days in advance. When making the appointment, indicate why you are interested in interviewing this person and the nature of the interview. The interview should not take more than 15–20 minutes.

✓ Write and send a thank-you letter to the interviewee.

✓ Write a one-page summary of your interview.

✓ Be prepared to discuss the traits with classmates.

LEARNING POINTS

✓ Perception is the process of observing the outer physical world and processing that information mentally into patterns meaningful to the brain, our inner world.

✓ The outer world consists of observable traits, verbal and nonverbal communications, context or situation, culture, and gender.

✓ The inner world involves metaperception or the awareness of others' judgment of ourselves, self-perception, the five senses, expectations, desire, interest, emotions, attitude, readiness, and tendencies.

✓ Metaperception, which is our view of what others think of us, regulates our social behavior.

✓ Self-talk, or evaluation and feedback we give ourselves, contributes to formation of our self-perceptions, belief systems, and performance.

✓ Expectation, the perception of our own level of performance in a given task or educational setting, can influence our performance.

✓ An example of perception influenced by the outer world is demonstrated by perceptions of who would make a good leader.

✓ Context or situation determines our perceptions.

✓ The feeling or attitude of the observer plays a major role in judging others.

✓ Perceptions are combined with experiences to form a belief system.

REFERENCES

Archer, D., Akert, R., and Costanzo, M. (1993). The accurate perception of nonverbal behavior: Questions of theory and research design. In B. D. Blanck (Ed.). *Interpersonal expectations: Theory, research and applications* (pp. 242–260). Cambridge, UK: Cambridge University Press.

Caine, R. N., and Caine, G. (1991). *Making connections: Teaching the human brain.* Alexandria, VA: Association for Supervision and Curriculum Development.

Eden, D. (1993). Interpersonal expectations in organizations. In B. D. Blanck (Ed.). *Interpersonal expectations: Theory, research and applications* (pp. 154–178). Cambridge, UK: Cambridge University Press.

Gissing, G. (1927). *The private papers of Henry Ryecroft.* New York: E. P. Dutton & Co.

Haney, W. V. (1979). *Communication and interpersonal relations: Text and cases* (4th ed.). Homewood, IA: Richard D. Irwin, Inc.

Hasler, L., and Zacks, R. T. (1979). Automatic and effortful processes in memory. *Journal of Experimental Psychology, 108,* 356–388.

Hastie, R., and Park, B. (1986). The relation between memory and judgment depends on whether the judgment task is memory-based or on-line. *Psychological Review, 93,* 258–68.

Hollander, E. P., and Julian, J. W. (1969). Contemporary trends in the analysis of leadership process. *Psychological Bulletin, 71,* 387–397.

Kenny, D. A. (1981). Interpersonal perceptions: A multivariate round robin analysis. In M. B. Brewer and B. E. Collins (Eds.). *Scientific inquiry in the social sciences* (pp. 228–309). San Francisco: Jossey-Bass.

Kenny, D. A., and DePaulo, B. M. (1993). Do people know how others view them? An empirical and theoretical account. *Psychological Bulletin, 114,* 145–161.

Kenny, D. A., and LaVoie, L. (1984) The social relations model. In L. Berkowitz (Ed.). *Advances in experimental social psychology* (pp. 18, 142–182). Orlando, FL: Academic Press.

Laing, R. D., Phillipson, H., and Lee, A. R. (1966). *Interpersonal perception: A theory and method of research.* New York: Springer.

Levine, K. G., and Lightburn, A. (1989). Belief systems and social work practice. *Social Casework, 70,* 139–145.

Lord, R. G. (1985). An information processing approach to social perceptions, leadership, and behavioral measurements in organizations. In B. M. Staw and L. L. Cummings (Eds.). *Research in organizational behavior* (pp. 7, 87–128). Greenwich, CT: JAI Press.

Lord, R. G., and Maher, K. J. (1991). *Leadership and information processing: Linking perceptions and performance.* Boston: Unwin Hyman.

Major, B., Feinstein, J., and Crocker, J. (1994). Attributional ambiguity of affirmative action. *Basic and Applied Social Psychology, 5,* 113–141.

Malloy, T. E., and Janowski, C. L. (1992). Perceptions and metaperceptions of leadership: Components, accuracy and dispositional correlates. *Personality & Social Psychology Bulletin, 18,* 700–708.

Markus, H., and Zajonc, R. B. (1985). The cognitive perspective in social psychology. In G. Lindsey and E. Aronson (Eds.). *The handbook of social psychology* (3rd ed.) (pp. 1, 137–230). New York: Random House.

Rosenthal, R. (1993). Interpersonal expectations: Some antecedents and some consequences. In B. D. Blanck (Ed.). *Interpersonal expectations: Theory, research and applications* (pp. 3–24). Cambridge, UK: Cambridge University Press.

Sorrentino, R. M., and Boutillier, R. G. (1975). The effect of quality on quantity of verbal interaction on ratings of leadership ability. *Journal of Experimental Social Psychology, 11,* 403–411.

Verderber, R. F., and Verderber, K. (1992). *Inter-act: Using interpersonal communications skills* (6th ed.). Belmont, CA: Wadsworth Publishing Company.

Wildman, B. G., and Clementz, B. (1986). Assertive, empathic assertive and conversational behavior: Perceptions of likability, effectiveness and sex role. *Behavior Modification, 10,* 315–331.

SELF-CONCEPT AND SELF-ESTEEM

Learning to love yourself is the greatest love of all.
—Whitney Houston, "The Greatest Love of All" (Arista Records)

Do you want to be a positive influence in the world?
First, get your own life in order.
—Tao Te Ching, quoted by Will Schutz in *The Human Element* (1994)

ADVANCE PLANNER: SELF-CONCEPT AND SELF-ESTEEM

When you complete this chapter, you will be able to:

✓ Identify the two elements that formulate individual self-concept.
✓ Differentiate between individual self-concept and individual self-esteem.
✓ Analyze how self-esteem influences individual behavior.
✓ Evaluate the functions of self-esteem in interpersonal communication.
✓ Describe five techniques for enhancing self-esteem.

To accomplish these objectives, you will complete some or all of these activities:

1. Analyze a case that reflects two students' views of themselves and others.
2. Read and discuss some of the characteristics of self-concept and self-esteem.
3. Identify significant people in your life.
4. Examine the sources of your self-concept.
5. Discover life experiences that were instrumental in developing your own self-esteem.

A CASE STUDY IN SELF-CONCEPT

A Tale of Two Students

Mary Williams graduated from high school last spring. She was class valedictorian and received a scholarship to attend her state's university. Her parents gave her a graduation party at which relatives and friends acknowledged their pride and admiration of her. Mary was thrilled with the love and acceptance she felt from everyone.

The pride and admiration extended to Mary seemed to be well-founded. She was courteous to everyone and consequently attracted people to her presence. She was an officer in many school organizations, and when teachers wanted student input on school issues, Mary's name was always suggested. Mary was equally popular with students. She was always willing to listen to anyone's problem without rendering judgment.

Currently, Mary is finishing her first semester at the state university. During this semester she pledged a sorority, joined a campus organization, and is working part time at a fast food restaurant. She has carried 15 hours of course work and, according to her estimate, is barely achieving the 3.5 GPA she needs to maintain her scholarship. She is feeling overwhelmed and tired (mentally as well as physically) a good deal of the time. She is discouraged that she has less time for people, and when she is around her friends she doesn't reflect the same energy she previously did. In fact, sometimes she's impatient and judgmental of their comments and actions.

Ann, Mary's roommate is also a very good student. Her background is similar to Mary's, but she seems to approach life from a different view. She is aware of what others accomplish and, if her achievement is less than theirs, she usually offers some cynical comment. In discussions with others, she often will counter others' achievements with her own. Mary has tried to understand Ann, but is finding it increasingly hard to do. Consequently, she spends less time with Ann and is considering a request to change roommates for the second semester. Ann has noticed Mary's avoidance, and has asked Mary if she thinks she's too good for her. As you may imagine, with finals approaching, both are feeling a great deal of stress.

Discussion Questions

1. What elements do you believe influenced Mary's self-concept when she graduated from high school? As a result, how would you describe her self-esteem? On what basis do you make your judgments?

2. Do you think Mary's self-concept or self-esteem may have changed during the first semester of college? Why or why not?

3. How would you describe Ann's self-concept and self-esteem? On what basis do you make this judgment?

4. What do you think will be the outcome of their discussion?

INTRODUCTION TO THEORIES OF SELF-CONCEPT AND SELF-ESTEEM

Self-concept is a description of how we perceive ourselves, and self-esteem is a description of how we feel about our self-concept. When we feel good about our self-concept, we have strong, positive self-esteem. For instance, if we see ourselves as personable (self-concept), we may be proud of that trait (self-esteem) (Schutz, 1994).

Sources of Self-Concept

Self-concept is a product of our own perceptions about ourselves and the reaction and response of others toward us as individuals. Physical appearance contributes to self-perception. If we like the way we appear, our self-concept is positively reinforced. Life experiences serve as a second source of self-perception. Positive life experiences in athletics, academics, relationships, occupational endeavors, etc., positively reinforce self-concept. The greater the opportunity for positive life experiences, the greater likelihood of positive impact on self-concept. This impact is intensified when the life experiences are in areas we highly value.

The reaction and responses of others serve as important validation to reinforce or alter self-perception. This is especially true of those considered to be significant others in our lives. Significant others usually include parents, siblings, spouse, or boyfriend or girlfriend. It is not unusual, however, for significant others to include close relatives, teachers, work associates, and friends. A significant other is usually someone you respect because of his or her integrity, to whom you can disclose personal information, and with whom you share a similar value base (Verderber & Verderber, 1995).

The sources of individual self-concept are rooted in an internal locus of control (self-perceptions) and an external locus of control (reaction and response of others). In regard to these sources, Silverberg (cited in Campbell, 1984) acknowledges that "both are important, but cautions the former [internal] is the steadier and more dependable; the latter [external] is always more uncertain. Unhappy and insecure is the person who, lacking an inner source for self-esteem, must depend for this almost wholly upon external sources."

Determining Your Own Self-Concept

How can you determine your own self-concept? One of the exercises at the end of this chapter provides a format for accomplishing this task. First, inventory your personal characteristics, identifying those traits that constitute who you are. (It might be wise to involve significant others in this task.) Examples of characteristics others have listed include: personable, physically attractive, intelligent, impatient, critical of others, and affectionate. After you've completed your inventory, assess whether you consider each characteristic to be a positive or negative attribute. Next, consider why that trait is included in your inventory. Is it because you consider it important as a component of who you are, or is it solely a source of validation from others that serves to enhance your self-esteem?

Development of Self-Esteem

Self-esteem is an expression of self-concept. Mruk (1995) contends that the basic components of self-esteem are *competence* and *worthiness* and their interaction provides a measure of one's degree of self-esteem. The element of competence is behavioral in nature, and can be measured in terms of whether the outcome of an action is effective or ineffective. Therefore, it can be fairly easily evaluated. Worthiness is more difficult to measure, because it is experiential and deals with more subjective phenomena associated with personal or social values. These two components are the bases upon which personal characteristics are evaluated and self-esteem develops.

Self-esteem is a lifelong developmental issue. Mruk (1995) describes the development of self-esteem as a three-stage process: 1) early childhood precursors of self-esteem, 2) emergence of self-esteem during middle childhood and adolescence, and 3) the role self-esteem plays in adulthood.

During the pre-verbal experience of early childhood (0 to 5 years), the components of competence and worthiness are treated as separate developmental precursors. The child is born into an environment of values about what is good, desirable, attractive, etc., defined by his or her significant others. The child learns to respond to significant others based upon their reactions to the child's presence, behavior, or achievements. This worthiness dimension occurs before the emergence of means-to-an-end activities such as walking or talking, which lead to a sense of competence or incompetence.

It is in middle childhood (6 to 12 years) that self-esteem emerges as a relationship between competence and worthiness. Children begin to evaluate their actions and attributes compared to standards or values. During this period, the social world of the child expands and significant others outside the family begin to introduce new values or standards of worthiness. At the end of this stage, self-esteem meaningfully affects the child's behavior by shaping perception, influencing experience, and forming identity.

The last stage, adulthood, becomes one of self-esteem management. It is the period in which a person lives up to personal or social values and works through problems that challenge individual abilities. These challenges include the formation of satisfying interpersonal relationships, career expectations, and other responsibilities that come with adulthood.

High, Medium, and Low Self-Esteem

Once we pass childhood, self-esteem becomes relatively stable. In fact, at this point it could be said that we create our style of self-esteem. This style (high, medium, low, or defensive) expresses our generally perceived level of worthiness and competence based upon our experiences in the world (Mruk, 1995). It influences our interpersonal communication through behavioral expression, the dialogue we choose to internalize, our selection of words and tone of voice, and our perception of others.

Two important behavioral influences are provided through our self-esteem: 1) a personal growth urge that calls upon an individual to demonstrate competence and worthiness leading to higher levels of functioning, and 2) a defense mechanism shielding against threats to the self-concept (Mruk, 1995). If we possess high self-esteem, challenges or changes in our routine are likely to be seen as opportunities for personal growth. An individual with low self-esteem, however, may view them as a threat to security, evoking actions of denial or avoidance. For example, two individuals are trying to adapt to the communication technology of e-mail. One has a positive self-concept about his or her competence with electronic technology and will be more likely to adopt e-mail as a communication mode than the other, whose self-concept about competence with the technology is poor.

There are times, however, when the world presents the possibility of threat, against which self-esteem acts as a shield. At those times we act to protect our sense of worthiness and competence by standing up for ourselves or resisting destructive criticism. In regard to the previous example with e-mail, an individual may place such a high value on personal contact and the importance of nonverbal interpersonal expression that he or she resists adopting the technology and risks the criticism of peers because of his or her self-esteem. Sometimes the ability to discern between poor self-concept and proactive use of self-esteem as a defense mechanism is difficult even for the individual expressing the behavior.

Affirmation we receive from others serves to reinforce our self-perception. This is especially true in childhood when self-esteem is developing. However, as our style of self-esteem stabilizes, it becomes more difficult for us to accept statements about ourselves with which we do not agree. We filter out those statements others make about us if we don't believe them ourselves. This may explain why it's difficult to use positive comments to influence someone with low self-esteem. He or she may not have had positive experiences that correlate with the positive comments, or may have developed a personal attitude that places low value on the positive behavior reflected in our comments. On the other hand, an individual with high self-esteem demonstrates behavior that elicits reinforcement the person can internalize and call upon for reassurance in times of criticism.

Individuals with positive or high self-esteem tend to select words and use a tone of voice that are positive and upbeat. This behavior may result from the attitude that experiences are opportunities for further growth and a higher level of functioning. This is especially true in the area of competition. Such a positive outlook tends to attract others. People naturally gravitate toward individuals demonstrating positive self-esteem. In contrast, people with low self-esteem often portray an attitude that says, "Why try? I'll just lose anyhow." Individuals with low self-esteem tend to belittle the accomplishments of others as well as themselves. They are full of self-criticism and self-doubt, and often talk in sarcastic or whining tones.

Whatever individuals see in themselves, they are likely to see or look for in others. Consequently, if our self-esteem is high, we are likely to associate with others with high self-esteem. The more accurately we see ourselves, the more accurately we perceive others, leading to more accurate, effective, and efficient interpersonal relations.

Maintenance and Enhancement of Self-Esteem

By the time we reach adulthood, the habits of self-esteem are deeply ingrained. To change or modify these habits requires both unlearning of the past and time for new learning. However, as research has shown, self-esteem can change, particularly during major life transitions such as graduation, marriage, death of significant others, divorce, etc. Mruk (1995) identifies these techniques for enhancing self-esteem: acceptance and caring, consistent and affirming feedback, assertiveness, modeling of others' behavior, and problem solving. The following is a synopsis of some of those techniques.

1. *Acceptance and Caring.* The presence of significant others in our lives is an important aspect of being accepted and cared about. With these people we generally feel most comfortable and likely to disclose information neces-

sary to evaluate and change our behavior. The safeness we feel with significant others is often a result of an established, nonjudgmental atmosphere in which we can discuss our behavioral concerns. We feel safe with the significant persons and a bond of trust exists between us.

It is fortunate that many of us have significant persons in our life. If we lack these, we need to look for ways to find significant others for ourselves or to assist others. Children need persons to admire, for instance, and special community programs may help provide these contacts. Adults seek mentors or develop or join support groups. A support group can be simply a close-knit group of friends or a group of people who have had similar experiences in their lives that draw them together. A support group provides for a rich mixture of diversity in perception, experience, and individual style. It allows the presentation of a greater number of safe challenges or opportunities to try out self-esteem-enhancing behaviors; provides greater opportunity for the presentation of social factors affecting self-esteem, such as positive feedback and effective modeling; and gives its members a sense of camaraderie.

2. *Consistent, Positive (Self-Affirming) Feedback.* Authentic feedback is the basis upon which self-esteem develops, whether it is internally based on our own evaluation or externally based on the affirmation of others. Feedback drives self-concept, which maintains self-esteem. To enhance self-esteem, for ourselves or for others, it is important to focus on positive rather than negative behavior. The logic behind this recommendation seems obvious. It is important for individuals to feel good about themselves and develop a strong sense of self as a basis for further enhancing self-esteem.

Accepting positive feedback from others can serve as the basis for developing a habit of positive self-talk, because it contributes to better self-awareness of competence and worthiness. As you perform tasks in life, take time to reflect on the competence you have demonstrated and accept the worthiness of your performance reflected in the comments of others. If you associate with positive people, your own sense of self will become stronger. Through observing the positive behavior of others and experiencing the feeling derived from that behavior, we can visualize the behavior we desire in ourselves. This is certainly another benefit that can be derived from support groups and mentors.

When relying on feedback as a source of affirmation, it is important to correctly sort authentic from non-authentic information. This is best accomplished through perception checking, the process of putting your perception into words, then checking with someone else to see if his or her interpretation agrees with yours. Some people feel safest checking perceptions with persons they know well, but it is a good habit to be able to ask for clarification of your perceptions with others you encounter in daily life. Frequent checking allows you to more accurately identify irrational thought patterns—which otherwise could lead to lowered self-esteem—and to challenge or replace them with a more realistic understanding of self, the world, and others.

3. *Natural Self-Esteem Moments.* Self-esteem can change significantly, particularly in periods of natural transition or at certain crucial turning points in life. Examples of such times are the breakup of a relationship, the consummation of a relationship (forming a partnership or marriage), the winning or losing of a popular election, or the announcement of cuts from and assignments to a competitive team. At these pivotal times we choose to see the events as either negative or positive. The more times we see them as positive, the more chance we have for personal growth. It is important to recognize the role self-esteem plays at these moments and take advantage of them.

Perhaps the greatest challenge of self-esteem moments is learning to derive positive growth from disappointing turning points in life. To do so, the key is to interpret the disappointment as strengthening our competence rather than reducing our worthiness. The additional strength added to our sense of competence comes from realizing how we need to grow so we may be more successful at the next turning point. Turning disappointment into advantage may require exercise of a physical skill, verbal accounting to ourselves or others, or increased spirituality and faith in a power greater than our own.

Natural self-esteem moments can also be created if you are aware of what inspires you to be open to the elevation of purpose and the energy to take the risks of personal growth. For some people this stimulation may come from reading the biography of a successful person whom they respect. For others, it may come from viewing art, seeing special movies, or listening to music, any of which may stimulate the esteem energy needed for personal growth. A method of increasing awareness of personal inspiration is to keep a journal regarding your self-esteem and what affects it in your life.

4. *Assertiveness.* The ability to stand up for your position and values is a basic source of self-esteem and success. It helps you avoid situations that might damage self-esteem and enables you to say no to negative treatment from others. Realizing that, as a human being, you have certain rights, and knowing how to use or exercise them, can lead to increased self-esteem.

5. *Goal Setting.* The attainment of personal goals enhances self-esteem because such successes allow you to take control of your life, and the associated accomplishments provide a sense of satisfaction, which increases self-esteem.

Identifying Significant People

Purpose To help you identify those people who can become part of your plans to enhance self-esteem.

Activity If you were to think of your life as a business and yourself as the Chairperson of the Board, who would you identify as members of the board (significant people) of your business? Around the table below, position yourself and your members of the board. Indicate positions by initials or names. After you have completed your drawing, answer the questions below.

Discussion

1. As chairperson, where are you seated? Why? Is there a reason you've placed members of your board in particular positions?

2. How have each of the people listed above affected your self-concept? (Be specific.)

3. Are there other people you'd like to add to your board of directors? Who are they and why?

4. Do you think you're a member of someone else's board of directors? If so, who, and how have you contributed to that person's self-concept?

5. Share your drawing and something about your board of directors with two other persons.

EXERCISE
Sources of Self-Concept

Purpose   To help you gain a better understanding of the characteristics making up your self-concept.

Activity   Complete this inventory by selecting personal characteristics that you possess or others see in you. You can identify them yourself, or ask for the opinions of significant others. To assist you in getting started, here are examples of characteristics people often list:

intelligent	perfectionist	thoughtful
physically attractive	caring	calm
patient	fair	direct
friendly	personable	jovial
trustworthy	flexible	trusting
honest	succinct	accepting
self-conscious	punctual	sharing

Personal Characteristics	Value (+ or −) Influence on Self	Influence on Others

EXERCISE
Ben's Dilemma: Impact on Self-Concept

Purpose To analyze a case for development of self-concept and to assess development of self-confidence and self-esteem in your own life experiences.

Activity This activity tells a story without an ending. It is a case that demonstrates how events in someone's life can influence self-concept and behavior. As you read the story and complete this activity, begin to think and reflect upon life experiences you've encountered that have affected your self-concept. They may be recent experiences or ones from the past.

Read Ben's Dilemma and answer the questions posed. You may want to read the questions before starting the story. Then be prepared to share something from your life that had an impact on your self-concept.

A Case Study—Ben's Dilemma

Ben was from a small community. He lived with his parents and an older brother. During his early school years, Ben frequently had teachers who had also taught his brother, Dan. These teachers usually acknowledged Ben's older brother, but never allowed that to interfere with the relationship they developed with Ben.

Ben was an extroverted person who enjoyed the company of friends. He had a few friends in all of his classes. In the classes Ben enjoyed and found interesting, he did very well. In other classes that he found less interesting, he did average work. Ben was a solid B student.

One day a situation developed in Mary Woods' physical education class, causing her to question the appropriateness of Ben's behavior. Ms. Woods' reaction to Ben was, "Why can't you behave more like your brother Dan did in my class?" This reaction caught Ben completely by surprise. No other teacher had ever compared him to Dan. Ben assured Ms. Woods that he was his own person and not like Dan. Ms. Woods responded that since Dan was such a fine student in class and never caused problems, it might be to Ben's advantage to try to be more like him.

Ben was distraught over Ms. Woods' comparison of him to his brother. Despite his feelings, he tried to be positive in subsequent classes and did quite well. At the same time he tried to emphasize to Ms. Woods that he was not like his brother.

At mid-semester the class finished a Cardio-Pulmonary Resuscitation (CPR) unit. Ben found the unit very interesting and enjoyed learning the information. He passed the performance part of the final unit exam, and decided to study with a friend for the written exam. Ben was motivated to do well on the test, and studied the day before the test with his friend Mike. Class members were allowed to sit on the gym floor as they took the test. Mike and Ben sat together. A week later when the tests were returned, Mike and Ben did not receive theirs. When Ben asked Ms. Woods about his test, she accused him and Mike of cheating since they had received two of the highest grades. Ms. Woods pointed out to Ben that his brother Dan would never have performed such an act of dishonesty, and then escorted Ben and Mike to the principal's office.

Ben and Mike stood by their story and, when asked about the closeness of their grades, explained that they studied together for the test. Ms. Woods did not accept their explanation, and asked that they retake the test. They did as she requested and received grades almost identical to the first test grades. Ms. Woods concluded the reason for the high test scores was that either one or both of them had access to the original test before it was given. She refused to accept their test scores.

From then on, Ben's behavior in the course changed drastically. For the remainder of the semester, he did everything in his power to make the class total misery for Ms. Woods. He started arguments with her and was repeatedly sent to the principal's office. The situation escalated to the point that one day Ms. Woods told Ben school was no place for him, and he would not amount to anything in life regardless of what he did.

Discussion Questions

1. How did Ms. Woods' reaction to Ben affect his self-concept?

2. Which of the two self-esteem determinants—competence or worthiness—did Ms. Woods' reaction to Ben most affect?

3. How did Ben use his self-esteem as a protection mechanism?

4. Have you ever experienced a situation like the one described in the case study? What was it like and how did you feel? Did your self-esteem suffer?

5. In pairs, describe experiences that led to development of your self-confidence and your self-esteem. You may choose both positive and negative experiences. Take turns practicing actively listening to each other's experiences.

FURTHER ACTIVITY

Independent Practice

1. Interview a young child about his or her self-concept. What images does the child use to describe himself or herself? Is anyone giving the child affirmation or positive feedback? Does he or she have any goals?

2. Interview someone who contributed to your own development. This person should be someone who has known you for a long time, perhaps since middle childhood—a parent, older sibling, family friend. What strengths did they see in you as a young child?

3. If you have a close circle of friends or a support group, discuss formation of self-concept and enhancement of self-esteem with them. Can these friends give you any pointers about yourself? Can you help them?

Journal Writing

1. Record the results of your interview with the child. Use concepts from your text (e.g., being accepted, receiving positive feedback, using natural moments) to analyze the development of self-concept and self-esteem in the child. Are there any significant gaps?

2. Write your reflections on your interview with the significant other person in your life. How did their comments about your early years open any new insights into your own development of self-concept and self-esteem?

3. Write your personal plan for enhancing your self-esteem.

4. Write a plan to support or affirm someone else's self-esteem. This should be a person in your life that you see regularly who may need some bolstering or special support.

LEARNING POINTS

✓ Self-concept is a collection of our perceptions about our physical, mental, and vocational abilities. It is derived from our own perception about ourselves and the reaction and response of others toward us.

✓ Self-esteem is an expression of how we feel regarding our self-concept.

✓ The basic components of self-esteem are individual competence and worthiness. Our expression of self-esteem is a result of the complex interaction of these two components.

✓ Self-esteem begins to emerge, expands, and shapes the individual during middle childhood. We spend the remainder of our life, adulthood, managing our self-esteem through our responses to life's challenges.

✓ The style or level of self-esteem (high, medium, low, or defensive) we choose to express influences the interpersonal interactions we have with others.

✓ Self-esteem is portrayed through our behavior, the dialogue we choose to internalize, our selection of words and tone of voice, and how we choose to see others.

✓ Our approach to self-esteem influences the way we react to change, and our ability to protect ourselves against destructive criticism or advice.

✓ We spend our adult lives managing our self-esteem within life's challenges. This task is one in which significant others play an important role.

✓ A successful self-esteem management program includes being accepted and cared about by others. Mentors and support groups can play an important role in this phase by providing an opportunity to check perception, as well as describing differing life experiences and modeling individual style preferences.

✓ Authentic feedback is the basis upon which self-esteem develops. A successful enhancement program includes providing ourselves with positive internal feedback and associating with positive people.

✓ Perception checking—testing our perceptions against others' views—is useful to validate our competence and worthiness within our interpersonal actions and is an important method of authenticating feedback.

✓ Natural self-esteem moments, occurring at pivotal points in our lives, are the times when our attention is most sharply focused on our self-concept. These times provide the greatest opportunity for personal growth. Whether it be from the ecstasy of achievement or the depression of failure, our awareness of self-concept is optimized. To optimize personal growth from either of these situations, it is important to focus on the positive results. It is also important to understand oneself well enough to know those events that inspire you (in elevation of purpose and energy) to take risks and create natural self-esteem moments. One method to develop self-awareness of these moments or events is journaling.

✓ The attainment of personal goals serves as a source of success and personal satisfaction, both of which increase self-esteem.

REFERENCES

Campbell, R. N. (1984). *The new science: Self-esteem psychology.* Lanham, MD: University Press of America.

Mruk, C. (1995). *Self-esteem: Research, theory, and practice.* New York: Springer Publishing Co.

Schutz, W. (1994). *The human element: Productivity, self-esteem, and the bottom line.* San Francisco: Jossey-Bass.

Verderber, R. F., and Verderber, K. S. (1995). *Inter-Act: Using interpersonal communication skills* (7th ed.). Belmont, CA: Wadsworth Publishing Co.

Chapter 6

VALUES

. . . David O. McKay taught, "The greatest battles of life are fought out daily in the silent chambers of the soul." If you win the battles there, if you settle the issues that inwardly conflict, you feel a sense of peace, a sense of knowing what you're about. And you'll find that the public victories—where you tend to think cooperatively, to promote the welfare and good of other people, and to be genuinely happy for other people's successes—will follow naturally.
—Stephen Covey, *The Seven Habits of Highly Effective People* (1989)

People who are self-aware, who have imagination and conscience, can see when the script they are living is not in harmony with their values— their life is not the product of their own design, but the result of a creation they have deferred to other people and circumstances. We need to approach our roles in life with values and directions clear, to rescript ourselves so the paradigms from which behavior and attitude flow are congruent with deepest values and in harmony with correct principles.
—Milton Rokeach, *Understanding Human Values* (1979)

ADVANCE PLANNER: VALUES

When you complete this chapter, you will be able to:

✓ Define values.
✓ Identify sources of values.
✓ Recognize the stages of values development and relate them to your own values development.
✓ Identify, evaluate, and clarify your own values.
✓ Describe and practice ways to impart values to others.
✓ Analyze reasons for changing adult values.
✓ Manage situations in which values conflict.
✓ Take actions based on values.
✓ Analyze the influence of values on your lifestyle choices.

To accomplish these objectives, you will engage in some or all of the following activities:

1. Analyze and discuss a case study.
2. Read and discuss a summary of theories related to values and values development.

3. Create a life map to demonstrate the role values play in your goals and major decisions.

4. Analyze symbols representing things you value.

5. Participate in a consensus-building exercise designed to help you see the relationship between what you value and how you act.

A CASE STUDY IN VALUES

The Test

You are one of 150 students enrolled in a required introductory course taught by a graduate student. You have struggled to stay interested in the course, but have missed several of the 7:30 a.m. class meetings. On the midterm you managed a low *C;* you also scored some low grades on quizzes that you thought were pretty unfair and for which you didn't have enough time to study. As a result, your grade going into the final is stuck on the border between a *C* and a *D.*

You have buckled down, though, and have studied quite a bit for the final, but you're afraid you may have been concentrating on the wrong stuff. You need at least a high *C* to hang on to a small scholarship you received from your hometown Chamber of Commerce, not to mention meeting your parents' expectations. Your roommate, who is aware of your situation, has a work-study job in the department that offers your course. As the two of you discuss your concerns, your roommate casually says, "You know, I saw the TAs from your section making copies of the final exam yesterday, and when the copier jammed, I helped them clear it and threw away at least two pages from the test that had been stuck in the copier. I know right where they are and can go get them if it will be any help . . . want me to?"

Discussion Questions

1. What values would seem to be reinforced if you take your roommate up on the offer to get you copies of the test pages?

2. What values seem to be in conflict with those?

3. Do you think it is right to cheat? Are there any circumstances in which cheating is okay?

AN INTRODUCTION TO THEORIES OF VALUES AND VALUES DEVELOPMENT

When was the last time you thought about your *values*—those qualities or standards that you believe are desirable, worthy, and important? Can't remember? Maybe never? You're probably not alone. Most people have a set of values, but they don't think much about them. Instead, their lives resemble a collection of habits—habits that developed when a situation arose that needed to be resolved. Some people think about values only when they are faced with a crisis that requires immediate action (Leatz, 1993). Yet your values are directly related to the kind of person you are, your goals and aspirations, the way you behave, and the way you relate to other people.

This chapter helps you look at values in a number of ways. It begins with a definition of values, then explores the typical sources of our values. It also discusses the stages of values development and describes some ways of clarifying values and managing values conflicts.

What Are Values?

Values coincide with personal beliefs about what is good and just, right and wrong, ethical and unethical, moral and immoral. Some common values include honesty, fairness, justice, patriotism, loyalty, equality, cooperation, autonomy, health, etc. Values are important because they influence our perceptions and preferences and motivate us to act (Hanna, 1995). According to Williams (1979), "Values are core conceptions of the desirable within every individual and society. They serve as standards or criteria to guide not only action but also judgment, choice, attitude, evaluation, argument, exhortation, [and] rationalization."

Frankl (1963) based his theories of logotherapy on the human striving to find meaning in life. But he cautioned that values do not drive a person— they pull rather than push. Implicit in the concept of pulling is the freedom of the individual to choose to accept or reject an idea. No one is driven to good behavior; in every instance we must *decide* to behave morally, not to satisfy some moral drive or to ease the conscience, but for the sake of some value to which we commit ourselves.

The goals we set for ourselves, the plans we map out for our lives, result from our value systems, but aren't necessarily the same things as our value systems. Gaus (1990) offers this suggestion to help distinguish a plan of life from a value system: "The plan concerns the organization of commitments to act that flow from one's value system. . . . Valuings imply action commitments; one who adopts a plan of action has organized his activity in light of his comparative valuings, resources, and circumstances. Understood thus, plans do not directly determine or organize what one values, but rather how one's value system translates into efficient action in particular circumstances" (p. 239).

For example, imagine that you are one of two high school graduates given a choice of either going to college or working as an apprentice mechanic in a well-established and highly successful garage. If you grew up in an atmosphere in which learning and intellectual pursuit were important components of your value system, your commitment to learning has probably shaped a life plan that includes a college education. On the other hand, if your value system more strongly focused on self-sufficiency and hard work, you might be more strongly committed to a life plan centered on starting early to develop a fulfilling and honest career.

It is difficult not to equate values with knowledge and belief, but values themselves derive from what we know and shape what we believe. Many years ago, knowledge of mental illness was limited; the mentally ill were believed to be possessed by demons and their illness was thought to be the deserved result of some moral failing. Communities valued as good certain punitive measures (imprisonment, commitment to asylums, etc.) to deal with the mentally ill and protect others. Thus the value judgment that insanity or mental illness was bad derived from the belief that the mentally ill were culpable and led to the belief that they should be punished accordingly. Of course, changes in knowledge have led to our current belief that mental illness is, indeed, illness. Because we value health and our responsibility to safeguard the health of those we love, we now see humane medical treatment as the good way of helping those who are mentally ill. The connections among beliefs, knowledge, and values are strong—changes in beliefs affect values and changes in values affect our perceptions of reality (Rokeach, 1979).

Sources of Values

None of us is born with a set of values. We learn them from others—parents, families, peers, schools, religion, government, the media, etc. The primary sources of values for most of us are family and parents. The things our parents valued shaped both the way they behaved as parents and their expectations for the ways their children would behave. You can expect that your values will affect the way you raise your children, too. The strength of the influence of parental values can be seen in the parent messages that keep replaying in our minds, even well into adulthood: "A penny saved is a penny earned," "Vegetables are good for you," "Buckle up for safety." The values we learned from our parents are reflected in conscience, too. Many years after leaving home, a person can still feel guilty pangs about buying something on impulse or occasionally missing church—an indication that her parents valued frugality and religion, and those values strongly influence her internal critic.

The value messages parents send can often be conflicting, as well. A child may hear that the parents value fairness and equality of all people, but when she brings home a new friend of a different race, she may hear another message. It's no wonder that children are confused—and that confusion carries over when as adults they attempt to clarify values (Hanna, 1995).

Messages from television, radio, and advertisements are powerful influences on values, too. Just consider the value messages those media send about youth and body image. Is it any wonder that our society tends to devalue aging, or that so many of us are obsessed with diet, sometimes to the point that obsession becomes illness?

Our own experiences also influence the development of our values. Personally experiencing betrayal or dishonesty may clarify for us the degree to which we value loyalty and honesty. The strong support of parents and siblings or friends will reinforce for us the value of family and friendship.

Not only do we develop personal values, we also develop collective values that we share with others in the societies to which we belong—within families, on the job, in school, and within geopolitical groups like neighborhoods, towns, states, and nations.

Values Development

As we mature in other ways, we also mature in building our system of values. Values take time to develop; research into values clarification has iden-

Stages of Value Development

Value Development Level	Description	Personal Development Level
Acceptance (Prizing)	Ascribing worth or value to something; prizing or cherishing it; willing to identify with it or publicly affirm it	External/Reactor (ages 0–8)
Preference (Choosing)	Seeking out and pursuing a value on one's own; freely choosing from alternatives after considering consequences	Shifting (ages 8–16)
Commitment (Acting)	Willing to act and take a stand on one's values; acting with consistency and repetition	Crystallized (ages 16–23)

tified three stages most people move through as they develop value systems: acceptance (prizing), preference (choosing), and commitment (acting) (Simon et al., 1972).

In the early stage of values development, we accept, prize, or cherish something largely because we have been influenced (by parents, media, experience, etc.) to value it. In the parallel stage of personal development, we are still largely focused on the external and tend to behave primarily in reaction to the actions of others. For example, a child of 6 or 7 identifies with going to church and considers it important only because it is important to his parents.

In the preference stage of values development, we choose to believe and behave in a certain way, not merely because of external influence, but because we have considered the alternatives and the consequences and have freely chosen to place value on the belief or behavior. This stage generally emerges between the ages of 8 and 16, when personal development is shifting from an external focus to an internal one. For example, at this stage a young person may value church attendance because he enjoys it and wants to go.

In the final stage of values development, our values are clear and ingrained and we feel a strong commitment to them. At this stage, we are willing to act in accordance with our values and beliefs, consistently and regularly, and would be ready to take a stand to protect them. Most people are ready to commit to values by the time they reach adulthood (ages 16–23), when their life focus has crystallized. For example, at this stage a person may attend church consistently because he values religion and finds church services spiritually fulfilling. An adult who tells you he values going to church because that's "just what you're supposed to do" probably has not developed a firm commitment to religion as a value. He has remained in the acceptance phase of the values development process.

Changing Values

As we mature, our values may change. That doesn't mean that our core values shift dramatically, but that things that once seemed to shape our lives no longer exert as strong an influence. In their place have emerged new values (or perhaps they were always there, just not as powerful as they are now) that reflect the new direction our lives are taking. For example, a mother of young children may highly value a strong public school system and will lobby for strong schools and an elementary curriculum that challenges and encourages children. When that same woman is in her forties and her children are attending college, the passionate value she placed on strong elementary schools may have waned. She still may believe in the value of a public school system, but her actions may now reflect a stronger passion for worthwhile and accessible college programs that will prepare her grown children for successful life careers. Her early values haven't evaporated altogether—the basic belief in education hasn't gone away—but the shape of her values in that regard has changed as her life circumstances have changed.

People often find themselves achieving victories that are empty, successes that have come at the expense of things they suddenly realize were far more valuable to them. People from all walks of life—doctors, academicians, actors, politicians, business professionals, athletes, and plumbers—often struggle to achieve a higher income, more recognition, or a certain degree of professional competence, only to find that their drive to achieve the goal blinded them to the things that really mattered most and now are gone (Covey, 1989).

Flexibility is vital to a strong and healthy value system, but strength doesn't imply unchanging, rigid values. Instead, it means we are able and willing to continually process values and in doing so, modify them or change their priority. Lack of flexibility makes us judgmental, closes doors, and dismisses the possibility that the value systems of others may be just as legitimate as our own. Without the flexibility to adjust our thinking, we may destroy good relationships or completely reject new relationships because the other person simply doesn't believe as we do (Hanna, 1995).

Managing Values Conflicts and Influencing the Values of Others

When our values coalesce to the point of clarity and action, we are ready to take a stand and act in accordance with them. Usually a stand emerges when our values are challenged, confronted, or attacked in some way. In the face of such a challenge (which may come from other people, the community, or new information we uncover about nature, people, or things), values that we might have held in the abstract suddenly are called forth in the form of concrete action. Say, for example, you value your environmental responsibility to pass the earth on relatively intact to future generations. You have only recently learned that the fluorocarbons in aerosol cans do serious damage to the ozone layer. So you take a stand to not use any products that come in aerosol cans. You act on that stand the next time you face a fierce flying insect and the only weapon available is a can of Raid. If you value your environmental responsibility strongly enough, you'll risk a sting rather than sending even a minute amount of fluorocarbons into the atmosphere.

Challenges sometimes evoke values we didn't realize we held dearly. For example, a young family has always spent time together on a regular summer vacation. This year, the oldest child is 10 years old and playing for the first time on a summer league softball team. It turns out that the scheduled games overlap the time the family had set aside for vacation. The family discusses the things it values that are relevant to this situation: sports play as a source of good health, teamwork as a means of learning to cooperate with and be responsible to others, as well as family togetherness and the mental and emotional benefits of a relaxing vacation. Ultimately, they take this stand: When they are in town, softball games get highest priority; but family trips are more important than attending every game.

We usually order our values hierarchically and use them to guide our behavior at certain moments. Because we view some values as more important than others, we often make trade-offs in our lives based on the relative importance we attach to certain values. For example, if you value intellectual development more than you value physical development, given a limited amount of time, you may spend it in the library studying rather than in the gym working out (Verderber & Verderber, 1995). Values are so fundamental to human behavior that when our personal values are not congruent with our other value sets or the values of others, we may experience serious conflict and the stresses that result can be difficult to manage.

Ethics or values conflicts are not always framed in the context of right versus wrong. More often we are confronted with value dilemmas that present something that is right on both sides—and we can't do both right things at the same time. The rightness on each side reflects two of our core values in conflict with each other. People who have no core values can experience no ethical dilemmas—they don't value any rightness and so are unaware of the ethical universe in which value-driven people live (Kidder, 1994).

Interpersonal conflicts driven by values are the most difficult to resolve. Because values are so closely tied to beliefs, and because beliefs are largely subjective, when we find ourselves in conflict that stems from a fundamental difference in values, the result is likely to be a standoff. Neither party to a conflict is likely to relinquish his or her hold on values (especially those that have crystallized for us and to which we are firmly committed), so argument or moralizing will have little effect on the conflict and will most probably make it more intense. So how can you manage a values conflict? How can you influence the values of another?

Confrontation is not the answer. But more subtle approaches may work. Simply modeling the values you want to see others adopt can be a powerful strategy. If you truly value human dignity, for example, you'll walk away from conversations that turn to demeaning women or people of other races. Reinforcing the values you hold dear can also influence the values of others. If you and a co-worker are at odds because you strongly value cooperation in the workplace and your colleague seems to value only his own well-being, you may be able to gradually influence that person to value cooperation if you compliment him each time he demonstrates even the slightest willingness to be pan of the team.

Sometimes you simply have to acknowledge that the other person's value system is different from yours. In some cases, the only resolution to a values-based conflict may be to agree to disagree and move beyond it.

Conclusion

We often form friendships by aligning ourselves with those who share our values; it is more difficult to develop an intense relationship with those whose fundamental values are different from our own. But just as we try to understand cultural differences that may initially seem to be barriers to interpersonal interactions, so too should we be open-minded enough to at least attempt to learn why someone else values things that we do not. Most likely we can find many common values in spite of differences on one or two value issues.

Values are fundamental to the way we interact with others. They are the foundation of the life goals we set for ourselves, the building blocks of self-concept and self-esteem, the guiding forces in our exertion of power and influence over others, the bases for many of the conflicts we experience (as well as the roots of conflict resolution). It is no wonder, then, that developing a value system is fundamental to interpersonal communication and interpersonal leadership.

EXERCISE
Mapping Your Life

Purpose   Everyone's life map is different. We all have taken different routes to get to the present. Your personal life map has a unique design and reflects your individual ups and downs, beginnings and endings. It can reveal a great deal about you: your values, your goals, your successes, your failures, and your hopes. Drawing your life map can help you see how your values have affected your choices and how they will affect your future. [Note: If you consider your life map highly personal, you don't have to share it with others, but you should use it as a basis for participating in the discussion that follows this activity. If you do not wish to present a personal experience as an example, you won't be pressured to do so. You may find it useful, though, to reflect on specific life events in your journal.]

You Will Need   A large piece of newsprint paper (the older you are the bigger the paper), a pencil, and some colored markers. If you would be more comfortable working with your paper on the wall, you'll need some tape.

Activity   *Part 1:* Using a pencil (you probably will need to alter your work—sometimes later events may trigger memories about earlier ones or vice versa), draw the map of your life, showing the peaks and valleys, the backtracking, the leaps, the detours.

Starting at the left edge of the paper, record your birth. (If you consider your birth a high point in the map of your life, mark it toward the top of the paper. If you perceive your birth as a fairly neutral occurrence, mark it at about the center of the left edge.) Draw a more or less continuous line that maps your life through the present and into the future. Think about the important events in your life (importance is a matter only for you to decide—it's your map; if the day your pet turtle died was an important milestone in your life, it ought to be on your map) and mark them down on your map, with the highs represented by peaks and the lows represented by valleys. For each important event, write your age when it happened.

Part 2: When you have finished sketching your map, add the following symbols. (You may use colored markers to help you easily identify the symbols.)

!   Where you took a great risk.

x   Where you encountered an obstacle that prevented you from achieving a goal.

O   Where someone else made a critical decision for you.

+   Where you made the best decision you ever made.

Where you made the worst decision you ever made.

?   Where you see an important decision coming up in the future.

Part 3: Look carefully at any patterns that seem to emerge from your map. What symbols appear most frequently near the valleys? Near the peaks? Are there any symbols that appear near both peaks and valleys?

Discussion

1. What values are reflected in the events that you consider important in your life? Are those values consistent from one end of the map to the other? If not, how and why did your values change as you grew older?

2. What values influenced you in the places you took risks? Did you have to deal with competing values (either a competition of values within yourself or a competition between one of your personal values and a personal value of someone else)?

3. Were any value issues involved when you encountered obstacles to achieving goals? Did the goals themselves derive from positive personal or social values? Did your values change in any way when you tried to overcome the obstacles?

4. Did you feel your own values were compromised when someone else made decisions for you? Or did those decisions reflect values you shared with the person(s) making the decisions?

5. When you made both the best and worst decisions of your life, what values led you to those decisions? In the case of the bad decision, why was it bad? Did it in some way involve a conflict of values? In either case, did your values change in any way after the decision was made?

6. What role do you expect current and developing values (your own and those of others) to play in future important decisions?

SMALL GROUP EXERCISE
Archaeological Study—
Your Values Symbols

Purpose   This brief exercise is based on the theory that the things you carry with you or the things you save can reveal your underlying values. If you are having trouble identifying your values in the abstract, this exercise may give you a more concrete starting point for identifying and examining your values.

You Will Need   Contents of your pockets, wallet, tote bag, briefcase, book bag, or purse

Piece of heavy paper

Marking pen

Tape

Desks arranged in a circle or chairs arranged around a table so everyone in the group can see the others

Activity   Select at least five things you carry with you almost all the time and that would cause you to panic if you lost them. Arrange those things on the desk or table in front of you. In addition, think of at least three things in your home or dorm room that you have moved with you or have saved—things you would never dream of throwing out. Use a marking pen to list those three (or more) items on a piece of paper and tape the paper to the front edge of the desk or table so others in the circle can see it.

Discussion

Select one person to be the first to submit his or her artifacts to the scrutiny of the group. Look at the items on the table and the list. Discuss what you think they say about the things that person values. When the group has finished discussing those artifacts, let the person who selected them answer these questions:

1. What meanings do the things you selected have for you?
2. What values do they represent?
3. What does that tell you about yourself?

Really think about underlying values when you talk about your reasons for selecting or listing certain items. For example, if you selected your driver's license from your wallet, you may have done so because you wish to continue driving. But beyond that, why do you value being able to drive? What important things would you sacrifice if you could no longer drive yourself? What values might be compromised or suppressed if you depended on someone else to provide your transportation?

Move to the next person and repeat the discussion. Did more than one person select or list the same items? Did they do so for the same reasons or different reasons?

Remember: Approach this exercise like an archaeologist, not an editor! Be descriptive in your assessment of what each item represents, not judgmental.

LARGE GROUP EXERCISE
Cave Rescue

Adapted from Francis and Young, 1979.

Purpose To help you identify some of the things you value and to help you correlate actions to values.

You Will Need Cave Rescue Briefing Sheet
Cave Rescue Biographical Sheet
Cave Rescue Ranking Sheet

Activity Read the briefing sheet and become familiar with the situation you have been asked to help with. The biographical sheet is explained in the briefing. Use the ranking sheet as instructed.

When you have completed your ranking sheet individually, work with others in a small group to reach consensus about your rankings. Once your group has reached consensus, select someone to announce your decision and your rationale to the rest of the class.

Cave Rescue Briefing Sheet

You are a member of a research management committee responsible for administering research projects in the behavioral sciences at State University. You have been called to an emergency meeting because of a catastrophe in one of the projects for which the committee is responsible.

The project, which is a study of human behavior in confined spaces, is conducting an experiment in a remote part of the country. The experiment involves seven people who have been living underground in a cave system for several days. The group's only outside contact is via a radio link to a research station at the cave entrance. The volunteers in the cave have issued a call for help: They have been trapped by falling rocks, and water is slowly rising; they expect it will eventually fill the cave.

The only available rescue team reports that rescue will be extremely difficult and, with the equipment available, only one person can be brought out each hour. It is quite likely the rising water will drown some of the trapped volunteers before they can all be removed from the cave.

Through the radio link, the volunteers have been informed about the impossibility of rescuing everyone. They are unwilling to decide the sequence by which they will be rescued. Your research management committee must decide the order of rescue. Lifesaving equipment will arrive at the cave in about 50 minutes. By that time, you must provide the rescue team with the rescue sequence.

The only available information about the trapped volunteers has been drawn from the project files. You'll find that information on the Cave Rescue Biographical Information Sheet. You can use any criteria you wish to help you make a decision.

Complete a Cave Rescue Ranking Sheet individually, then work with members of your group to reach a consensus about the best order of rescue. Once your group has made its decision, complete another Cave Rescue Ranking Sheet for the group and select a spokesperson to announce your decision and your rationale.

Cave Rescue Biographical Sheet

Helen: White, female, American, age 34. Married, homemaker, four children, aged 7 months to 8 years. Husband is city council member. Was a promising psychology student when she left university to marry. Lives in suburb near university. Hobbies are ice skating and cooking. Became involved in the volunteer project through association with Owen, another volunteer. Project coordinator suspects Helen and Owen have developed a covert sexual relationship.

Tozo: Female, Japanese, age 19. Single, sociology student at State University. Parents live in Tokyo, father is wealthy industrialist and national authority on traditional Japanese mime theater. Outstandingly attractive, has dated several men from the upper crust. Recently featured in TV documentary on Japanese women.

John: Black, male, American, age 37. Married, five children, aged 6 years to 19 years. Campus coordinator of Catholic Social Services at State University. Worked full time while attending school; earned master's degree in social work. Heavily involved with black militant group for several years. Hobbies are camping with his family and photography.

Owen: White, male, American, age 47. Unmarried, physical education instructor at University High School. Served in Army right after high school, was infantry platoon leader in Vietnam, earned several distinguished decorations. Medical discharge due to serious leg wound (recovery complete except for occasional pains). Earned master's degree in physical education, using GI Bill benefits. Life is a bit unsettled, drinking problem. Hobbies: modifying and driving stock cars.

Paul: White, male, English, age 47. Divorced (six years), no children. Medical research scientist at University Hospital. Recognized world authority on treatment of rabies. Currently testing a new experimental, low-cost rabies treatment, but much of his research data are still in working notebooks. Hobbies are classical music and sailing. Some emotional difficulty related to divorce and ex-wife's recent remarriage. Twice convicted of indecent exposure (last occasion was 11 months ago).

Edward: White, male, American, age 59. Married, two grown children, seven grandchildren. General manager of small factory (71 employees) that produces rubber belts for machines. Recently negotiated a large contract for his company that, if signed, would create 85 new jobs for the company; will complete details when he returns to work. Socially and politically active; senior freemason and city council member. Hobbies: spelunking (cave exploration). Plans to write a book on the subject when he retires.

Jean: Black, female, Jamaican, age 72. Unmarried, no relatives. Living in U.S. since 1979, but has not sought American citizenship. Ph.D. in biological sciences; working with a government grant to explore biological organisms that live in caves. Most recent work with tree organisms has led to development of experimental vaccine that could be the forerunner to an AIDS vaccine. Recent Peabody Award winner from Stanford University. Assignment in current project: Study the behavior of people in confined spaces and gather microbes for future medical research.

Cave Rescue Ranking Sheet (Individual)

Instructions: Rank the seven people trapped in the cave in terms of the value of rescuing them. List names in the left-hand column in priority order. (Number 1 gets out first, etc.) Complete this sheet on your own, then complete another sheet with your group.

	Name	Primary Reason for Ranking
1		
2		
3		
4		
5		
6		
7		

Cave Rescue Ranking Sheet (Group)

As a group, you must arrive at consensus about your rankings. This doesn't mean you have to agree unanimously, but the majority of your group should be able to live with the final order you come up with. When you determine the order, select someone to present your decision to the class.

	Name	Primary Reason for Ranking
1		
2		
3		
4		
5		
6		
7		

What procedures did you use to determine consensus?
What were the principal criteria you used to rank the trapped volunteers?

FURTHER ACTIVITY

Journal Writing

Consider the following situation: A close friend would like to be an artist, but hasn't experienced much success with art as a career. He can't understand why his work isn't selling. Knowing that you pursued an undergraduate minor in art history, he asks—and genuinely wants—your opinion of his chances of being a successful artist. You honestly think his art is atrocious and that he has very little chance of making good in a career in art. But you know he is likely to find your opinion quite painful to hear. What would you do?

Write in your journal about your response to this situation. Think about similar values issues in your life.

Have you ever lied to protect someone's feelings? What were the consequences?

Have you ever told the unvarnished truth in spite of the effect you knew it might have? What were the consequences?

Is there such a thing as a "little white lie?"

What does *honesty* mean? Does it mean the same thing to everyone?

What happens when our sense of honesty conflicts with our sense of loyalty?

What other values conflicts have you experienced, either within yourself or with someone else? How did you resolve them?

LEARNING POINTS

✓ Values are qualities or standards we believe to be important, that help us form personal beliefs about what is good, just, right and wrong, moral and immoral.

✓ Goals and perceptions grow out of our value systems.

✓ Values aren't the same as beliefs, but they can grow out of beliefs, as well as lead us to beliefs.

✓ We learn values from parents, friends, and teachers; media like television and advertisements both reflect and influence our values.

✓ Values develop through three stages: acceptance, preference, and commitment.

✓ Values are not rigid and unchanging; changes in life circumstances may lead us to new values.

✓ Taking a stand on values means acting in a manner consistent with the values.

✓ Challenges to our values usually force us to take a stand.

✓ Values conflicts can be internal: two values we hold seem to be at odds with each other and we cannot act on one value without compromising another.

✓ Values conflicts with other people are difficult to resolve because of the subjective nature of values and their close ties to belief systems.

✓ We can influence the values of others by modeling the values we profess and reinforcing valued behavior in others.

REFERENCES

Covey, S. R. (1989). *The seven habits of highly effective people.* New York: Simon & Schuster.

Francis, D., and Young, D. (1979). *Improving work groups: A practical manual for team-building.* San Diego: University Associates.

Frankl, V. E. (1963). *Man's search for meaning.* New York: Washington Square Press.

Gaus, G. F. (1990). *Value and justification: The foundations of liberal theory.* Cambridge: Cambridge University Press.

Hanna, S. L. (1995). *Person to person: Positive relationships don't just happen* (2nd ed.). Englewood Cliffs, NJ: Prentice Hall.

Kidder, R. M. (1994). *Shared values; troubled times: Global ethics for the twenty-first century.* E. N. Thompson Forum on World Issues, University of Nebraska-Lincoln. Lincoln, NE: Cooper Foundation and University of Nebraska-Lincoln.

Leatz, C. A. (1993). *Career success/personal stress: How to stay healthy in a high-stress environment.* New York: McGraw Hill.

Rokeach, M. (Ed.) (1979). *Understanding human values: Individual and societal.* New York: The Free Press.

Simon, S. B., Howe, L. W., and Kirschenbaum, H. (1972). *Values clarification: A handbook of practical strategies for teachers and students.* New York: Hart Publishing Co.

Williams, R. M. (1979). Change and stability in values and value systems: A sociological perspective. In Rokeach, Milton (Ed.). *Understanding human values: Individual and societal.* New York: The Free Press.

Verderber, R. F., and Verderber, K. S. (1995). *Inter-act: Using interpersonal communication skills* (7th ed.). Belmont, CA: Wadsworth.

Chapter 7

CREATING THE VISION AND ESTABLISHING GOALS

The future belongs to those who believe in the beauty of their dreams.
—Eleanor Roosevelt

The people who get on in this world are the people who get up and look for the circumstances they want, and, if they can't find them, make them.
—George Bernard Shaw

Obstacles are those frightful things you see when you take your eyes off your goals.
—Unknown

People with goals succeed because they know where they're going.
—Earl Nightengale

ADVANCE PLANNER: VISIONING AND GOAL SETTING

When you complete this chapter, you will be able to:

✓ Define vision statement, goal statement, and strategic action steps.

✓ Compare and contrast vision statements, goal statements, and action steps.

✓ Write and evaluate goal statements.

✓ Create your own personal vision statement.

✓ Analyze a case study and resolve problems by applying the class concepts of vision statements, goal statements, and strategic action steps.

To accomplish these objectives, you will complete some or all of these activities:

1. Discuss a case study that illustrates the value of goal setting.

2. Read and discuss some theories of goal setting that lead to success.

3. Complete a vision statement worksheet, a vision statement, goal statements, and strategic action steps.

4. Plan a celebration as a reward for completing action steps and fulfilling goals.

CASE STUDY IN GOAL SETTING

No Goals, No Go

Jane and John Dolan run a small business from their home 15 miles from town. They have three children: Jim, who is a first-year student at the State University but lives at home; Sara, a junior in high school; and Betsy, a fifth grader. Jane has dedicated much of her life to raising her family. During 20 years of marriage, Jane has primarily been in charge of the house, cooking, child raising, and the family bookkeeping. John has helped when possible, but his overall business responsibilities leave him little time for additional work. John is also a charter member of a statewide small business association and spends three days each month in the state capital on association business. Both Sara and Betsy participate in several school and out-of-school activities.

Recently, Jane enrolled in a junior college program to fulfill a lifelong dream of becoming a legal assistant. The college she attends is 30 miles from home. Needless to say, things at home have changed and there is considerable tension. Everyone but Betsy wants to use the family car, and conflicts about transportation flare up daily. (John uses a vehicle leased by their small business.) The house is not always cleaned, the meals are not always cooked, the records are not always current. Jane needs more time to study, Sara resents having to take care of Betsy, Jim feels guilty about being involved in college classes and activities and not helping at home, and John, while encouraging Jane to go to school, wants life to be more normal and less hectic.

Discussion Questions

1. Have any of the Dolans identified a life vision?

2. Have individual members of the Dolan family clearly defined their goals? Have they shared their goal statements with each other?

3. Try to adopt the perspective of each of the Dolans and write a family vision statement.

4. What are some goal statements that might support the vision statement you just wrote?

5. What should this family do to reduce conflicts and help each other create opportunities for success? Analyze the situation and devise a plan.

6. Have the Dolan family members accepted each others' goals?

INTRODUCTION TO THEORIES OF VISIONING AND GOAL SETTING

She was the twentieth child in a black family of 22 in Clarksville, Tennessee. A weak and sickly infant, she was continually afflicted with childhood diseases, and at four she contracted polio. She was unable to walk without steel braces until she was nine, and continued to wear a supportive device in her shoes until age 11.

Both she and her mother were strong believers that fate was not something you had to resign yourself to, but that people could create their own vision and destiny. Together mother and daughter began a training program for those skinny, wobbly legs. Soon she was running. With renewed energy she began to formulate her own goals with a strategy plan. It did not take long until she was the fastest kid on the block . . . and then in the city, in the state, and even the nation.

At age 16 she qualified for the U.S. Olympic team and in 1956 she won a bronze medal in the 100-meter dash. In the 1960 Olympic games she won three gold medals, for the 100- and 200-meter events and the 400-meter relay. In all three races she broke world records and established herself as the fastest woman on earth.

When asked how she did it, Wilma Rudolph answered, "No one has a life where everything that happened was good. I think the thing that made my life good for me is that I never looked back. I've always been positive no matter what happened" (Weldon, 1984).

The story of Wilma Rudolph illustrates every aspect of building a road to success. First, she created an inspiring life vision by converting stumbling blocks into stepping-stones. Second, she wrote and committed herself to goal statements. Finally, she was willing to take the necessary action steps to complete her goals and realize her vision. This process is the formula for success. These three essential steps work for both organizations and individuals. If you are looking for personal achievement and attainment, these three steps can change your life.

Starting on the Road to Success: Step One—Creating the Vision

What Is a Vision Statement?

A vision statement states what you truly want out of life—not what you predict will happen in your life. Most important, a vision statement defines the kind of person you want to be. It details your principles and beliefs. A vision statement gives you the power to create and design your life around your personal values. It clarifies what is important to you and defines where you are willing to commit your time, energy, and effort.

On August 28, 1963, between 200,000 and 250,000 people assembled in Washington, D.C., to peacefully demonstrate on behalf of the civil rights struggle. The highlight of the day was Martin Luther King, Jr.'s now famous "I Have a Dream" speech, in which he delivered his vision statement for America: "I say to you, my friends, that in spite of the difficulties and frustrations of the moment, I still have a dream. It is a dream deeply rooted in the American dream. I have a dream that one day this nation will rise up and live out the true meaning of its creed; we hold these truths to be self-evident: that all men are created equal."

Dr. King made other vision statements as he continued his speech. "I have a dream that one day on the red hills of Georgia the sons of former slaves and sons of former slave owners will be able to sit down together at the table of brotherhood. . . . I have a dream that my four little children will one day live in a nation where they will not be judged by the color of their skin but by the content of their character. . . . With this faith we will be able to work together, to pray together, to struggle together, to go to jail together, to stand up for freedom together, knowing that we will be free one day" (King, 1963).

Dr. King's words addressed the future and provided hope through an inspirational message built on faith. This is the core of a vision statement: It clarifies your reasons for living, sets a course of direction, and defines what is important to you. A vision statement is energizing, motivational, and inspiring to you; it represents the best that is within you. Dr. King's speech raised the American consciousness and created the force for passage of the 1964 Civil Rights Act.

Keep in mind that your vision lays the foundation for your future and for all your goals and objectives. John Scully, former president of PepsiCo, describes the moment he learned that Pepsi was number one and had at last outperformed Coke: "We always believed, since the early seventies when Pepsi was widely viewed as the perennial also-ran, that we could do it. All of us started out with that objective, and we never took our eyes off it." The objective he talks about is his vision for PepsiCo (Ford & Lippitt, 1988, p. 8).

Why Are Vision Statements Necessary?

Your vision statement puts a fire in your heart. It becomes your compelling image of what you want in life and helps you create the energy to accomplish what you want to do.

Your vision statement gives direction to your life. It is like a compass that keeps you from getting lost in the world and provides you with the right direction.

Your vision statement allows you to live life with a purpose. It helps you answer the questions: Who am I? Where am I going? What kind of a life do I want to create? What kind of person do I want to be? and What commitments am I willing to make? Some people live life haphazardly, not knowing where they are going and tending to be influenced by what others think and do. Your vision statement is like a magic formula for success. It allows you to become the master of your destiny. Life is no longer a matter of chance, but a matter of choice. With a vision statement you become empowered. A vision statement puts you in charge of your life.

Your vision statement creates a positive vision of your future. It gives you the ability to see beyond the present and to create what does not yet exist. Charles Kettering, CEO of the Kettering Institute, said, "Pay attention to the future because that is where you will spend the rest of your life" (Neal & Christensen, 1990). Your vision is your dream in action.

Your vision statement allows you to live your life to its fullest potential. Scientists have concluded that people generally use only about five percent of their brain power. As you begin working with your vision statement, you will soon realize the depth of your being. You will have numerous challenges and some failures, but throughout the process of living you will gain courage, tenacity, perseverance, and confidence. The Japanese have a saying: "If life knocks you down seven times, then get up eight." If your vision is strong and your commitment deep, you will always "get back up."

The Power of Vision

If you choose to really succeed in reaching your full potential, then a personal vision statement is essential. Covey (1994) says the power of vision is incredible. Research indicates that teams and organizations with a strong sense of vision significantly outperform those without the strength of vision.

It is also important to remember that as you create the life you desire, you must be willing to let go of your past. Givens (1993, p. 27) says, "Where you is, is where you is. . . . The more time you spend dwelling on the past, the more the past limits and controls your future. In taking control of your life you begin with a clean slate. It is all too easy to get caught up and trapped in the magnitude of what happened to you in the past, whether in your childhood or the day before yesterday." Let go of the past and begin living your new life today.

Continuing on the Road to Success: Step Two—Writing Goal Statements

What Are Goal Statements?

Your vision statement is the big picture of your future. The vision statement answers the questions: What do I want to do and what kind of a person do I want to be? Your goal statements are the specific ways you plan to direct your time and energy to create your vision. Your goal statements make things happen. Written goal statements ensure your vision will be realized.

Consider a group of good friends gathered in a living room on New Year's Eve several years ago. Everyone took a turn sharing hopes, plans, and worthy ambitions for the year ahead. The group pledged to meet again on January 1 the following year to tell of their successes. One year later the eight gathered for their annual celebration. When the topic of last year's resolutions came up, the room grew silent. With quiet laughter people disclosed that they couldn't even remember their pledges from a year ago. They were clueless as to whether the resolutions had been accomplished. As the conversation continued it became clear that in order for people to be successful, goals must be written with specific action steps.

Why Have Goal Statements?

Goal statements provide you with excitement, motivation, energy, and enthusiasm. Weldon (1984) relates this story about a championship basketball game. Both teams were ready and fit. As they were waiting to take the floor, one team gathered around the coach and began to shout, "Who's gonna win? We are! We are!" The teams thundered onto the court. Immediately, the home team took possession of the ball. A quick pass to a speedy guard, the ball went up, arching perfectly toward the basket . . . but it fell to the floor. There was no hoop on the backboard! Everyone was confused, then frustrated. After a few minutes of chaos, the game was canceled, because without hoops the referees could not keep score, the players would not know if they hit or missed, and the fans would never know how well their teams played.

Playing a championship basketball game is like playing the game of life. It provides you with excitement and motivation; however, life without goals is like a basketball game without hoops. "You not only can't keep score, but you probably won't even play the game" (Weldon, 1984).

Goal statements establish your direction and keep you on track. For Dave Thomas, growing up during the depression meant growing up hungry. By the time he was eight years old, Dave told people he wanted to own a restaurant so he would never be hungry again. Orphaned at birth, he never had a stable home life, but he remained faithful to his goal. When he was 12, Dave Thomas got a job in a diner. He worked his way up to busboy and eventually became the manager. Throughout his life he remained in the restaurant business, but always working for others. He turned around four failing chicken restaurants, and eventually became a CEO of a national restaurant chain. Finally, he opened his first restaurant in Columbus, Ohio, and named it after his daughter Wendy. Today Dave Thomas owns over 3800 restaurants all over the world. When asked about the key to his success, Dave stated that he just concentrated on his goal and kept on track (McGarvey, 1992).

Goal statements ensure greater success. A recent study of college graduates who have been out of school for ten years attempted to determine how graduates were progressing toward achieving their goals (Givens, 1993). The study showed 83 percent of the graduates had set no goals at all. This group reported that they were working hard and staying busy, but they had no specific goals. Another 14 percent had goals, but their goals were mental, not written. This 14 percent was earning, on the average, three times the income of those who had no goals at all. Only three percent of the entire graduate group had written goals. They were earning ten times as much as the group who had no goals at all.

Goal statements create self-confidence. Henry Ford was one of America's most successful entrepreneurs. He is often called the genius of mass production; however, some of his early Model Ts were not dependable. Early in this century many new car owners, stuck in muddy ruts, were assailed with remarks like, "Get a horse!" Most thought the car was just a passing fancy and could never replace the more reliable horse and buggy. But Henry Ford had a vision. He thought the car was the wave of the future. Henry Ford also had a goal: Mass produce cars so every family could afford one. Ford's empire moved into high gear, and his Model T became the most popular car in America. Within a few short years, however, Ford came under attack by critics who said his cars lacked imagination and creativity. After producing 15,000,000 Model Ts, Henry Ford closed his factory doors.

People were shocked. Ford said his doors would not reopen until he created a new model. People said it couldn't be done and Ford would be bankrupt within a year. They said he could never regain the market or create a car as great as the Model T. Within 18 months, a new Ford, the Model A, rolled off the production line, and within a few months it was the number one selling car. Reporters who interviewed Henry Ford about his new success asked how he found the confidence to close his factory for a year and a half. Ford said, "If you think you can, or you think you can't, you are right." He said he never had a doubt about his success, because if you find success one time, you will always find it again.

Henry Ford truly believed that success is not a matter of luck, but of effort and strategy. As you write goal statements and take your first victorious step, the next step becomes much easier. Success is doing those things you know need to be done, and doing them to the best of your ability. Achievements and accomplishments are not accidents; they are outcomes of a pattern of success. Careful planning, thoughtful strategy, and faithful execution are the main features of this pattern (Rouillard, 1993).

Goal statements increase opportunities. Opportunities are everywhere, but you need to see them. Givens (1993) asks you to imagine yourself in a 10 x 10 room. Every minute a $100 bill floats down from the ceiling, and all you have to do is reach out, grab the bill before it hits the ground, and the bill is yours. Within a five-hour time period, you could have $30,000. It sounds easy, and seems a nice way to walk away with a large sum of money. The only hitch to this story is that you are blindfolded! You cannot see the opportunities, and for most people the bills would float to the ground untouched.

Goal statements help you remove the blindfold. Goal statements help you know exactly what you are looking for. Goal statements help ensure your success. Goal statements give you the vision to increase your opportunities to catch the $100 bills. Goals create dynamic personal growth; without goals people are only half alive (Robbins, 1991).

How to Write Goal Statements

When water turns into steam, it expands to about 1700 times its original size. Steam has tremendous potential. When steam is directed purposefully it can generate enough power to light city streets or to pull a train over a mountain. However, if steam is left to boil on its own with no aim or purpose, the water will eventually disappear and the potential for greatness evaporates into thin air. Goals in people's lives are like focused steam—the full power and potential can be realized only if there is direction and purpose.

When writing your goal statements, let the word STEAM suggest five basic guidelines.

S = *Specific*. Goal statements need to be specific. They should be clear and concise.

T = *Time Determined*. Goal statements need to allow the proper amount of time to accomplish a goal. If you allow too much time, you won't be challenged. If there is not enough time, you will be frustrated.

E = *Ensure Success*. In order to achieve success your goal statements need to be realistic and achievable. While the purpose of goal statements is to challenge you to reach a higher level of performance, you also want to ensure success by knowing that with your time and energy you can accomplish your goal.

A = *Action Oriented*. Goal statements indicate that you are willing to take detailed action to accomplish your goal.

M = *Measurable*. Goal statements should be quantifiable. You need to know when you have reached the goal, and you must be able to measure or evaluate the success of your efforts.

EXAMPLE: Angela is a member of her college golf team. After graduation, Angela's goal is to play on the women's professional golf tour. Currently Angela has a five handicap. Her goal is to lower her handicap to a three.

Using the *STEAM* guidelines, Angela wrote the following to create her goal statement:

S = I will lower my current golf handicap by two points (specific).

T = I will follow my plan for six months (time determined).

E = I have the energy and am willing to invest the effort to achieve this goal. I am a good golfer with great potential. With dedication I am capable of achieving this goal (affirmation that the goal is realistic and achievable; success is ensured with determination).

A = I will accomplish this goal by practicing 20 hours each week and playing a minimum 100 rounds of golf in the next six months. My chipping and putting need greater attention. During practice I will spend 75 percent of my time on my short game (detailed action).

M = I will know I have accomplished my goal when my computerized golf handicap printout is a three (measurable source of evaluation).

After Angela completed the *STEAM* process she wrote the following goal statement: In 6 months I will lower my golf handicap from 5 to 3. I will accomplish this goal by playing 100 rounds of golf in 6 months devoting extra attention to chipping and putting. I will know I have succeeded in accomplishing my goal when my handicap is 3 on the computer read-out sheet.

Persevering on the Road to Success: Step Three—Committing Energy to Strategic Action Steps

How Do People Accomplish Goals?

Wilma Rudolph overcame many obstacles on her way to winning three Olympic gold medals. Many people initially questioned her abilities and doubted her resolve, but she remained focused and determined. Martin Luther King, Jr. and the people who worked with him in the civil rights movement in the 1960s endured horrible resistance, but nothing could deter their efforts. You must recognize that you, too, will have to overcome obstacles to achieve your goals and will need persistence and tenacity. One way to ensure that you accomplish your goals is to keep them visible and focused in your mind.

The value of keeping your goals in the forefront of your mind instead of letting them become obscured by obstacles is illustrated by the story of Florence Chaddick, the first woman to swim the English Channel both across and back. On a foggy day in July 1952, Florence set out to accomplish another swimming feat: To be the first woman to swim from Catalina Island to the coast of California. The going was rough. The cold water made her muscles ache, and sharks had to be frightened off by rifle shots. As the fog became increasingly dense, Florence could barely see the support boats alongside. She could see nothing but endless water. She began to doubt she could meet the challenge, even though her mother and trainer kept telling her she was close to completing the goal. The obstacles seemed too overwhelming. She finally asked to be pulled from the water.

Sitting in the boat with her body still shaking from the cold, Florence was shocked to learn that she was only half a mile from the California shore. The fog had defeated her. She simply could not see her goal. Florence was convinced she could reach her goal if she could just keep the vision clearly focused in her mind. Two months later in dense fog, Florence set out again. The vision was clearly set in her mind, and even though she struggled against the same obstacles that defeated her the first time, this time Florence Chaddick made it. Her hand touched the California coast in record breaking time—beating the men's record by two hours (Weldon, 1984).

Florence Chaddick, Wilma Rudolph, Martin Luther King, Jr., and many other successful and dedicated people and organizations all recognized the importance of keeping goals clearly focused. The odds against achieving some goals may seem overwhelming, but with endurance and persistence the goals are within reach.

A second way to accomplish goals is to write and follow strategic action steps, the short-term procedures that help ensure success. For some people the first step is the most difficult to take. Strategic action steps help people overcome hesitancy and inertia. Each completed action step builds confidence and dedication by diminishing doubts and uncertainties and reaffirming commitment and belief in the goal.

Strategic action steps, written after you write your goal statement, detail the step-by-step procedures you plan to follow to accomplish the goal. Return for a moment to Angela who wrote this goal statement about lowering her golf handicap to three: *In six months I will lower my golf handicap from five to three. I will accomplish this goal by playing 100 rounds of golf in six months, devoting extra attention to chipping and putting. I will know I have succeeded in accomplishing my goal when my handicap is three on the computer read-out sheet.*

Angela can now begin to devise a specific plan with more details. Her first strategic action steps might be to: 1) talk to coach on Tuesday for some hints on improving putting; 2) practice one hour on putting after instruction; 3) play first round (out of 100), record score, and evaluate.

Strategic Action Steps Keep People Motivated

Strategic action steps keep people motivated because completing one small step provides an immediate sense of accomplishment. (A clear illustration of the saying, "by the yard it's hard, by the inch it's a cinch.") Keep your action steps realistic. Just as you wouldn't eat a 12-ounce steak in one bite, but would cut it into small pieces, each life goal must be cut into a manageable bite size (Waitley, 1994).

Two other features of strategic action steps keep people inspired:

Why do I want to do this? When writing your strategic action steps, also write down the answer to the question, "Why am I doing this?" to help you stay motivated and renew your energy.

Plan small celebrations. Every so often you need to celebrate your accomplishments. The type of celebration you plan is up to you; the important thing, however, is to do something to reward yourself.

Completing the Process

Goal setting follows this simple four-step process: Write your goal statement; answer the question "Why do I want to do this?"; write your strategic action steps; and plan your celebrations.

Here is a simple illustration of the goal setting process:

Goal Statement: I will lose eight pounds (specific) in two months (time determined). I have the energy and determination to accomplish this goal. I have proven will-power and the weight loss is important to me. With my efforts, my plan is realistic and achievable (ensure success). I plan to accomplish this goal by eating low-fat, low-calorie foods and by exercising. I will limit my fat intake to 35 grams per day, and my caloric intake to 1500 each day. I will exercise a minimum of three times a week (action). I will know I have reached my goal when two months from today I get on the scale and it reads eight pounds lighter (measurement).

Why I Want to Do This	Strategic Action Steps	Celebration
1. Look better	1. Buy low-cal snacks	1. Rent favorite video
2. Feel better	2. Eat 3 fruits a day	2. Go to the park
3. Improve health	3. Walk all stairs	3. Browse the mall
4. Build confidence	4. Drink 8 glasses of water a day	4. Visit friends

Conclusion

If the Chinese proverb "The longest journey begins with a single step" is true, then the first step of the journey to a successful life is to create a vision statement. The vision statement will clearly help you design the type of future you want. The second step is to write goal statements to direct you on a path toward commitment and success. The goal statements will make your vision a reality. The third step is to write strategic action steps—the things you can do daily, weekly, and monthly to make your goal statements become reality. When writing goal statements answer the question, "Why do I want to do this?" and grant yourself minor victory celebrations.

The small decisions people make create their destinies. You are in charge of your life. You are in charge of your decisions and actions. By following these three steps you can realize your full potential. And when you reach the end of your road of life, you can look back and say, "This was a job well done."

Writing a Personal Vision Statement and Goal Statements

Purpose To help you develop a personal vision statement that will help you clarify what is important to you so you can identify goals that will make your vision a reality. To write goal statements that will clearly move you toward your vision.

You Will Need Pen or pencil

The worksheets on the following pages

Activity To create a vision statement and related goal statements, begin by answering the series of questions listed in the worksheets. This will take time, energy, and reflection, but you and your future success are certainly worth the effort.

Vision Statement Worksheet

List five things you are happy about in your life.

1. _____
2. _____
3. _____
4. _____
5. _____

List five things you are committed to in your life.

1. _____
2. _____
3. _____
4. _____
5. _____

List five things you are doing right now to use your full potential.

1. _____
2. _____
3. _____
4. _____
5. _____

Place your name in the designated box. Write your five most important roles in the five large circles. Examples of your current roles could include: student, friend, son, daughter, team member, grandchild, employee, roommate. After you have identified five major roles then add five adjectives that describe your behavior in each of these roles.

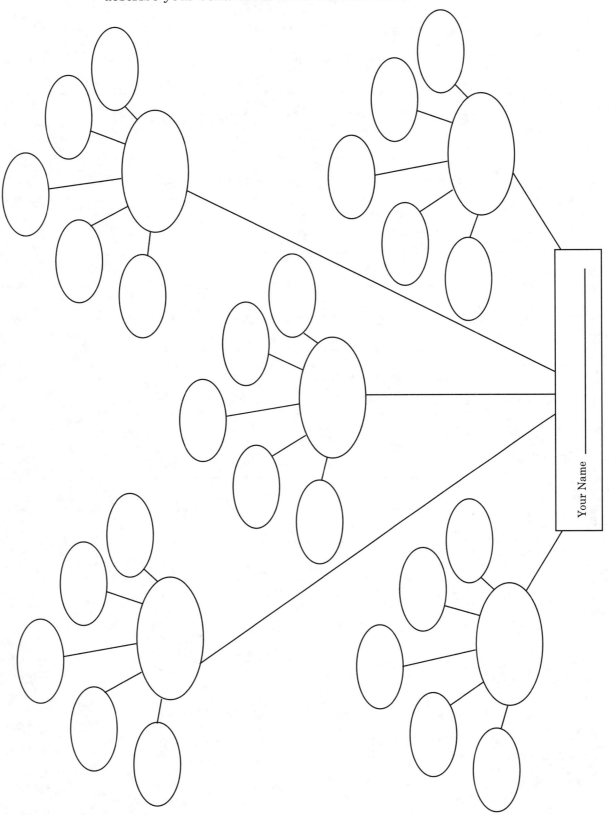

Your Name

Now repeat the same process using five roles *you anticipate* you will have in your future. Examples might include: parent, civic leader, wife, husband, professional.

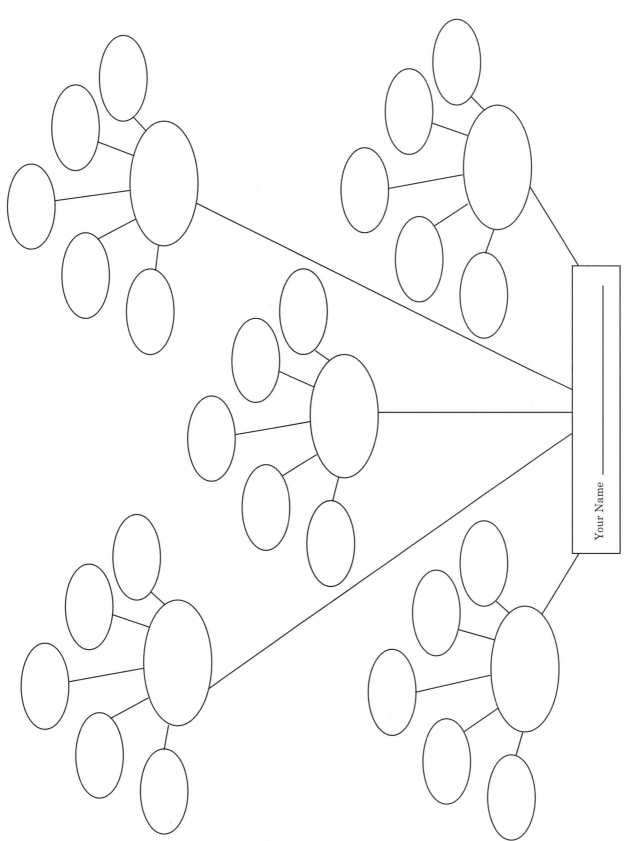

Your Name

List your five priority values.

1. _____

2. _____

3. _____

4. _____

5. _____

List your ten greatest strengths.

1. _____

2. _____

3. _____

4. _____

5. _____

6. _____

7. _____

8. _____

9. _____

10. _____

List five things you would like to do to make a difference in the world.

1. _____

2. _____

3. _____

4. _____

5. _____

List five things you really enjoy doing. Include items on your list that you would like to do even if you don't think you have the money or the time. (For example, travel, skiing, restoring an old car, etc.)

1. _____

2. _____

3. _____

4. _____

5. _____

In one paragraph, write what you would like someone to say at your funeral.

Review the answers you gave to the previous questions. After analyzing your answers, summarize your ten life-guiding principles (values) and core beliefs. Examples of principles and core beliefs could include such things as: responsibility, loyalty, the Golden Rule, hard work, tenacity, faith.

1. _____

2. _____

3. _____

4. _____

5. _____

6. _____

7. _____

8. _____

9. _____

10. _____

Example of a Vision Statement

Here is an example of a vision statement that takes into account the principles and core beliefs discovered during the previous visioning process:

I pledge to live my life to its fullest potential. I will continually look for opportunities and new experiences that will enrich my life and provide for greater growth. I will be a lifelong learner. I prize curiosity. I want to be well informed. My ultimate goal is to learn from my life events so sometime in my later years I will have gained wisdom.

I find great joy in five specific areas of my life: wife, parent, difference maker, friend, and professional in my chosen career. In fulfilling my roles I want to be loyal, competent, sturdy, trustworthy, and responsible. Hard work, honesty, tenacity, and faith will be my guideposts in helping me make decisions. I will always seek to do my best in each of these areas.

✓ As a wife I am supportive, caring, and loving. My marriage vows are sacred. My husband is my best friend and my confidant. We laugh, share, plan for our future, and enjoy each day together. While we are two separate individuals who help each other grow and flourish, we are of the same roots and provide support for one another.

✓ As a parent I provide both roots and wings. It is my responsibility to teach my children to be good citizens of the world. My husband and I have instructed our children in the virtues and values we think are essential for a productive and happy life. A wise person once said that children are on loan to us. When the time comes they must be set free to fly. I will encourage them to fly with the eagles.

✓ At the end of each day I want to reflect on what I have done to make a positive difference in the world. The differences I make may be of word or deed, but I will find a way each day to be a positive force in the world.

✓ I promise to be a good friend. I will be there when needed. I will be empathetic, trustworthy, and loyal. I will laugh with my friends in the good times, and I will cry with them in the trying times, but I will be there. I will listen.

✓ As a professional I vow that I will be a hard worker, someone who is never satisfied with mediocrity. I will take advantage of different learning situations and continue to grow. I will provide positive leadership. My world of work also includes a volunteer segment. I will contribute time, energy, and efforts to assist others in need.

Each of these roles enables me to use my skills, talents, abilities, and knowledge. I vow to continue to use my abilities now and to develop new skills and interests for the future.

I believe one day I will be a mother-in-law and grandparent. When that time comes I pledge that I will be a supportive mother and mother-in-law. I will also be an incredibly loving grandparent, because like parents, grandparents provide the roots for children to grow.

I thoroughly enjoy traveling and learning about other cultures. I will be a good steward of my money and invest it wisely to accommodate my future travel plans. I will lead a healthy lifestyle because I plan on living a long time.

I have a strong internal locus of control. I value my personal freedom and autonomy. I will maintain a positive view of the future. I will continue to flourish and help others plant and grow. I will make a difference—and when I die my wish is to have others say, "She was a wonderful, loving wife and mother. She knew how to have fun and she was a great friend. She made a contribution by helping others who were in need, and we will miss her. She cared. She made a difference in the world, but she was a woman of faith and we celebrate with her today."

Writing Your Vision Statement

You are now ready to write your personal vision statement. Writing your vision statement has many advantages: Writing helps you crystallize your thoughts; at any time you can read your statement to keep you focused and motivated; you can revise your statement as you desire; writing it makes your vision become yours.

A vision statement is usually about a page long, but it can be longer. Remember your vision statement represents the best that is within you. Your statement will address what you want out of life, as well as what type of person you want to be.

One final note: Take the word *try* out of your vision statement. This statement represents what you want and what you are willing to do. Trying won't cut it.

Write a draft of your vision statement here:

Goal Statements Worksheet

Using the *STEAM* principle, write two goal statements in the spaces provided. Then complete the following charts. Meet in groups of three to critique. Is each statement specific? Does it have a realistic time schedule? Is success ensured? Are action steps included? Is there a measurement tool? Are the strategic action steps specific? Does the person really desire this goal? Are there planned celebrations?

Goal Statement:

Why I Want to Do This	Strategic Action Steps	Celebrations

Goal Statement:

Why I Want to Do This	Strategic Action Steps	Celebrations

LEARNING POINTS

✓ Vision statements help define what we want out of life and define the kind of person we want to become.

✓ Vision statements are grounded in values (principles and beliefs).

✓ Goal statements are the means by which vision statements become operational in our everyday lives.

✓ Goal statements are positive, short- and long-term plans that energize and inspire us.

✓ To provide direction and purpose, goals statements must be: specific, time-determined, ensuring of success, action-oriented, and measurable (STEAM).

✓ Action steps break goal statements into specific procedures, which when properly executed, build toward goal attainment and eventually bring the vision statement into reality.

REFERENCES

Covey, S. R. (1994). *First things first.* New York: Simon & Schuster.

Ford, G. A., and Lippitt, G. L. (1988). *Creating your future: A guide to personal goal setting.* San Diego: University Associates.

Givens, C. J. (1993). *Super self: Doubling your personal effectiveness.* New York: Simon & Schuster.

King, M. L. (August 1963). *I have a dream* [Online]. Available FTP: mrcnext.cso.uiuc.edu Directory: gutenberg/freenet File: i-have-a-dream.

McGarvey, R. (June, 1992). Get what you want out of life. *Reader's Digest,* 105–109.

Neal, B. (Producer), and Christensen, R. D. (Director). *Power of vision* [Videotape]. Burnsville, MN: Charthouse International.

Robbins, A. (1991). *Awaken the giant within.* New York: Simon & Schuster.

Rouillard, L. A. (1993). *Goals and goal-setting.* Menlo Park, CA: Crisp Publications.

Waitley, D. (1994). *Flextactics: The new dynamics of goal-setting.* [Cassette recording]. New York: Simon & Schuster Audio Division, Nightengale-Conant Corporation, Sound Ideas.

Weldon, J. (1984). *Unlimited times.* Scottsdale, AZ: Joel Weldon and Associates.

8

TIME MANAGEMENT

Ordinary people think merely how they will spend their time; a person of intellect tries to use it.

—Arthur Schopenhauer

Doing more things is no substitute for doing the right things.

—Anonymous

ADVANCE PLANNER: TIME MANAGEMENT

When you complete this chapter, you will be able to:

✓ Organize yourself more effectively.

✓ Prioritize action steps that are important to you.

✓ Prevent interruptions in your life.

✓ Meet deadlines that are important to you.

✓ Manage procrastination through concentration.

In order to accomplish these objectives, you will complete some or all of these activities:

1. Conduct a preliminary time management assessment to help you determine your present time management skills.

2. Discuss a case study to help point out key concepts in managing your time.

3. Run an individual time log to identify your major time-consumers.

4. Identify specific ways in which you would use extra time if it were available to you.

5. Complete an exercise to help you improve your use of time by setting goals.

6. Discuss ways to increase your skills in managing your time more effectively.

CASE STUDY IN TIME MANAGEMENT

Alarms, Demands, Warning Signs, and CNN

Mornings would be great if weren't for alarms, Rory thought, reaching up and tapping the snooze alarm for ten more minutes of rack time, but already the old worries were invading the brain. I've really dug myself a deep hole to crawl out of this semester. How did I get in this position? I'm in trouble with my housemates, classes look terrible, people at work aren't even excited to see me come in, and I need to start looking for a permanent job when (or if) I graduate next semester.

Rory rationalized: Okay, so my roommates don't get it. I never cleaned up after myself and really don't plan on doing it. Somebody else can put my dirty dishes in the dishwasher and as long as I can find a clean towel, who really cares? I can't believe some of my housemates are such neat-niks they don't want to have friends over just because the place looks like a pit. They need to lighten up!

Now classes—unfortunately this was to have been a no-brainer semester, Rory thought. Only one science course scheduled, meaning only one lab and some extra time that hadn't been available in past semesters, but where did it go? Rory studied once in a while, but surely you didn't have to read all those assignments. And some of the professors were sticklers on attending class.

Maybe I would be doing better in my classes if I had gone to more classes, Rory reflected, but a couple of them cut into some prime television time, and who wants to miss *The Young and the Restless*? And the assignments. In past semesters professors could be persuaded to lower the grade only one letter for turning assignments in late. This semester a couple of profs were unreasonable: It was in on time or forget it. Zeros really sink your grade fast and literally hammer your GPA!

Then there was work. The first year Rory used a work-study grant to work for a department on campus about ten hours a week. The next year, work-study didn't come through, so the department paid a straight hourly salary. The money was okay and the work wasn't too hard. Then one of the secretaries quit and the department was slow about hiring somebody. Because of budget cuts they didn't replace the secretary and asked Rory to work more hours—which led to working some nights and weekends trying to keep up. Rory kept hearing Mom's constant question: "Rory, are you an employee or are you a student?" Maybe a different job was the answer; some people at the department were beginning to get upset because Rory refused to continue to work so many hours.

Even worse than all this was the thought of looking for a position to begin after graduation. Maybe Rory just didn't want to admit that the GPA was going to be a stumbling block to even applying for some of the positions at the Placement Office on campus and showing those recruiters the old "Rory-fied" enthusiasm and drive. Their loss, right? Two close friends had already been through senior check and had started interviewing. One had a second interview already. Yeah, but Jamie's borderline retentive, Rory thought. I'll get over there eventually. But Rory was nagged by the memory of the poster in the Placement Office that said: "Coming to see us after you graduate is like studying after finals." Okay, I'll get there before I graduate, Rory promised, but not today.

The snooze buzzer sounded again and Rory finally decided to get up, feeling more tired than the night before. In the harsh light of the bathroom, Rory looked in the mirror. Wow, what a mess. Rory went through the morning routine: Brush the teeth, stumble out to the kitchenette, grab some cereal from the cupboard. There were no clean bowls to be found, so Rory retrieved one from the living room, rinsed it out, and filled it with cereal and milk.

Wandering into the living room, Rory turned on the television to CNN and soon became engrossed in some interesting news sequences they were running. When Rory looked at the clock again, the bad news sunk in: I just missed my science lecture. Oh well, I can get the notes from somebody. Sometimes life is just overwhelming, Rory mused, settling in to watch a morning of television.

Discussion Questions

1. Rory's inability to manage time has begun to affect relationships. Which relationships are being affected and why?

2. Do you know someone (or perhaps it is you) who is struggling to decide if he or she is a student or employee first?

3. Once someone (or you) makes the decision to be a student or employee first, how does that affect the way time is managed? How would such a decision affect Rory's time management?

4. Many decisions we make today have a long-term impact on our future. What decisions has Rory made today that will affect the future?

INTRODUCTION TO THEORIES OF TIME MANAGEMENT

We have tried to capture time on calendars, measure it by the clock, extend it by daylight savings time, speed it up, and slow it down. But the simple key to good time management is to work smarter, not harder, in every phase of your life. Determine what is important in your life through visioning, writing goal statements, and taking action steps that will focus in on the goals.

There are three possible approaches to time management. First, you can increase the amount of your available time. This approach means you must stretch the hours of each day as much as possible, a strategy that could result in fatigue, lack of efficiency, and sometimes depression. A second approach is to do more work in the available time. This approach assumes that if you can pack more work into your day, everything will work out great. Likely results, however, include high stress and burnout. The third strategy is to do only the important work in the available time. This approach suggests that a scale of priority be assigned to the use of your time. It also reflects a commitment toward only essential matters. This approach necessitates an action-oriented strategy, and is clearly the best way to manage your time.

Each of us has a clear sense of the importance of various demands on our time. What is important for one person may not be as important for another. But the first rule of effective time management is for you to decide where your priorities lie. If you could save five hours per week or month, how would you use the time? What important activities and tasks would you wish to accomplish? Assigning your own value to tasks and actually completing them will allow you to feel less stressed and more satisfied that you have done something worthwhile.

Researchers into time management identify ten keys to managing time that will give you more focus, less stress, and more control of the important things in your life:

1. Run a time log to help you pinpoint and eliminate one time-consumer each month.
2. Identify priorities each day.
3. Set realistic goals.
4. Use some system for planning.
5. Establish deadlines for yourself.
6. Delegate, when feasible.
7. Plan meetings carefully.
8. Develop procedures for gathering data.
9. Group similar work tasks during uninterrupted time blocks.
10. Schedule some personal time each day.

Let's look at each of these strategies individually. All of them may not work for you, but practicing even one or two can make a significant difference in the way you manage time—and can prevent time from managing you.

1. Run a Time Log

A time log identifies your current use of time to help you discover where you are spending time, both wisely and unwisely, so you can become more effective in completing tasks. A time log is the foundation for building sound time management habits. You cannot begin to improve the ways you budget time until you know where you currently spend it.

Your time log should record all activities you perform, including sharpening pencils, chatting with friends or classmates, studying, using the telephone, etc. To keep a useful time log, you need to make notes as you go through the day. Do not allow more than 15 minutes to pass before adding to your time log record. It is amazing how many things we do, many of them so unconsciously that we forget about them literally moments after we have completed them.

No one needs to see your time log except you, so it can take any form you wish. A basic time log has two columns, one to list the times of the day and another for descriptions of the activities you engage in at those times. It's best to keep a time log for five days in a row, to give you a feel for your habit patterns.

After five days, trace your habit patterns to find your most obvious time-consumers. Make a concentrated effort to eliminate or modify your top three major time-consumers. Don't try to deal with all negative patterns at once. After you feel you have effectively improved your time management skills for your top three concerns, focus on the next group of three time-consumers and try to eliminate them, and so on.

Even though keeping a time log may appear to be time-consuming in itself, you must be willing to give it the effort it deserves and complete it honestly. Time spent at this point is time saved later.

2. Identify Priorities Each Day

We all use different criteria to establish priorities for tasks we must accomplish each day. Some of these criteria are:

✓ personal feelings toward the project or individuals with whom we must work to complete it;

✓ our degree of interest in the task and our sense of how much fun it will be;

✓ its importance for us and others it may affect; and

✓ our sense of the task's urgency in relation to ourselves or to others.

Bliss (1991) prefers to set priorities in terms of importance. You must examine each item on your list of things to do in light of the question, "Does this task clearly contribute to the achievement of my lifetime goals or my short-range objectives?" If it does, put a star by it. Continue until you reach the end of your To Do list. Then number the starred items in the order in which you would like to do them. After you have ranked your starred items by priorities, do the same thing with your less important items. You now have a game plan.

Lakein (1973) says, "No list is complete until it shows priorities. Whenever you make a list, finish the list by setting priorities." Lakein suggests using the ABC priority system. Write a capital letter A to the left of those items on the list that have a high value; a B for those items on the list that have a medium value; and C for those with low value. By comparing the items to one another, you will come up with the ABC priority choices for every entry on your list. You will get the most out of your time by doing the A's first, and saving the B's and C's for later. You can break down your A's, B's, and C's further so that they become A1, A2, A3, B1, B2, C1, etc.

3. Set Goals

One common thread running through all self-help literature is the idea of the power of goals. We've been told to set long-term goals, short-term goals, daily goals, monthly goals, personal goals, organizational goals, ten-year goals, and lifetime goals. Covey (1994) says "goal-setting is obviously a powerful process. It's based on the same principle of focus that allows us to concentrate rays of diffused sunlight into a force powerful enough to start a fire. It's the manifestation of creative imagination and independent will. It's the transformation of vision into achievable, actionable doing. It's the common denominator of successful individuals and organizations."

When writing your goals be sure that they are realistic, specific, comprehensive, and understandable.

4. Use a System for Planning

Each individual has a system for planning that works for her or him. A plan is an orderly means to establish effective control over your own future. A good plan is logical, comprehensive, flexible, action-oriented, future-driven, formal, and people-focused. According to McGee-Cooper (1993), "One important element in sticking with the plan is to stay refreshed with daily fun and renewal. When you are joy-starved, you become unmanageable. When you stay balanced with ample fun, exercise, and relaxation, you look forward to your daily planning."

The 10/10 Rule is a simple one to follow: If you spend 10 minutes per day planning you will become 10 percent more effective in your life.

5. Establish Deadlines

Remember Parkinson's Law: "Work expands to fill the time available for its completion." You can greatly increase your effectiveness if you simply give yourself a deadline for each task and do your best to stick. to it. Bliss (1991) indicates that most people work better under pressure, and a self-imposed deadline can provide the pressure you need to keep at your task until it is completed.

Until you set a deadline for a project, it isn't really an action program; it is more like a vague wish, something you intend to do someday. The problem, however, is that someday is not a day of the week. It will never arrive and the task will never get done.

6. Delegate

To delegate is to appoint someone else to act on your behalf. In other words, delegation means asking someone else to do something that falls within your area of responsibility. There are many advantages to delegating: spreading the workload, taking advantage of someone else's expertise, building the capabilities and responsibilities of the other person, motivating the other person, and freeing yourself for other important tasks.

Remember, however, that delegation has some associated risks, as well, many of which revolve around the capability and commitment levels of the persons to whom we delegate. Key questions delegators need to ask are: Does this person have the ability to learn the skills needed to complete the task? Does this person have the commitment to be propelled through to task completion?

Delegating to someone who is not capable or who does not share the delegator's commitment level can lead to unmet expectations on the part of one or both. When we delegate, we are asking someone to do something on our behalf; a lackluster performance, therefore, can have a negative effect on others' perceptions of the delegator. The key to delegation, then, is to be objective about the talents and shortcomings of others and to use that knowledge to delegate wisely.

7. Plan Meetings Carefully

For meetings to be effective, an agenda must be developed and shared before the meeting so participants can be prepared. The meeting needs to always start and end on time; everyone attending the meeting should participate in the problem-solving and decision-making processes; and there needs to be a follow-up of action taken.

Bliss (1991) gives us insight into meetings as we plan before, during, and after. The most important part of a meeting happens before it even starts—the preliminary planning that too often is done haphazardly or not at all. Before scheduling a meeting, ask yourself if a meeting is really needed. If the answer is yes, plan the meeting carefully and prepare a clear agenda. Start the meeting on time, stay on track (according to the agenda you have made), and summarize. After the meeting, record what was decided, what assignments were made, and the deadlines for action.

8. Develop Procedures for Gathering Data

Because so many resources (books, people, magazines, professional associations, seminars, computers, etc.) are available to us, we can easily become confused about what information is really necessary to help us carry out our important tasks. Each one of us has a method we rely on to gather data. Good time management demands that we become aware of our personal information gathering process and evaluate it critically so we can increase the effectiveness of our daily lives.

There are a number of systematic approaches to help you gather data and manage. Examples of these systems include Day-Timer, the Franklin Planner, and Day Runner.

9. Group Similar Tasks during Uninterrupted Time Blocks

You can't eliminate interruptions. Still, you can minimize the number of interruptions you have to deal with. Indeed, you must keep interruptions to a minimum if you wish to operate effectively, because one hour of concentrated effort is worth more than two hours of interrupted segments.

Start by identifying your most productive times during your day. This is the time when you need to do your most important tasks, your highest priorities on your To Do list, those things that you must do. Next, find an area where you can work without interruption and stick to the most important tasks you have to complete at this moment. You can implement this plan for studying, researching, being alone, making telephone calls, or being with friends.

10. Schedule Personal Time Each Day

"Most timelocked schedules need loosening, not tightening. What conventional time management too often does is make us more clock-conscious than ever, more wedded to the notion that our schedules can be sub-divided and re-organized" (Keyes, 1991). Such techniques seldom invite us to reflect, to question the categories themselves, and to remain flexible enough to move as the future demands. We need to set aside one hour each day for ourselves. This gives time for relaxing, meditating, creating, and restoring the energy so vital to our future.

Conclusion

We all know people who seem to get more "life out of their time." These people are wise time managers who have learned to use the skills of prioritizing, goal setting, planning, setting and adhering to timelines, effectively delegating, and scheduling personal time. Through practice, these skills can become part of our daily lives. We, too, can share the quality and quantity of life that wise time managers enjoy.

EXERCISE
Discover Your Time Management I.Q.

Purpose To help you discover how bright you are when it comes to managing your time.

Activity Read the following statements and respond to each with often, sometimes, or rarely.

1. I hold planning sessions with myself every day to draft the next day's To Do lists. ✗Often Sometimes Rarely

2. I tackle the biggest, most important tasks first. Often Sometimes ✗Rarely

3. I regularly finish all the things on my daily To Do list. Often ✗Sometimes Rarely

4. I meet deadlines with plenty of time to spare. Often Sometimes ✗Rarely

5. My room and desk are well organized. ✗Often Sometimes Rarely

6. I can quickly and easily find items that I put away long ago. ✗Often Sometimes Rarely

7. I know when and how to cut short unexpected interruptions, such as drop-in visitors. Often ✗Sometimes Rarely

8. Following interruptions, I am able to resume my work right away. Often ✗Sometimes Rarely

9. I am able to delegate tasks with ease. Often ✗Sometimes Rarely

10. I regularly critique my time management techniques. Often ✗Sometimes Rarely

How to Arrive at Your Time Management I.Q.

Score your answers as follows:

3 points for "often" 9
2 points for "sometimes" 10
1 point for "rarely" 2
Add your total points = ___21___

28–30	You're doing a great job.
25–27	Keep up the good work, but apply your timesaving techniques more consistently.
✗19–24	There's room for improvement. Start by analyzing weaknesses in your technique and work to eliminate them one by one.
16–18	Discipline yourself to avoid overcommitment.
Below 16	Get back to basics. Organize yourself and learn to plan ahead.

Extra Time

Purpose   To become aware of the number of important things you will do when you have extra time, and to be able to prioritize each item.

You Will Need   Pencil or pen

Paper

Activity   Individually list the things you would do if you had extra time. Work for three minutes. When time is up, in small groups of 3–5 persons, discuss your lists.

Discussion   What types of things do each of you have on your list? Do they involve other people? If they do involve other people, discuss how they are involved. If you have listed more than one item, how will you prioritize them? How important to you are the items you placed on the list? (Rate them as very important, important, somewhat important, and not important.)

EXERCISE
Getting Things Done

Purpose To develop an understanding of why you are not getting more things accomplished.

You Will Need Time Consumer Form

Pencil

Activity Individually check the list indicating your major time consumers (if you have a job, also check the list relating each time consumer to the job). Determine the major time consumers of the class. Prioritize the class list and use the top four time consumers in this activity. Divide into four groups and assign one of the four major time consumers to each group.

Discuss and record reasons for the problem and ways to correct the problem. Elect a leader from each group who will report back to the whole group when individual discussions are finished.

Discussion

Identify reasons for each time consumer and possible solutions to each problem.

My Major Time Consumers

On the Job		Off the Job
❏	Procrastination	❏
❏	Lack of organization	❏
❏	Misplaced items	❏
❏	Interruptions	❏
❏	Waiting for information	❏
❏	Attempting to do too much	❏
❏	Taking too many naps	❏
❏	Meetings without goals	❏
❏	Inability to say "No"	❏
❏	Failure to plan	❏
❏	Socializing	❏
❏	Ineffective delegation	❏
❏	Confused choice of priorities	❏
❏	Unrealistic time frames	❏
❏	Negative attitudes	❏
❏	Poor communication	❏
❏	Other people's mistakes	❏
❏	Understaffing	❏
❏	Lack of feedback	❏
❏	Too much drinking	❏
❏	Perfectionism	❏
❏	Handling paperwork	❏
❏	Too many goals	❏
❏	Conflicting deadlines	❏
❏	Worrying too much	❏

Action Steps

Purpose To develop a plan of action with commitment regarding one or two of the time management techniques discussed in this chapter.

You Will Need Paper

Pencil or pen

Activity Individually list the action steps you wish to take to increase your time management skills. Share with one other person in the group to get commitment in following through. Determine a date by which you will take action steps and agree with one other person to call each other by that date to see if you have completed your tasks.

Discussion

Determine if the action steps are realistic, specific, understood, and comprehensive enough to be meaningful.

FURTHER ACTIVITY

Journal Writing

Periodically during each day make entries in a Time Log to identify the tasks you are doing and the time it takes to complete them. Keep the log for 14 twenty-four hour days. After completing the time log, look for those things that consumed most of your time, the habits that have developed that you wish to correct, and the strong points that you wish to build upon. Prioritize the list of things you wish to do to correct problems. Correct one problem (and only one) per month. Work with it to make sure you are comfortable with the changes before you undertake additional things.

LEARNING POINTS

✓ Pinpointing specific ways in which you are more organized will assist you greatly in the future.

✓ Prioritizing your day and week will create success.

✓ Writing action steps that help you complete your plan will reduce stress in your life.

✓ Taking steps to reduce one interruption in your day will result in great satisfaction.

✓ Managing procrastination by quickly setting deadlines to complete action steps takes concentration.

✓ Determining what is important versus what is urgent is the key to focusing your life.

REFERENCES

Bliss, E. C. (1991). *Getting things done: The ABC's of time management.* New York: Macmillan Publishing Company.

Covey, S. R. (1994). *First things first.* New York: Simon & Schuster.

Keyes, R. (1991). *Timelock: How life got so hectic and what you can do about it.* New York: Harper Collins Publishers.

Lakein, A. (1973). *How to get control of your time and your life.* New York: David McKay Company, Inc.

McGee-Cooper, A. (1993). *Time management for unmanageable people.* Dallas: Bowen and Rogers.

Chapter 9

HANDLING STRESS

Rule No. 1 is, Don't sweat the small stuff.
Rule No. 2 is, It's all small stuff.
—Robert S. Eliot, M.D.

ADVANCE PLANNER: HANDLING STRESS

When you complete this chapter, you will be able to:

✓ Discuss the definition of stress and its link to personal change.

✓ Explain the three possible personal reactions to stress.

✓ Recognize the nature of stress as a positive force.

✓ Develop personal stress reduction strategies using the Five-Step Task Response Procedure, Stress Inoculations, and 52 Proven Stress Reducers.

To accomplish these objectives, you will complete some or all of these activities:

1. Read and discuss a brief summary of theories about the nature and implications of stress.

2. Discuss a case study and identify alternative actions for responding to stressors.

3. Complete a stress task response procedure.

A CASE STUDY IN HANDLING STRESS

The FSI Company Peer Salary Management Plan

Food Supplement Incorporated (FSI) is a medium-sized business listed on the NASDAQ stock exchange. It produces an emergency relief food product for sale to both public and private companies worldwide. When mixed with water, about eight ounces of the product will maintain a 150-pound adult for one day. Because it is low in fat and high in protein, the food product could be reformed to appeal to the health-conscious American consumer.

FSI employs 1,264 workers in three primary categories. Forty-three planners, engineers, and decision makers make up the management team. The sales and supervision workforce accounts for another 149 employees. The remaining 1,072 workers are hourly employees. At a recent meeting, the stockholders endorsed a plan to produce and sell food products directly to the public. Such an endeavor will require motivated and change-receptive management, and those responsible for leading the company into new markets are to be rewarded. The company president, at the Board of Directors' request, will implement a TQM (total quality management) process to encourage present management to plan the new venture. Those who will best know who is contributing to the company's future success are the 43 management team members, who have elected a committee of five to evaluate the good work and good ideas of team members to determine merit salary raises. The plan has been named Peer Salary Management (PSM), but some team members say the acronym stands for Peer Stress Maker.

The plan requires each team member to complete a written self-evaluation of the past year's accomplishments. Only a few people submitted reports by the original deadline. The Board of Directors declared no one would receive any raise unless he or she filed a self-evaluation report. Consequently, all but two team members submitted reports. (One of the two does not think PSM is the American way; the second has been hospitalized for a heart condition and is expected to recover completely in a few months.)

The merit panel has convened and ranked the 41 self-evaluations it received. The president has asked the panel what to do about those who did not submit self-evaluations and how to distribute the company's salary raise funds. (Current salaries of the 43 management team members range from $45,000 to $165,000. Salary increases will be based on five percent of the total salaries of the team.) The responsibility for the program's success rests heavily on the merit panel, and has created some stress among its members. Let's look in as the company president meets with the committee of five.

The company president is a well-respected manager who takes a sincere interest in the welfare of each person who works for FSI. He deals with all issues and concerns with a personal touch and his door is always open. He asks the team members to express their views about the new salary plan.

Marty is always on time and ready to do what is good for the company; she believes merit should be rewarded based on performance of assigned tasks. "I don't like the idea that I am responsible for determining merit. I don't get paid to award salary raises. I wish the boss would do it for us."

Ashad is a company engineer who has been responsible for developing many innovative products in the laboratory. "I agree with Mary; I have enough enemies. This new procedure will make everyone dislike me."

Larry is a hustler, always ready to try new ideas when old methods fail. "I think we should get on with it. If you do not have the guts to evaluate your peers you should work someplace else."

Marty is the most likable of the group and does not want to be responsible for hurting anyone's feelings with a poor evaluation. "I do not want to be an evaluator of my fellow team members."

Lucy had previously worked for a progressive company that rewarded good ideas with salary increases. Lucy was recruited by FSI partly because of her excellent record in team motivation. "If we don't do this, our best workers will quit and our jobs may be in jeopardy."

The president says, "If we do this right, we will all be more secure in our positions with FSI. I am asking each of you to suggest guidelines to use with our PSM program."

Mary is the first to speak. "I don't think it's fair that some get a lot more salary than others. I believe this is a chance to increase the salaries of those of us at the lower end of the salary scale. We should divide the total salary raise fund by 43 and let each person have a fair share. We are all members of the same team. I think those of us who do the work we are asked to do should receive equal raises."

Larry speaks. "Without good ideas and people willing to try them, we soon will become just an average company trying to survive. Those with good ideas and the guts to try new moves should receive a reward for taking risks. I believe we should designate a portion of the raise funds for equal distribution and award the balance to those who were responsible for innovations."

Ashad says, "I can live quite well with my present salary and think we all can. The president knows who deserves a raise and I believe we should follow the recommendation of our boss."

Marty replies, "We all worked hard last year, but some contributed more than others. I believe salary increases should be awarded in increments, based on the ranking from one to 41. The two who did not submit evaluations should not get a raise, as the Board of Directors suggested."

Lucy observes, "I am the only one who has been through an experience like this before. I suggest we recommend an average 2.5 percent pay raise for all team members. The balance of the raise funds can then be distributed on the basis of this committee's rankings."

The president is pleased with the input from the group. "I suggest the following plan. Salary raises will be distributed in a range from one to ten percent using the panel ranking of one to 41 to determine the percentage. Most raises will be in the range of three to seven percent. Also the hospitalized person should receive a five percent raise and the nonparticipant be treated as the Board recommended."

Discussion Questions

1. What were the sources of stress for each of the panel members?

2. How did the president's recommendation help alleviate stress for each person?

3. How do you handle stress in your life?

INTRODUCTION TO THEORIES OF STRESS MANAGEMENT

During the past two decades one of the topics most studied by sociologists and psychologists has been human stress. Behavioral researchers have determined stress to be a major factor in our lives (Hobfoll, 1989; Lazarus & Folkman, 1984; Reynolds & Shapiro, 1991) and have demonstrated clear links between stress and mental and physical well-being.

Early researchers (Selye, 1950) regarded stress as a response to a stimulus. More recent research models (Hobfoll, 1989) focus on the identification of those elements of yourself, your life, and your social interaction that seem likely to cause stress. Models such as those described by Cox (1978) and Fischer (1986) generally agree stress is defined in three parts: 1) external stressors, 2) individual internal processes regarding the stressor, and 3) responses to the internalization of the stressor.

Regardless of your inclination to view stress as a response to an event or to see the event as an inherent stressor, we all experience stress. This chapter will help you to discover methods of dealing with stress and hopefully to see the potentially positive and necessary role stress plays in our lives.

This chapter's treatment of stress is based on two theories:

✓ The three elements of stress are 1) the presence of an external stressor, 2) individual internalization of stress and 3) a response to the stressor.

✓ A close relationship exists between change and the presence of stressors.

What Is Stress?

Stress is anxiety, strain, or tension caused by a new burden or outside force. Stress results in an internal struggle that often causes apprehension, misgiving, or uneasiness (*Webster's Dictionary*). Stress is often viewed as an unwanted situation. Stress can, however, be a positive force in our lives. Much everyday stress is caused by occurrences that make life interesting. Your personal definition of stress may say much about how you react to new situations. How do you define it? Do you view stress as a negative element or do you see opportunity as change occurs? Look at the four examples of stressors below. Are they all problems or do some seem like opportunities?

✓ A job seeker is notified to begin a new job in a distant city.

✓ Parents receive information that their teenager is a substance abuser.

✓ A mid-level manager has been asked to develop a plan to distribute profit-sharing funds for a five-member sales staff team.

✓ A farmer faces planting time decisions during a season when soil moisture is low.

All four situations contain stressors, but notice that stressors do not have to be negative. Your reaction to a stressful situation will determine if the stress is negative or positive. A certain amount of stress is inevitable and we should never expect to live in a completely stress-free environment. We need a certain amount of stress to provide impetus and motivation for important things we need to accomplish. The key is to keep stress at levels that do not inhibit your ability to function or become so severe as to cause you physical or psychological harm.

Most people react to stress in one of three ways: 1) anxiety; 2) anger or un-realistic responses; or 3) selection of an appropriate task response. The most productive response is selecting a task appropriate to the stressor. Later in this chapter we will explain a five-step procedure for responding to stress systematically. Let's take a more detailed look at the three possible reactions to stress.

Anxiety

Anxiety is a nervous state that prevents us from anticipating our next action. When something stressful happens or might happen, nervousness and un-certainty are common responses. We worry about doing the right thing or simply don't know what to do. Later in the chapter we will show how to deal with stress by practicing responses to mild stress events. Such practice ses-sions are called stress inoculations.

Anger

Becoming angry or unrealistic is another possible response to stress. Want-ing something done your way or not at all could be unrealistic, even when it is the best way to achieve a goal. If someone else becomes stressed because of your demand, he or she may respond with fear and unexpected actions. Unrealistic responses to stress often create a stress cycle that affects others and actually can increase your personal stress.

Task Response

Taking a considered approach to a stressor is the most desirable means of re-sponding to stress. You must determine what the stressor is and consider mutually exclusive alternative responses before acting on the best alterna-tive. This procedure provides accountability by allowing supervisors as well as peers and subordinates to know specifically how and why you reacted to a stressor.

If your reaction was appropriate, others can document your procedure and emulate your actions. If your action did not produce the desired results, you can study what you did and seek help from others in identifying alter-natives you did not consider or factors you did not rate as important.

Remember, of the three possible reactions to stress, the selection of a task appropriate to the stressor is the only response likely to reduce rather than increase the amount of stress you are experiencing. It is the one re-sponse that allows you to use the stress positively for motivation or problem reduction. Becoming angry or behaving in an unrealistic fashion may in-crease your stress, while the inaction of anxiety can lead to physical and mental problems associated with the inability to handle stress.

Consider this example:

You are leaving your 11 a.m. class. It is time for lunch and you offer to drive two fellow students to a fast-food restaurant. When you get to your car you find the windshield has been smashed. What is your response?

Anxiety: Someone must be mad at me and broke my windshield. Maybe if I go to my dorm room I'll be safe. What did I do to make someone do this to my car? I don't know what to do.

Anger: Some dummy did this and when I find them! I bet it was Joe. He was mad at me for laughing at his suggestion last week. I'm going to kick the @%!★ out of him and his car!

Task Response: I'll call the police and see if we can find out what happened. You guys go to lunch if you want to; there is nothing you can do to help while I wait for the police. Yeah, please bring me a sandwich, too.

Later the police determine that earlier that day, a telephone construction crew was working on lines above your car. With the police you confront the crew. They will not admit damaging your car, but both you and the police believe they did. Your last appeal is to notify the crew supervisor, who denies responsibility. You are disappointed in people who are unwilling to admit what they have done, but you realize you can accomplish nothing if you continue to confront the phone crew. Instead, you call your car insurance company and let your comprehensive policy pay for the damage.

If you respond with anxiety, you could remain worried for weeks about who might be out to get you. If you respond with anger, you are ready to do battle with Joe. The task response leads to the best solution. It fixes your windshield and even gets you lunch.

Stress Management Strategies

According to Abraham Maslow, the stresses humans experience emanate from either wants or fears. Maslow believes we will react positively to stress derived from wants and negatively or unpredictably to fear-related stress. According to Maslow, the trick is to change fears to wants and we will react more positively (Maslow, 1970).

On the negative side, stress has been shown to cause headaches, sleeplessness, indigestion, back pain, chest pain, and high blood pressure (Zarrow, 1986). The positive side of stress is a feeling of accomplishment after we have resolved a stressful event. Popular theorists believe that with the ability to recognize stress, we can develop stress control techniques that will enrich our lives.

Based on the model of stressor, internalization, and response, many studies have been completed that measure the ability of techniques and substances to control the body's physical reactions to stress.

A study typical of research that measures responses to stress reduction techniques was completed by Forbes and Pekala (1993) in the area of nursing at Thomas Jefferson University in Philadelphia. They assessed the effectiveness of deep breathing and hypnosis as stress reduction techniques for nurses. The measures of stress were skin temperature and pulse rate. Hypnosis had no effect on either, while deep breathing produced significant reductions in both.

Similarly, Barton et al. (1994) studied the long-term results of in-home counseling and group counseling as means of reducing stress in child-abusing families. Both counseling methods resulted in reduced stress. One study of university students to determine the therapeutic effect of popping air capsules or balloons as a stress reduction technique showed popping reduced students' stress (Dillon, 1992). Another study of the same technique, however, reported no stress reduction (Taylor et al., 1994).

We are often encouraged to think before reacting to stress. Counting to ten is an example of the many stress control techniques we are encouraged to use. Although this age-old axiom for controlling anger and stress sounds simple, it does reflect the underlying need to use self-control and self-management techniques to control our lives. Because stress results largely from individual perceptions, techniques for managing it must be suited to the individual, too. What works for one person might not work for another. The common element of stress control, however, is to make a considered response to stress, which we refer to as the *Five-Step Task Response Procedure for Stress Reduction.*

The Five-Step Task Response Procedure for Stress Reduction

This five-step process is a planning technique that results in a measured response to stressors. The key to the procedure is to recognize alternative responses to stress. The five-step process is based on Maslow's theory that fears can be changed to wants (Maslow, 1970) when positive alternatives to stressful situations are identified. The five steps are:

1. *Recognize the Stressor:* Clearly identify the stressor. Know what the problem is, or identify what decision needs to be made. Identifying the stressor is especially important when several individuals are involved. All involved in the stress situation need to agree about the nature of the stressor.

2. *Identify Alternatives:* Identify alternatives to reduce or eliminate stress. Alternatives, by definition, are mutually exclusive actions that can relieve or remove the stressor. Allow time for each person involved in the issue to recognize the stressor. Then determine what alternative actions you might take to resolve stress.

3. *List Related Factors:* List circumstances and conditions that may affect your course of action. Focus on reasons an eventual resolution will be effective.

4. *Make a Choice:* Determine the best approach to resolving stress. Also list in order of usefulness the alternative stress responses you identified. You will need the list if your first choice is not effective in resolving stress. In addition, others may want to know why you resolved stress as you did. The list of alternatives helps support your choice.

5. *Rank Importance of Related Factors:* Identify the order of importance of the factors that influenced your action. This step allows you and others to analyze your decision-making process.

Using Stress Inoculations to Prepare Yourself for Stress

Reacting to stress is something we need to learn to handle as a routine activity. The idea of stress inoculation is to gradually introduce you to the type of stress you are likely to encounter. Just as inoculations prepare the body to handle physical disease, we can give ourselves stress inoculations to increase our mental and emotional capacity to handle stress situations.

Stress inoculation is used extensively in military training to prepare soldiers for stress-filled missions. After soldiers have experienced practice stress situations, they are better prepared to complete missions with unknown stress situations. Exposure to realistic simulated battle situations prior to real combat enables soldiers to deal with actual battle stressors.

Another example of stress inoculation is found in the training programs that prepare future teachers to handle discipline problems. The student teaching experience exposes future teachers to classroom discipline problems and allows them to try discipline strategies with the backup of a master teacher in the room. Eventually the future teachers can handle discipline on their own.

College professors who have witnessed student speeches and presentations are aware that many students feel enormous amounts of stress when required to speak in front of a group. They approach this task certain in the knowledge that they will either throw up, pass out, or die, perhaps all three in just that order. Although it is likely that some of us will never feel totally comfortable in a public speaking environment, one strategy some professors use is to slowly expose students to the experience, rather than requiring them to speak in front of the entire class on the first day. At the beginning of the semester, students may be asked to give a presentation to just one other student, perhaps later on to the members of their class learning group, and then finally to the entire class. The underlying theory is that if we approach the experience in small approximations we may be somewhat desensitized to the stress. One of the reasons most college curriculums require extensive student speeches and presentations is the hope that students who have sufficient experiences of *not* throwing up, passing out, or dying may feel less frightened and will learn to control their stress when required to give presentations as part of their jobs. You should consider the multitude of speaking opportunities that present themselves to you as part of your education as a chance to inoculate yourself to the stresses associated with the experience. Ironically, the more stress you feel about public speaking, the more important it is for you to do it!

Here is another way to practice stress inoculation on a practical level. If you view waiting in long lines as a stressor, the next time you are in a supermarket, choose to stand in the longest checkout line and be aware of your reactions to waiting. Be sure to pick an occasion when you have time to wait. During the inoculation wait, notice how others in line are reacting. Think about how you would like to react to the wait and train yourself to reduce stress by focusing on something that reduces your anxiety about waiting. You might use the time to balance your checkbook or read a book. Pick a task you can focus on that reduces anxiety. If you are successful handling a long wait, you'll be better prepared to handle the stress of waiting in a long line of traffic or in a crowd at the airline ticket counter.

52 Proven Stress Reducers

Sometimes simple solutions are the best for resolving stress. You may discover that a great deal of stress originates in habitual behavior you are not even aware of. Small changes in behavior, then, may go a long way to reducing stress. This list of ideas for reducing stress (52 Proven Stress Reducers, 1991) provides many options. Some will work for you and some won't, but you have plenty to choose from.

Behavioral psychologists generally suggest that it takes two weeks to practice a new behavior or attitude before it becomes one you will value. So do not give up after the first day. Stick with a new behavior or value for at least two weeks.

It can also be difficult to alter more than one behavior or value at a time. If you want to adopt several of the stress reducers listed here, try them one at a time. You also may want to share your new idea with a close friend. The friend will be a source of support as well as a reminder of your commitment to the change in behavior or value.

1. Get up 15 minutes earlier in the morning. The inevitable morning mishaps will be less stressful.

2. Prepare for the morning the evening before. Set the breakfast table, make lunches, put out the clothes you plan to wear.

3. Don't rely on your memory. Write down appointment times, when to pick up the laundry, when library books are due, etc. ("The palest ink is better than the most retentive memory"—old Chinese proverb.)

4. Do nothing which, after being done, leads you to tell a lie.

5. Make duplicates of all keys. Bury a house key in a secret spot in the garden and carry a duplicate car key in your wallet, apart from your key ring.

6. Practice preventive maintenance. Your car, appliances, home, and relationships will be less likely to break down or fall apart at the worst possible moment.

7. Be prepared to wait. A paperback can make a wait in a post office line almost pleasant.

8. Procrastination is stressful. Whatever you want to do tomorrow, do today; whatever you want to do today, do now.

9. Plan ahead. Don't let the gas tank get below one-quarter full, keep a well-stocked emergency shelf of home staples, don't wait until you're down to your last bus token or postage stamp to buy more, etc.

10. Don't put up with something that doesn't work right. If your alarm doesn't work, or your wallet, shoe laces, windshield wipers, whatever, are a constant aggravation, get them fixed or get new ones.

11. Allow 15 minutes of extra time to get to appointments. Plan to arrive at an airport one hour before domestic departures.

12. Eliminate (or restrict the amount of) caffeine from your diet.

13. Always set up contingency plans, just in case. ("If, for some reason, either of us is delayed, here's what we'll do." Or, "If we get separated in the shopping center, here's where we'll meet.")

14. Relax your standards. The world will not end if the grass doesn't get mowed this weekend.

15. For every one thing that goes wrong, there are probably 10 or 50 or 100 blessings. Count 'em!

16. Ask questions. Taking a few moments to repeat back directions can save hours.

17. Say no! Saying no to extra projects, social activities, and invitations you know you don't have the time or energy for takes practice, self-respect, and a belief that everyone, every day needs quiet time to relax and to be alone.

18. Unplug your phone. If you want to take a long bath, meditate, sleep, or read without interruption, drum up the courage to disconnect temporarily.

19. Turn needs into preferences. Our basic physical needs translate into food, water, and keeping warm. Everything else is a preference. Don't get attached to preferences.

20. Simplify, simplify, simplify.

21. Make friends with nonworriers. Nothing can get you into the habit of worrying faster than associating with chronic worrywarts.

22. Get up and stretch periodically if your job requires that you sit for extended periods.

23. Wear earplugs. If you need to find quiet at home, pop in some earplugs.

24. Get enough sleep. If necessary, use an alarm clock to remind you to go to bed.

25. Create order out of chaos. Organize your home and work space so that you always know exactly where things are. Put things away where they belong and you won't have to go through the stress of losing things.

26. When feeling stressed, most people tend to breathe in short, shallow breaths. When you breathe like this, stale air is not expelled, oxidation of the tissues is incomplete, and muscle tension frequently results. Check your breathing throughout the day and before, during, and after high-pressure situations. If you find your stomach muscles are knotted and your breathing is shallow, relax all your muscles and take several deep, slow breaths. Note how, when you're relaxed, both your abdomen and chest expand when you breathe.

27. Writing your thoughts and feelings down can help clarify things and give you a renewed perspective.

28. Try the following yoga technique whenever you feel the need to relax: Inhale deeply through your nose to the count of eight. Then, with lips puckered, exhale very slowly through your mouth to the count of 16, or for as long as you can. Concentrate on the long sighing sound and feel the tension dissolve. Repeat 10 times.

29. Inoculate yourself against a feared event. Example: Before speaking in public, take time to go over every part of the experience in your mind. Imagine what you'll wear, what the audience will look like, how you will present your talk, what the questions will be, and how you will answer them, etc. Visualize the experience the way you would like it to be. You'll likely find that when the time comes to make the actual presentation, it will be old hat and much of your anxiety will have fled.

30. When the stress of having to get a job done gets in the way of getting the job done, diversion—a voluntary change in activity or environment— may be just what you need.

31. Talk it out. Discussing your problems with a trusted friend can help clear your mind of confusion so you can concentrate on problem solving.

32. One of the most obvious ways to avoid unnecessary stress is to select an environment (work, home, leisure) that is in line with your personal needs and desires. If you hate desk jobs, don't accept a job that requires that you sit at a desk all day. If you hate to talk politics, don't associate with people who love to talk politics.

33. Learn to live one day at a time.

34. Every day, do something you really enjoy.

35. Add an ounce of love to everything you do.

36. Take a hot bath or shower (or a cool one in summertime) to relieve tension.

37. Do something for somebody else.

38. Focus on understanding rather than on being understood, on loving rather than on being loved.

39. Do something that will improve your appearance. Looking better can help you feel better.

40. Schedule a realistic day. Avoid the tendency to schedule back-to-back appointments; allow time between appointments for a breathing spell.

41. Become more flexible. Some things are worth not doing perfectly and some issues are appropriate to compromise upon.

42. Eliminate destructive self-talk: "I'm too old to . . .," "I'm too fat to . . ."

43. Use your weekend time for a change of pace. If your work week is slow and patterned, make sure there is action and time for spontaneity built into your weekends. If your work week is fast-paced and full of people and deadlines, seek peace and solitude during your days off. Feel as if you aren't accomplishing anything tangible at work? Tackle a job on the weekend that you can finish to your satisfaction.

44. "Worry about the pennies and the dollars will take care of themselves." That's another way of saying: Take care of the todays as best you can and the tomorrows will take care of themselves.

45. Do one thing at a time. When you are with someone, be with that person and with no one or nothing else. When you are busy with a project, concentrate on doing that project and forget about everything else you have to do.

46. Allow yourself time every day for privacy, quiet, and introspection.

47. If an especially unpleasant task faces you, do it early in the day and get it over with. Then the rest of your day will be free from anxiety.

48. Learn to delegate responsibility to capable others.

49. Don't forget to take a lunch break. Try to get away from your desk or work area in body and mind, even if it's just for 15 or 20 minutes.

50. Forget about counting to 10. Count to 1000 before doing something or saying anything that could make matters worse.

51. Have a forgiving view of events and people. Accept the fact that we live in an imperfect world.

52. Have an optimistic view of the world. Believe that most people are doing the best they can.

EXERCISE
Loan Associate Sweet Meets the Klumps—A Case Study

Purpose This case gives you practice analyzing the stressors in a situation and prescribing appropriate task responses.

Activity In a small group setting, read the following case study. Apply the Five-Step Task Response Procedure for Stress Reduction to the example stressors in the case study. Use the Student Worksheet for Loan Associate Sweet Case Study to develop a written record of the five-step process for one stress example in the case study and prepare to present your findings to the class for further discussion. Example stressors are printed in bold print.

The Case David Sweet is a loan associate for Happy Valley Bank. People in Happy Valley respect David for his personal service and ability to plan family and business budgets to meet client needs. Sweet has received a request to meet Margaret and Harold Klump to budget their business and family financial needs and has filled his briefcase with examples of family recordkeeping and financial planning alternatives. It is a rainy day in Happy Valley as Sweet drives out to Junction Road to visit the Klump home. The **rain turns to snow and sleet** as Sweet pulls into the Klumps' driveway. He dashes for the front door as **a large dog** races from the barn to block his entrance to the front porch. Sweet sidesteps the beast with a soothing "Good dog, nice dog" and continues to the door. The dog lets him pass, but keeps vigil. The **doorbell does not work;** a firm knock pushes the door open. **No one is home.** Sweet extracts his appointment book from the briefcase and discovers he is **one week early.** Sweet, accompanied by the dog—still wary, but tolerant— walks to the garage. No sign of the Klumps. So he returns to the front porch to wait. At least the porch roof keeps the rain at bay.

Finally he hears a noise in the driveway, and the Klumps arrive home. The Klump's limo-like auto pulls around Sweet's subcompact and unloads: Father Klump, Mother Klump and seven Klump children. The car trunk opens (automatically) to reveal the fruits of the day's shopping: clothes, food, toys, a new computer, tennis equipment, an exercise machine, weights, in-line roller skates, and a six-foot teddy bear.

Loan Associate Sweet gasps at the sight and reminds the Klumps that they scheduled a home financial visit because they wanted to curb unnecessary spending, as he helps them unload the car. Margaret Klump invites Sweet into the dining room to visit, while she directs Harold and the little Klumps to put the new purchases away. "You won't believe it," Margaret says. "We just got an unexpected inheritance check for $2,500. We had such a good time getting something new for everyone."

Sweet reminds her that unpaid bills were the reason for the visit. Harold brings tea for all. "Yes," he says. "We are $6,000 behind on bills and two months late on our $1,200 a month business loan payment and behind on the car loan, too, so **we really need you to fix our financial problems.**"

Sweet shows them a new family planning computer budget and cash flow analysis program. "No, **don't have time to learn that,**" says Harold, "always busy working outside." Margaret agrees, but observes, "We have to do something to get a handle on our money." "Yes," chimes in Sweet, "you have the money to have fun and pay your bills; you just need to be more systematic in budgeting and aware of your daily cash funds so you can pay bills as they come due."

"Okay," say the Klumps in unison, "where do we start?" Sweet works at getting the new computer program up and prepares the family's first monthly record. It's obvious the car has to go. "Okay," says Harold, "but it just won't be much fun driving around town anymore." Sweet notices the time—nearly 6 p.m. "Oh no. I'm **late for a meeting** at the Bryans'. I should have been there an hour ago. Would you call them for me?"

As Sweet dashes off, he accepts a dinner invitation for the next week to complete the Klumps' budget. "Now make sure you keep your records up to date each day," he calls as he jumps in his car and races down the road to another exciting episode of personal financial management counseling.

Student Worksheet for Loan Associate Sweet Case Study

1. Stressor your group is discussing:

2. Stressor alternative solutions (list at least two):

3. Factors that will influence your selection of a stress relief task:

4. Task solution your group believes will be most effective:

5. Order of importance of the factors listed in item 3:

FURTHER ACTIVITY

Journal Writing

Identify three or four of the stress reducers from the list of 52 Proven Stress Reducers that you think sound interesting. In your journal, write about what you think the effects of the stress reducers are likely to be. In what circumstances might you use these stress reducers? Which of the reducers are the most likely to be useful and why?

Practice some stress reducers for a week or two. Write in your journal about the experience. Do you think they helped reduce stress? If so, why? If not, why not?

LEARNING POINTS

✓ A relationship exists between change and stress. For most people the choice is not whether to have stress but how to handle stress.

✓ Stress is defined as anxiety, strain, or tension caused by a new burden or outside force.

✓ The three common reactions to stress include anxiety, anger, or a task response.

✓ General ideas for success in handling stress include using stress control techniques and learning to change fears to wants. (See list of 52 Proven Stress Reducers.)

✓ The five-step task response procedure for handling stress includes identifying the stressor, determining mutually exclusive alternative responses, listing important factors regarding the stressor, placing the alternatives in order of choice, and listing the factors in order of importance. This process provides a task (what to do) response to stress and allows the individual to quickly pick an alternative if a first choice is not effective in resolving the stressor.

✓ Stress inoculation, the process of deliberately introducing yourself to stressful situations in small doses and under circumstances you can control, can be an effective means of preparing professionals to handle work environment stressors.

REFERENCES

Barton, K., Baglio, C., and Braverman, M. (1994). Stress reduction in child-abusing families: Global and specific measures. *Psychological Reports, 75,* 287–304.

Cox, T. (1978). *Stress.* London: Macmillan Press.

Dillon, K. M. (1992). Popping sealed air capsules to reduce stress. *Psychological Reports, 71,* 243–246.

Fisher, S. (1986). *Stress and strategy.* London: Lawrence Erlbaum Associates.

Forbes, E. J., and Pekala, R. J. (1993). Psychophysiological effects of several stress management techniques. *Psychological Reports, 72,* 19–27.

Hobfoll, S. (1989). Conservation of resources: A new attempt at conceptualizing stress. *American Psychologists, 44*(3), 513, 524.

Lazarus, R., and Folkman, S. (1984). *Stress, appraisal and coping.* New York: Springer.

Maslow, A. (1970). *Motivation and personality* (2nd ed.). New York: Harper and Row.

52 Proven Stress Reducers (1991). *PM Magazine,* May, 26–27.

Reynolds, M. S., and Shapiro, D. A. (1991). Stress reduction in transition: Conceptual problems in the design, implementation and evaluation of worksite stress management intervention. *Journal of Human Relations 44* (7), 717–732.

Selye, H. (1950). *The physiology and pathology of exposure to stress: A treatise based on the concepts of the general-adaptation syndrome and the diseases of adaptation* (1st ed.). Montreal: Actta.

Taylor, K. A., Purser, K. C., and Baluch, B. (1994). Could popping air capsules affect state anxiety? *Psychological Reports, 75,* 161–162.

Webster's new world dictionary of the American language, 2nd college ed., S. V. "stress."

Zarrow, S. (1986). The achiever's guide to a tranquil mind. *Prevention Magazine,* March, 72–76.

Chapter 10

LEVELS OF COMMUNICATION

I don't like that person. I'm going to have to get to know him better.
—Abraham Lincoln

The reality of the other person is not in what he reveals to you,
but in what he cannot reveal to you.
Therefore, if you would understand him, listen not to what he says,
but rather to what he does not say.
—Kahlil Gibran

ADVANCE PLANNER: LEVELS OF COMMUNICATION

When you complete this chapter, you will be able to:

✓ Name and describe each level of communication discussed in the chapter.
✓ Name and give examples of each of the four levels of self-disclosure.
✓ Recognize the appropriateness of self-disclosure.
✓ Describe the benefits of healthy self-disclosure.
✓ Diagnose a situation and choose the appropriate level of communication to use.
✓ Practice self-disclosure in your own life.
✓ Work through appropriate levels of communication in your own interpersonal relationships.

To accomplish these objectives, you will complete some or all of these activities:

1. Participate in an exercise in self-disclosure and appropriate feedback.
2. Discuss a case study to help illustrate some key points of levels of communication.
3. Read and discuss a brief introduction to some theories of levels of communication.
4. Take a quiz designed to help you determine your self-monitoring abilities.
5. Identify the levels of communication you use in your relationships with others.

6. Write in your journal about the levels of communication in which you engage in your day-to-day living.

A CASE STUDY IN LEVELS OF COMMUNICATION
A Day in the Life . . .

When LaShon awoke this morning, she had a feeling today was going to be a bad day. After the argument last night with her roommates, however, things couldn't get much worse. Although they had lived together all last semester, her roommates still did things that drove her nuts! She tried to make suggestions about how to improve the situation, but she didn't want them to think she was difficult. After all, they did have to live together, and LaShon didn't want to make things any worse.

"Well, I guess I'll just go to class and deal with this later," she thought as she got ready. As LaShon crossed campus, her mood didn't improve, although she gave a cheerful "Hi" or "What's up?" to people she met. Finding a seat in her first lecture of the day, LaShon was glad to see Ryan. They had become acquainted during the first two weeks of class and always sat together. "Hey, LaShon!" Ryan called from the back of the auditorium as he approached his seat. "How's it goin'?" LaShon sighed and replied, "I need to find a new place to live." "Why?" asked Ryan in surprise. That was all the invitation LaShon needed to unload all her problems on Ryan. "My roommates are awful, my grades are falling, the rent is too high, and the neighbors are weird!" Ryan began to feel uncomfortable and actually looked forward to the start of the lecture.

After class, LaShon's already bad mood just got worse when she realized she had no idea what was discussed in last hour's lecture, because she couldn't take her mind off her problems. "Ryan didn't seem interested in my problems at all," she mumbled to herself as she walked to work. "And I thought he seemed like such a nice guy."

LaShon was happy to see Thuy at work when she arrived. She and Thuy had worked together for three years. In between customers, LaShon was able to talk to Thuy about her problems. "Both Joanne and Nicole like to stay up later than I do, but the TV keeps me awake," LaShon said about her roommates. Thuy listened but offered no solutions for LaShon.

LaShon returned home from work and immediately went to her room, dodging her roommates' clothes on the floor and dirty dishes in the sink. She slammed her door and sat on her bed. LaShon decided to call her parents. Her mother answered the phone, and LaShon immediately started to cry. "I just don't know what to do, Mom," LaShon sobbed. "My roommates don't care about how I feel. I think this situation is starting to affect my performance at school. My grades are falling and I'm upset all the time. I'm really scared about school and whether I belong here or not."

"I understand you are upset, confused, and scared right now," her mother replied. "We all feel like that at some time in our lives. I felt like that when I started college, too. You just need to be honest with your roommates and tell them how you feel. Things will get better, and you know you can always talk to your father and me if you need to."

Discussion Questions

1. In what different contexts did LaShon communicate throughout her day? How do different contexts affect the way people communicate? How do different contexts affect your communication?

2. What is the correlation between the kind of communication and the type of relationship LaShon shares with the person with whom she is speaking?

3. People choose to share their feelings for various reasons. Why did LaShon do so?

4. When was LaShon's sharing of thoughts and feelings appropriate? Inappropriate? Why?

INTRODUCTION TO THEORIES OF LEVELS OF COMMUNICATION

An effective interpersonal relationship is built on a series of positive interactions between two individuals. Developing positive relationships with others takes an investment of time and effort from both parties.

Although no two relationships develop in exactly the same way, all relationships tend to follow similar patterns of development. As our relationships develop, the ways in which we communicate change. Researchers in this area differ about numbers and names of stages of communication, but all agree that each of us moves back and forth through all levels of communication as we meet and become acquainted with new people. A high level of trust must be established before reaching completely open and honest communication with another individual (Dodge, 1986).

Five Basic Levels of Communication

The five levels of communication described in this chapter are adapted from Powell's book *Why Am I Afraid to Tell You Who I Am?* (Powell, as cited in Dodge, 1986). The levels are listed here in order of least revealing to deepest sharing, but the list order is not meant to imply that any one level is better than any other in all situations.

Cliché Conversation

Cliché conversation, as its name implies, is a form of communication that occurs in the casual exchange of cliché or common phrases. This is the weakest and lowest level of communication. We often use this level in chatting with people in the hall before class or in the aisle at the grocery store. Such clichés as "Hi, how are you?" and "What's up?" are common. We do not expect a response of more than a word or two. A more detailed response would be either surprising or frustrating, because we do not intend at this level to take the time to have a lengthy, meaningful exchange. Communication at the level of cliché conversation is superficial and offers no real sharing.

Reporting Facts about Others

At the reporting level, communication is limited to an exchange of information about another person or a situation. In conversation, we are satisfied to merely report facts about others and what they have done; we share nothing of ourselves. For example, if you and a friend are walking across campus and you see a third person, you might merely report what you know

---

Levels of Communication

✓ Cliché Conversation
✓ Reporting Facts about Others
✓ Individual Ideas and Judgments
✓ Individual Feelings and Emotions
✓ Peak Communication

about her: "That's Jesse. She's from my hometown." You limit your level of communication to a set of facts, but offer no judgments or personal commentary on the facts.

Individual Ideas and Judgments

At the level of individual judgment, we communicate some personal information, although it is highly censored. We are willing to share ideas and judgments, but we watch carefully for reactions, to be sure our ideas and judgments are accepted and shared by others, For example, you and a friend may be driving in an area of the city that has become more heavily traveled and you might say, "I used to ride my bike on that road, but now I think it's too dangerous." In this case, you are offering a judgment about the safety of the road, but with some reservations and most likely with the expectation that your friend will agree with your judgment.

Individual Feelings and Emotions

At the gut level of individual feeling, we want to communicate in a way that will let another know who we really are. We are willing to share the feelings behind our ideas, judgments, and beliefs. A high level of emotional honesty and trust is involved in communication at this level. When you can say to a friend, "I don't think you're telling me how you really feel, and that upsets me," you are communicating at the level of individual feeling and emotion.

Peak Communication

At the level of peak communication, we approach absolute openness and honesty. We are aware of the emotional risks of revealing ourselves completely to someone else, but to achieve peak communication, we must strive for perfect empathy with each other. In spite of the risks associated with emotional openness, if your relationship with someone is strong enough, peak communication is occurring when you can say things like, "It makes me angry that you won't open up to me. I can tell you're upset."

The Role of Trust in Communication

It is apparent that trust plays a larger role in how we communicate with others the further we move up through the levels of communication. Covey (1989) emphasizes the importance of trust in communication when working with others. If we trust those with whom we work, we are more likely to share our interests, goals, dreams, concerns, backgrounds, and frames of reference. It takes time for people to get to know each other well and to develop trust, but in the end, we work together better and are willing to share ideas, concerns, and challenges. Trust leads to relationships that are synergistic.

Synergism (or synergy) is the simultaneous action of separate units, which together have a greater total effect than the sum of the individual effects—the essence of synergism is that the whole is greater than the sum of its parts. The ideas we come up with as a group will most likely be more exciting and workable than the ideas we could come up with individually.

The key to achieving synergy is to build relationships on a basis of trust. The degree to which trust is operative in a relationship is reflected in levels of communication. The lowest level of communication in a low-trust situation can be characterized as *defensive*. When we do not trust those we must work with, our level of cooperation and productivity remains low. The middle position is *respectful* communication. We have respect for each other but want to avoid confrontation, so we communicate politely but not empathetically.

We may understand each other intellectually, but we really don't understand the assumptions and values underlying others' positions, keeping us from being open to new possibilities. At the highest levels of trust and cooperation, *synergistic* communication occurs. The group is able to provide better solutions than any one individual, and group members appreciate this. Everyone genuinely enjoys the creative enterprise (Covey, 1989).

As the level of trust increases, we want the other person to know us and appreciate us. We feel more comfortable sharing personal information. While sharing is important in a relationship, it is also important to be aware of what, when, and how much we share with another person.

Self-Monitoring and Self-Disclosure

Self-monitoring, or the manipulation of the image that we present to others (DeVito, 1992), is important in interpersonal interactions. High self-monitors adjust their behaviors according to the reactions of others. Low self-monitors, on the other hand, are not concerned with the image they present. They communicate their thoughts and feelings openly, without trying to manipulate the impressions they create. Most of us lie somewhere between the two extremes (DeVito, 1992).

We all engage in self-monitoring behavior to some degree, depending upon the situation. In an interview for a job, we would most likely highly monitor our behavior, dressing and speaking professionally, asking only pertinent questions about the position, and politely thanking the individual after the interview. At home with friends, we would be more likely to tell jokes, wear casual clothes, and speak freely about our ideas and opinions, not highly monitoring our behavior.

In other situations, however, for most of us the degree of self-monitoring falls along the continuum between high and low. It is ridiculous to think we should be totally open, disclosing everything to everyone in every situation. It is just as ridiculous to think we should never share anything with anyone. There are no absolutes when deciding what and how much information to share with others. There are, however, guidelines we can use to help us determine what is appropriate to share in a relationship. The next few paragraphs will focus on self-disclosure in relationships.

Self-disclosure is defined as "making the self known; you reveal yourself so that others can see and understand you. Individuals disclose verbally and nonverbally" (Hanna, 1995, p. 219).

Reasons for Self-Disclosure

Self-disclosure has the potential to improve and expand your relationships, but serves other functions as well. The following are some reasons individuals choose to self-disclose:

✓ *Catharsis,* or getting things "off your chest."
   I am so disappointed with the way things are going at work.

✓ *Self-clarification* of your beliefs, opinions, attitudes, and feelings. Talking it out often happens with many people from hairdressers to therapists.
   Maybe I'm not ready to start my own business right now after all.

✓ *Self-validation,* with the hope of getting agreement from another. You are seeking validation of a behavior or confirmation of a belief you hold about yourself.
   I think I can handle this project. My desktop publishing skills have really improved.

- ✓ *Reciprocity,* or hoping to encourage another to self-disclose.
  I'm not sure if I agree with Frank's attitude about land preservation.

- ✓ *Impression formation,* in the effort to make ourselves more attractive to others. We may try to impress another or to share information in a showing of support of another's situation.
  I just got a great promotion with a huge raise!
  I went through a situation like that a couple of years ago. If you need help, let me know.

- ✓ *Relationship maintenance and enhancement,* to eliminate misunderstandings as well as show and gain a high level of trust with another person. For relationships to remain healthy, a certain level of self-disclosure must occur.
  I felt patronized because of the way you explained how to start the computer.

- ✓ *Social control,* or using the revelation of information to increase your power in a situation or over a certain person.
  I've been offered another job. Are you prepared to reconsider that promotion?

- ✓ *Manipulation,* a calculated act of self-disclosure to achieve a desired result.
  I feel uncomfortable going on this date. I wish I knew someone we could double with.

We disclose for different reasons in different situations. In an established relationship, our reason may be to maintain and enhance the relationship. With an acquaintance, our reason may be reciprocity, in the hopes of the other also self-disclosing, or for impression formation, if we do not know the other well.

Degrees of Self-Disclosure
Self-disclosure can be categorized into degrees that parallel Powell's levels of communication described earlier (Hanna, 1995). That is, the information you disclose about yourself moves through levels, too.

- ✓ *Basic data:* biographical and demographic information, like your age, address, where you go to school, your major.

- ✓ *Preferences:* your likes and dislikes, what you would rather do or not do, such as: I don't like having to work part-time; I enjoy vacationing in Florida; My favorite food is Italian.

- ✓ *Beliefs:* thoughts, opinions and attitudes, such as: I believe school teachers are underpaid; I think students should pay less tuition.

- ✓ *Feelings:* disclosures about emotions, like: I'm happy to see those around me succeed; I'm scared to talk to the instructor; I'm worried about our finances this month.

The degrees are listed in order from least to most difficult to disclose, although different individuals may disagree about the ranking. These degrees of self-disclosure can be useful in checking how open you are in your relationships. Ask yourself to what degree you are comfortable in disclosing yourself to others, in what situations, and why. As you think about what you are comfortable disclosing to others, you also must consider what others are comfortable with in regard to your self-disclosure, what you are comfortable with in regard to the self-disclosure of others, and what is appropriate in a given situation.

Risks and Rewards of Self-Disclosure

When we choose to self-disclose we must consider the amount of risk we are willing to take and what the consequences may be if the self-disclosure is inappropriate. Remember that communication is irreversible; we cannot take back something we say and we cannot erase impressions and conclusions others form about us based on information we choose to self-disclose.

While there are risks in self-disclosure, there many rewards. A few of the rewards are briefly described here:

✓ *Keener awareness of self.* Self-disclosure gives us a deeper understanding of ourselves. Selective self-disclosure, or self-disclosure in moderation, seems to characterize the well-adjusted personality (DeVito, 1992).

✓ *Improved ability to deal with problems.* The ability to self-disclose painful information and be supported may help to alleviate any guilt we may have associated with that information.

✓ *Improved communication effectiveness.* If we know people well, we are able to better understand them and the messages they send. We know when to take them seriously, when they need to talk, and when to leave them alone. Self-disclosure is an essential component in getting to know another individual.

✓ *Closer, more meaningful relationships.* By self-disclosing we are, in effect, saying that we trust the individuals with whom we form relationships, respect them, and care enough about them and the relationship to share information with them.

✓ *Less vulnerability to illness.* The effort it takes to hold one's burdens seems to interact with the effects of the trauma to create stress that can lead to illness. Self-disclosure relieves stress that comes with traumatic situations, thus reducing one's susceptibility to illness (DeVito, 1992).

Guidelines for Practicing Self-Disclosure

"What now?" you ask. You are aware of the benefits and risks involved in self-disclosing. Now you need to decide for yourself when it is appropriate to self-disclose. Here are some guidelines to use in determining an appropriate amount of self-disclosure in interpersonal encounters (Verderber & Verderber, 1992).

1. *Self-disclosure should begin with the kind of information you want others to disclose to you.* When getting to know another person, we look for information freely shared with others, such as hobbies, interests, and current events. This type of self-disclosure should occur early in a relationship. "I'd like to try roller-blading. Maybe we should rent the equipment this weekend."

2. *Self-disclosure of more intimate information should come when you believe the disclosure represents an acceptable risk.* As discussed earlier, there is always some amount of risk involved in self-disclosure. We must determine how safe we feel sharing this information with this person. Our assessment of the safety factor may be based on the level of trust we share with the person, or, ironically, on the anonymity of our relationship with the other person.

Some people feel quite safe about intimate self-disclosure if they believe they will never interact with the person again (e.g., a bartender or persons they meet in an airport). You may, for example, be equally comfortable sharing information about a personal experience either with someone very close to you whom you can trust or with a bartender in a faraway city, realizing that she or he will never see you or anyone involved in the situation again.

3. *Self-disclosure should move gradually to deeper levels.* Receiving self-disclosure can be as threatening as giving it. People may become uncomfortable if the level of self-disclosure exceeds their expectations. As the relationship develops, the degree of self-disclosure increases. For example, you may share general information in the beginning of the relationship, then move on to self-disclosure about more personal issues or problems farther into the relationship after you have received some indication from the other person that he or she is prepared for you to self-disclose (i.e., the other person has disclosed something to you).

4. *Intimate or very personal self-disclosure is most appropriate in ongoing relationships.* Revealing deep feelings to an acquaintance may be considered high-risk behavior for the discloser while potentially embarrassing for the receiver. A bond of trust must be established before disclosing such information. For example, unless you are involved in an ongoing relationship with someone, it is risky to express love for that person, either verbally or nonverbally.

5. *Intimate self-disclosure should continue only if it is reciprocated.* Lack of return generally suggests that the person does not feel the relationship is at a level where extensive self-disclosure is appropriate. You'll know, for example, not to continue self-disclosing behavior if you share a deep secret in a staff workshop and the only response you get is a sarcastic, "Thanks for sharing."

6. *Individual attitudes about self-disclosure vary, so what you would consider appropriate or inappropriate may not be so to someone else.* If the response to your self-disclosure indicated that it was inappropriate, ask why. Learn from your mistake so you can avoid it in the future. Here's one way to check your perception that self-disclosure was inappropriate: "I noticed the look on your face when I shared this information with you, and you seemed very uncomfortable. Is this an accurate perception? Why did this information make you uncomfortable?"

The Rhythm of Relationships

One of the realities of life, particularly in adulthood, is that situations and relationships don't last forever. Some relationships diminish in intensity because of changes in circumstances (e.g., promotion, relocation, marriage, divorce, birth). Others change because of death. Regardless of the situation, it is important to acknowledge that much like the tides, relationships have an ebb and flow. Changes in relationships can be exciting and invigorating or disconcerting, stressful, and even debilitating.

The way in which we conduct ourselves in the relationship often determines our reaction to the change. Take the situation of a roommate transferring to another school. This individual may be someone you have trusted, and the roommate likewise has trusted you. You consider yourself to be at peak communication with this person, and both of you have had no reluctance in sharing your innermost thoughts and feelings. This situation will likely be altered due to the change in frequency of contact.

What will not change is the quality of the relationship before the change. If both you and your roommate have been honest and open and have trusted one another, hopefully both of you know how important you are to each other. Therefore, it would be critical to share both your feelings of loss at the roommate's moving and your desire to continue the relationship. By doing so, you both share in the responsibility of maintaining communication with each other. Not sharing feelings of loss and a sincere desire to remain in contact may likely confuse the other person in the relationship and will leave you with guilt over the feelings you did not share (Viorst, 1987).

Conclusion

Effective communication is vital in healthy relationships, whether they be with family, friends, or co-workers. Trust and the ability to listen to others are essential tools in communicating effectively. As relationships develop and change, so does the manner in which we communicate.

EXERCISE
Do You Self-Monitor?

Purpose This exercise will help you discover the degree to which you monitor your self-disclosure. It is designed only as a starting point to help you assess your level of self-monitoring and as a basis for discussion about your level of comfort with your current level of self-monitoring.

You Will Need Pen or pencil

Self-monitoring quiz

Activity The statements on the self-monitoring quiz ask for personal reactions in various situations. No two statements are exactly alike, so consider each one carefully before answering. If a statement is true, or most likely true, as it applies to you, circle T. If a statement is false as it applies to you, circle F.

When you have completed the self-monitoring quiz, follow the instructions for scoring. Be prepared to discuss the questions below when your instructor asks you to.

Discussion

With one other person (or in a larger group), discuss your score on the self-monitoring quiz.

1. Were you surprised by your score? Why or why not?
2. What one or two statements did you find most revealing about your ability to self-monitor?
3. What did this quiz tell you about your self-monitoring behavior?
4. Are you comfortable with your current level of self-monitoring?
5. What changes would you like to make in your self-monitoring?
6. How will your behavior change as a result of changes in your self-monitoring?

Self-Monitoring Quiz

Adapted from DeVito, 1992.

These statements concern personal reactions to a number of different situations. No two statements are exactly alike, so consider each statement carefully before answering. If a statement is true, or most likely true, as applied to you, circle the T. If a statement is false, or not usually true, as applied to you, circle the F.

1. I find it hard to imitate the behavior of other people.   T   F
2. I guess I do put on a show to impress or entertain people.   T   F
3. I would probably make a good actor.   T   F
4. I sometimes appear to others to be experiencing deeper emotions than I actually am.   T   F
5. In a group of people, I am rarely the center of attention.   T   F
6. In different situations and with different people, I often act like very different persons.   T   F
7. I can only argue for ideas I really believe.   T   F
8. In order to get along and be liked, I tend to be what people expect me to be rather than who I really am.   T   F
9. I may deceive people by being friendly when I really dislike them.   T   F
10. I am always the person I appear to be.   T   F

Scoring Your Self-Monitoring Quiz

For each question, circle the number in the column that corresponds to your response. Add the numbers in the true and false columns, then add those two totals to arrive at your score.

Question Number	True	False
1	0	1
2	1	0
3	1	0
4	1	0
5	0	1
6	1	0
7	0	1
8	1	0
9	1	0
10	0	1

Total _____ + _____ = _____

Interpreting Your Score

7 or higher   Highly self-monitoring—You easily and often manipulate the image you present to others in interpersonal interactions, by adjusting your actions based on the reactions of others.

between 3 and 7   Moderately self-monitoring—You fall somewhere between the two extremes.

3 or lower   Rarely self-monitoring—You are rarely concerned with the image you present, and express thoughts and feelings openly without trying to manipulate the impression you create.

EXERCISE
Johari Window

Adapted from Luft, 1984.

Purpose A healthy interpersonal relationship is based on a balance of *self-disclosure,* or sharing information about yourself, and *feedback,* the messages you receive from others about the messages you send. In order to keep your relationships healthy and growing, you need to regularly examine the amount of self-disclosure and feedback you engage in. This exercise can help you determine if you and another are sharing enough to keep the relationship healthy and growing (Verderber & Verderber, 1992).

Background

The Johari Window (named for its creators, Joe Luft and Harry Ingham), actually a combination of four windows, is a visual representation of the relationship between self-disclosure and feedback. As one window changes, so do the other three. Whatever happens in one window affects all windows. The following descriptions of the four windows will help you understand how to create your own Johari Windows to reflect self-disclosure and feedback in specific relationships.

Open Window. The first window (upper left) is the open window. It contains information about yourself that is known to you and can also be known to others, and that you are comfortable sharing with others. Information that might fit into your open window includes your hobbies, your address, and the kind of car you drive.

Hidden Window. The second window (lower left) is the hidden window. It contains information known to you but not known to others. Such information may range from the hiding place for your extra house key to your deepest, darkest secret. This window may become smaller as you get to know another person and feel more comfortable sharing such information. In that case, the information moves into the open window, making that window larger and the hidden window smaller.

Blind Window. The third window (upper right) is the blind window. It contains information that is not known to you but is known to others. Your blind window may contain, for example, the information that you have bad breath or snore when you sleep or tend to interrupt others when they are speaking. As others give you feedback on your messages or behaviors, you become aware of the information and it moves into the open window, making the blind window smaller.

Unknown Window. The fourth and final window (lower right) is the unknown window. This window contains information that is known neither to you nor to others. For example, if you have never been to a ballet, you would not know what your reaction would be to a performance of *The Nutcracker,* nor would anyone else. You may hate it and leave at intermission, or you may love it and buy season tickets. Once you have experienced ballet, your feelings will be known to you and probably to a few other people, so information about your reaction to ballet would move to another window.

The diagram on the next page shows an example of a Johari Window in which all windows are equal.

	Known to Self	Not Known to Self
Known to Others	Open	Blind
Not Known to Others	Hidden	Unknown

Activity

After your instructor has explained the Johari Window concept and everyone feels they understand it, pair off with someone you don't necessarily know well.

Construct two Johari Windows:

1. A window that represents your perception of your relationship with the other person.

2. A window that represents how you think the other person perceives her or his relationship with you.

After you have constructed both windows, compare your windows with those drawn by your partner and discuss any differences.

Discussion

1. How do your windows compare?

2. What do the windows tell you about your relationship with your partner?

3. Do the windows suggest that your perceptions about your relationship are different?

4. How can you change the dimensions of the windows? Do you want to?

EXERCISE
Levels of Communication

Adapted from Dodge, 1986.

Purpose To examine the connection between levels of communication and your personal relationship with others.

You Will Need Pen or pencil

Levels of Communication Matrix

Activity After discussing levels of communication and acquaintanceship, brainstorm a list of types of relationships you share with various people (such as parents, roommates, best friend, significant other, classmates, etc.).

Think of some people in your life who fall into these categories. As you think about your relationship with them, also think about the level at which you communicate with them.

Once you have identified the category an individual falls into, write his or her initials in the box on the matrix that most closely correlates to the level at which you communicate with him or her. (For example, you might put the initials of your best friend, J. S., in the friendship column at level 5, peak experience.)

Discuss with one other person (as you wish to self-disclose) whom you placed in the various categories and why.

Discussion

Once everyone has completed the matrix and discussed it with one other person, share your impressions with the larger group:

1. Is it possible for a person to move through the matrix? Can that movement occur in more than one direction? Why?

2. What do you consider the ideal look for a Levels of Communication Matrix? Is it better to have relationships of all types and all levels? Is it better to have more intimate relationships at level 5? Is it okay for relationships to change over time?

3. Are the people you have identified all males, all females, or a mix? What is the gender mix at each level?

Levels of Communication Matrix

Level	Acquaintance	Friendship	Intimate
5. Peak Experience (Open)			
4. Feelings			
3. Ideas			
2. Facts			
1. Cliché			

Based on concepts found in Dodge (1986) and Verderber & Verderber (1992).

FURTHER ACTIVITY

Journal Writing

1. Over the next week, pay attention to and write about situations in which you disclosed information to another individual. With whom did you share information? What is your relationship with that person? What was their reaction to your disclosure of information?

2. Write about three communication situations you have experienced, in which you engaged in three of the five levels of communication. Describe your relationships with the other people involved in the situation.

3. Write about a situation in which you were uncomfortable with another person's self-disclosure. Why was it uncomfortable for you? What did you do or say in response to that person?

Independent Practice

1. Draw Johari Windows for several important relationships in your life (parent, roommate, advisor, significant other) and compare them. Do you see differences in degree of self-disclosure that depend on the nature of your relationship?

2. Complete a Levels of Communication Matrix for just one person you have known for a long time. Instead of recording only your current relationship and level of communication, write in dates that reflect the evolution of the relationship and level of communication at different periods of time. What pattern do you see in the development of your relationship with that person and the levels at which you communicate with him or her?

LEARNING POINTS

✓ We communicate with people differently, depending upon the type of relationship we have with them.

✓ We operate within five basic levels of communication: cliché communication, reporting facts about others, individual ideas and judgments, individual feelings and emotions, and peak communication.

✓ When we self-monitor, we manipulate the image we present to others in our interpersonal interactions. We all self-monitor to differing degrees.

✓ Self-disclosure involves revealing yourself so that others can see and understand you. People self-disclose for many reasons. A number of rewards and risks are involved in self-disclosure.

✓ Trust plays an important role in how we communicate and in how much we disclose to another person.

REFERENCES

Covey, S. (1989). *The seven habits of highly effective people.* New York: Simon & Schuster.

DeVito, J. (1992). *The interpersonal communication book* (6th ed.). New York: Harper Collins.

Dodge, G. W. (1986). *Priceless people: A guide for human resources development* (2nd ed.). Lincoln, NE: Nebraska Human Resources Research Foundation.

Hanna, S. L. (1995). *Person to person: Positive relationships don't just happen.* (2nd ed.) Englewood Cliffs, NJ: Prentice Hall.

Luft, J. (1984). *Group processes: An introduction to group dynamics.* Palo Alto, CA: Mayfield Publishing.

Powell, J. *Why am I afraid to tell you who I am?* cited in Dodge, G. W. (1986). *Priceless people: A guide for human resources development* (2nd ed.). Lincoln, NE: Nebraska Human Resources Research Foundation, p. 6.

Verderber, R. F., and Verderber, K. S. (1992). *Inter-act: Using interpersonal communication skills* (6th ed.). Belmont, CA: Wadsworth.

Viorst, J. (1987). *Necessary losses.* New York: Fawcett.

Chapter # 11

TRUST: THE FOUNDATION ELEMENT IN LEADERSHIP

> *The decline of trust in the United States is evident in any number of changes in American society: the rise of violent crime and civil litigation; the breakdown of family structure; the decline of a wide range of intermediate social structures like neighborhoods, churches, unions, clubs, and charities; and the general sense among Americans of a lack of shared values and community with those around them.*
> —Francis Fukuyama, *Trust* (1995)

ADVANCE PLANNER: TRUST: THE FOUNDATION ELEMENT IN LEADERSHIP

When you complete this chapter, you will be able to:

✓ Define trust.

✓ Identify the characteristics of trust that are evident in observed relationships.

✓ Describe a trusting relationship.

✓ Compare relationships in which trust is evident with those in which trust is not evident.

✓ Evaluate the trust that has been established between you and others.

✓ Implement steps to regaining trust in a relationship.

✓ Explain why trust must be the foundation for leadership.

✓ Practice strategies for establishing trust in relationships.

To accomplish these objectives, you will complete some or all of these activities:

1. Discuss characteristics of healthy relationships in which trust is evident.

2. Analyze your own characteristics for gaining and maintaining trust.

3. Complete an exercise that illustrates the potential for breakdown in trust.

4. Discuss steps to regaining trust.

5. Write various journal entries about your observations and evaluations of instances in which you see exhibitions of trust.

6. Critically review a conversation, noting characteristics that contribute to or break down trust.

7. Participate in getting-to-know-you-personally sessions.

A CASE STUDY IN TRUST

Hostility Turns to Trust

North Clackamas School District was formed in 1971 by consolidating five smaller districts. Not unexpectedly, many problems were associated with the creation of the new district. During the first year, 1972–73, the teachers voted to strike. They wore black armbands and picketed in front of the administration building during school board meetings. Settlement was reached just hours before the strike deadline, and only because the school board made what they considered to be major concessions. The following year the situation was much the same. Again the teachers wore black armbands and demonstrated; however, settlement was reached at fact-finding (a process that introduced a number of undesirable items into the contract).

During these years of conflict and confrontation, Donald Charles, then assistant superintendent and administration representative to the bargaining table, wrote: "During those two years the Board employed a professional negotiator to represent them at the bargaining table. While that procedure has been widely used and advocated by most observers, the outcome was not good. The negotiator's presence seemed only to make the association more argumentative and unyielding in their demands."

In 1974 the superintendent left the district, and Charles was appointed to replace him. One of Charles's highest priorities was to change the hostile atmosphere that had developed among school board, administration, and teachers.

At a conference that summer, Charles listened intently to a speaker who suggested that teachers do not want to run school districts, but they do want to be treated with professional respect and to receive fair pay. Following the conference and three days of one-on-one with the speaker, Charles commented, "The proposal that was written and accepted was really so simple that it was kind of embarrassing."

1. Each side would bargain for itself with no outside help at the bargaining table.

2. Each side would have a team of eight.

3. Teachers would bargain only those issues pertinent to people in North Clackamas District.

4. The teams would meet monthly to discuss any problems.

5. By mutual agreement, they could negotiate the contract whenever a problem was found, or when they felt it was desirable.

Betty Drew, past president of the North Clackamas Education Association, who was on the bargaining team when the proposal was implemented, pointed out that the association was working to try to change the confrontational situation by developing another approach. They were not able to get very far, however, until Donald Charles met them halfway.

The proposal was implemented that year, 1974; it has been successful since that time. In 1985 Drew stressed that feelings of trust and cooperation between teachers and administrators had deepened and grown stronger over the years (Pheasant, 1985).

Discussion Questions

1. What problems associated with trust might be expected when consolidating five school districts?

2. In this situation, with new teachers coming together for the first time, what would be the advantages of hiring an outside negotiator to be present at the bargaining table? What would be the disadvantages of hiring an outside negotiator?

3. Mr. Charles had served at the bargaining table prior to becoming the superintendent. Did this make a difference in the teachers' willingness to accept his proposal? Did they trust him? What characteristics do you think Mr. Charles might have exhibited at the bargaining table that now allowed the teachers to accept his proposal?

4. Is the proposal simple? In establishing trust, what are the advantages to keeping it simple?

INTRODUCTION TO THEORIES OF TRUST

"No trust—no beginning," wrote Rohnke (1984) as the first step in his education formula that was distilled from many years of experience with educating people. Rohnke believes that "If students don't trust you, your purpose, their peers, or the approach, program time will be limited to hassles, bickering, reluctance, and a huge waste of time" (p. 10). Did Rohnke's theory hold true in North Clackamas?

In the case study *Hostility Turns to Trust*, the bottom line was that teachers, for the first time, had the opportunity under the proposal to negotiate using a problem-solving approach as opposed to the traditional competitive approach that was widely used by schools to negotiate contracts during that time period. Let's briefly examine these approaches and the potential each holds for establishing trust.

According to Magenau (1976), in a problem-solving approach there is sharing of information about needs and priorities in an effort to find a mutually accepted solution. Using a problem-solving approach can develop each individual's awareness of decision making, potential for leadership, responsibility and obligations, and personal strengths. When everyone participates in a problem-solving approach, a sense of combined mental strength, morale, and camaraderie can be established.

In the competitive approach, an effort is made to push one party toward another's goal. Tactics such as threats, positional commitments, and put-downs have been known to be used during the competitive approach. Magenau contends that the problem-solving approach is preferred, but will be chosen and used to its fullest potential only when all key players can be trusted. When there is a perceived lack of trust, there is less information exchange, thus less ability to find commonality, thus less movement toward the goal. In other words, "no trust—no beginning."

Understanding Trust

Trust is defined as firm reliance on the integrity, ability, or character of a person or thing; confident belief. The American Heritage Dictionary traces the word back to the Old Norse *traust*, confidence, firmness (p. 1378).

Consider the following vignette (Fukuyama, 1996):

The recession of 1983–1984 that ravaged America's industrial heartland also hit the Nucor Corporation very hard. Nucor had just entered the steelmaking business by building mini-mills using new German continuous-casting technology. Its mills were built in places like Crawfordsville, Indiana, outside the traditional rust belt, and were operated by nonunionized workers, many of them former farmers. To deal with the drop in revenues, Nucor put its employees—from the CEO to the lowliest maintenance worker—on a two- or three-day workweek, with a corresponding cut in pay. No workers were fired, however, and when the economy and the company recovered, it enjoyed a tremendous esprit de corps that contributed to its becoming a major force in the American steel industry.

Workers at Nucor were willing to accept severe cuts in their weekly pay because they believed the managers who devised the pay cut plan were hurting as well and were committed to not laying them off. This community was a cultural one, formed not on the basis of explicit rules and regulations, but out of a set of ethical habits and reciprocal moral obligations internalized by each member. Trust paid off. Nucor workers were motivated to give their company an extra measure of effort once the recession was over.

Now, consider this situation:

In contrast to German practice, the French shop foreman's relations with his or her workers are regulated by a thicket of rules established by a ministry in Paris. This comes about because the French tend not to trust superiors to make honest personnel evaluations of their workers. The formal rules prevent the foreman from moving workers from one job to another, inhibiting development of a sense of workplace solidarity and making very difficult the introduction of innovations (Fukuyama, 1996, p. 10).

The problem is one of a deficit of "the ability of people to work together for the common purpose" (Fukuyama, 1996, p. 10). Coleman (1988) argues that in addition to the skills and knowledge needed in the workplace, a distinct portion of workplace success has to do with people's ability to associate with each other. The ability to associate, Coleman contends, depends on the degree to which people share norms and values and are able to subordinate individual interests to those of larger groups. Out of such shared values comes trust, and trust has a large measurable value.

Elements of Trust

In *A Handbook of Structured Experiences for Human Relations Training* (Pfeiffer & Jones, 1981), ten specific behaviors are identified as components recognized in a climate of trust. Following is a list of those behaviors, with descriptions and examples of what one might do to demonstrate each specific quality.

Sharing: telling and listening about personal events such as family matters and feelings.
People who have difficulty sharing their feelings may be heard saying, "I leave my personal problems at home." What is wrong with appropriate self-disclosure? Is it possible that briefly sharing a personal feeling with the people around us will tell them that the problem is not with their performance but instead is within us?

Vulnerability: the extent to which the leader is perceived as having the capacity to be susceptible; to err is human.
Ellis and Harper (1961) wrote, "It is irrational to believe that you should be thoroughly competent, adequate, and achieving in all respects. . . . Be prepared to accept small failures as undesirable, but not dreadful. Success is important, but it has nothing to do with your intrinsic value as a human being."

Loyalty: commitment to consistent goals of the organization (or unit) and its leaders (or authority figures).
Loyalty and trust seem to go hand in hand; loyalty can be cultivated by demonstrating trust. If individuals want people to trust them, they must trust others. For example, in the workplace, is it necessary to insist that employees punch a time clock or sign in? By trusting people to get the work done, loyalty will be established.

Accepting others: welcoming the unique behaviors of individuals.
The diversity around us must be celebrated, rather than viewed as problematic. Identifying and isolating personal biases from our interactions and recognizing that there is more that one right way to accomplish the task are important behaviors if productivity is to occur.

Involving others: using others for input or decision making.
"Consensus seeking is a powerful decision-making process, and the whole notion of involving others in decisions that will affect them makes sense" (Rothberg, 1984, p. 20). One problem with this type of shared decision making is that some individuals view the process of involving others as giving up power.

Valuing: willingness to exchange ideas and ideals with others.
Do we value the opinions of others? Open behavior (not overbearing, defensive, or threatening) that values the opinions of others appears to be important in the establishment of a trust relationship and thus a positive climate.

Awareness: sensitivity to the needs of others.
How well do we read people? Our relationships are often determined by the needs of those with whom we associate. One individual might be self-motivated and need little direction while another might be less committed and need more management. An understanding of such individuals, interactions, and group processes involving interpersonal skills can assist in our quest for improving this climate of trust.

Communicating: giving clear communications, both oral and written.
Clear two-way communication—oral and written—is vital for developing trust relationships. Schmuck et al. (1977) identified these communication responses that appear to be vital in establishing trust:

✓ Listening attentively.

✓ Paraphrasing.

✓ Seeking information to understand the other better.

✓ Offering relevant information.

✓ Describing observable behaviors that influence you.

✓ Directly reporting your own feelings.

✓ Offering opinions, stating your value position.

Responses reported to reduce trust are:

✓ Changing the subject without explanation.

✓ Criticizing.

✓ Trying to advise and persuade.

✓ Vigorously agreeing or strongly objecting.

✓ Commanding or demanding.

Openness: willingness to explore new experiences.
"A person genuinely interested in developing a climate of trust needs to be open and have a willingness to explore new experiences" (Rothberg, 1984, p. 21). Being open, however, means accepting change as opposed to maintaining the status quo; but change can be uncomfortable. Having a

positive self-concept is a prerequisite to openness; can I be open and trusting to someone else if I am uncomfortable with who I am?

Honesty: avoidance of deceit.

Honesty implies interactions that are both fair and equal. Have you ever worked for someone who told you one story and told another employee something different? What happened to your level of trust? It is to our advantage to share fairly and equally the information or resources in our possession. Doing so will elicit understanding, support, and trust.

Losing Trust

Trust can be damaged or lost in a second by thoughtlessness, carelessness, or inconsiderate behavior (Rohnke, 1984). Consider the story of Wang Laboratories (Fukuyama, 1996, p. 69–75):

> *Wang Laboratories, a manufacturer of computer equipment, at one time employed 24,800 people, making it one of Boston's largest employers. Its founder An Wang had emigrated to the United States from Shanghai. When Wang prepared to retire in the mid 1980's, he insisted that his son, Fred Wang, take over the business. Fred Wang was promoted over the heads of several more senior managers with proven track records. The blatant nepotism evident in his promotion alienated a string of American managers who quickly left the company.*
>
> *Why would a conscious, successful businessperson risk his company by placing it in the hands of a less-experienced son as opposed to a veteran administrator of the company? The answer lies in trust. The story of Wang Laboratories reveals a fundamental truth about Chinese business: there is a very strong inclination on the part of the Chinese to trust only people related to them—family. As a result of the lack of trust for nonfamily, more senior managers, Wang Laboratories posted its first loss the year after Fred Wang assumed leadership. In 1992 the company filed for bankruptcy, leading to a devastating breach of trust within the family; the elder Wang was forced to fire his son.*

Regaining Trust

✓ Have a clear understanding of your job.

✓ Understand the relationships of others within the working environment.

✓ Practice what you preach; portray a professional image.

✓ Give clear instructions.

✓ Show respect for people; criticize behaviors, not people.

✓ Be fair; apply rules consistently.

✓ Show honest appreciation.

✓ Be approachable—help those within the working environment solve problems.

✓ Keep in touch with what others are doing.

✓ Be patient.

Building Trust in Leadership

Trust is essential and powerful in laying the foundation for leadership. When people are able to say, "Yes, let's try that," to believe information has been presented accurately and completely, to feel it is safe to share ideas without being ignored or ridiculed, and to feel supported for their efforts even if their plans fail, then trust has been achieved. At this point, positive leadership can engage us and move us physically and emotionally toward efficiency and productivity.

Summary

A group of people who exhibit the elements of trust individually—sharing, vulnerability, loyalty, accepting others, involving others, valuing, awareness, communicating, openness, and honesty—and who surround themselves with positive experiences and successes, will discover that trust will grow in proportion to the building of personal confidence. As human beings, we often need supportive feedback from valued others to achieve a satisfactory self-image (Giffin & Patton, 1976). Thus as self-confidence increases we allow ourselves to communicate more freely and openly, to self-evaluate more confidently, and to practice our human relations skills in more diverse settings. Through each of these behaviors we are trusting more and are therefore being trusted.

Trust is a delicate commodity. We must make every effort to cultivate and protect the trust that others are willing to place into our care.

Hog Call

Adapted from Rohnke, 1984.

Purpose Knowing each other on a personal level and calling each other by name is an important dimension in establishing trust. Here is a means of breaking the ice.

You Will Need Blindfolds

Activity In a large room (or move this activity outside), your group will be divided into pairs—make sure you are paired with someone you don't know. Each member of the pair should select a one-syllable word or sound and pair it with the word or sound selected by the partner to create a unique set of words or sounds; e.g., shoe-foot, peanut-butter, fooz-ball, tweet-tweet (although your combinations will be more creative than these). Each pair should announce its choice in order to enjoy the humor of the more inventive selections, and more specifically to make sure there are no duplications.

One student from each pair will move to opposite ends of the room (gym, field, parking lot). Once there, scramble around so you are no longer opposite your partner, then put on a blindfold. The objective is to find your word partner by speaking and listening. Shout your partner's word or sound and listen for your partner to shout yours. For example, "peanut" will yell "butter" over and over until they find one another and become "peanut-butter."

Everyone should assume the bumpers-up position (hands up, palms out) for protection and to avoid dangerous collisions while moving around sightlessly.

When you find your partner, you may remove blindfolds and ask each other's name, where you are from and other information. When all are finished, everyone moves into a circle and introduces his or her partner to the group. Move around the circle until all have been introduced.

Yeah, But. . .

Adapted from Rohnke, 1984.

Purpose To develop trust within a group.

You Will Need Blindfolds

Activity Stand at one end of a large room or gymnasium (or take this activity outside) with your back to the wall. Everyone will assume the bumpers-up position (hands up, palms out) for protection. One person is blindfolded and must jog toward the far wall at a steady, unchanging pace.

The rest of you spread out in a line with backs to the wall that the jogger is approaching. Your job as spotters is to stop the jogger before he or she encounters the wall. (No fooling around, spotters; trust is a fragile commodity and is easily broken.) Be as quiet as possible in order to increase the commitment of the jogger. A few spotters should stand about three-fourths of the way down court on the sidelines to prevent wildly disoriented joggers from running into side walls or other objects.

EXERCISE
Developing Trust: A Leadership Skill

Adapted from Pfeiffer and Jones, 1981.

Purpose To examine behaviors and personal qualities that affect the process of establishing trust in relationships; analyze current behaviors and attitudes related to establishing trust in relationships; and increase awareness of how one is perceived by others in regard to behaviors that enhance the building of trust.
   Time required: Approximately two hours

You Will Need A copy of the Developing Trust Analysis Sheet

A copy of the Developing Trust Inventory Sheet (Self)

One or more copies of the Developing Trust Inventory Sheet (Other)

A pencil or pen

Physical Setting A room large enough for participants to move about freely and conduct semi-private conversations.

Activity

1. The facilitator will discuss with you the goals of the activity and the general importance of trust in effective interpersonal relationships.

2. Complete the Developing Trust Analysis Sheet according to the instructions provided.

3. Break into small groups of three or four members each and discuss your rankings of the items on the Developing Trust Analysis Sheet.

4. At your instructor's cue, disband your groups and complete the Developing Trust Inventory Sheet (Self) and put it aside for later use.

5. Find a partner. Work independently to complete the Developing Trust Inventory Sheet (Other) with regard to the way you believe others perceive your behaviors.

6. Exchange inventories and discuss your ratings with your partner.

7. Return to your original discussion groups (from step 3) to discuss the activity.

8. Focus on key things you have learned about how you establish trust in relationships. Take turns completing the sentence, "Something I learned/relearned/am learning about trust is. . . ."

9. Work independently to develop behavioral goals to increase your effectiveness in establishing trust in relationships.

10. Return to your discussion group and read your goals to each other; help each other clarify and refine them if necessary.

Developing Trust Analysis Sheet

Current theories and research concerning leadership stress the situational aspects of leadership effectiveness. In other words, leaders must take into account the particular dynamics of the organization, the existing social conditions, the characteristics of the followers, and their own leadership style. This means that effective leadership cannot be viewed as an isolated component. Leadership is relative, subjective, and interactive.

One component of leadership that appears germane to all leadership roles is relating. Relating, as a leadership skill, involves a variety of behaviors, including a particularly important one: establishing trust relationships.

Some of the behaviors and qualities involved in establishing a climate of trust are:

Sharing: telling and listening about personal events such as family matters and feelings.

Vulnerability: the extent to which the leader is perceived as having the capacity to err.

Loyalty: commitment to consistent goals of the organization and its leaders.

Accepting others: welcoming the unique behaviors of individuals.

Involving others: using others for input or decision making.

Valuing: willingness to exchange ideas and ideals with others.

Awareness: sensitivity to the needs of others.

Communicating: giving clear communications, both oral and written.

Openness: willingness to explore new experiences.

Honesty: avoidance of deceit.

Take a few minutes right now to think about these items. You will probably become aware that some of the items on the list mean more to you than others. You may want to add to the list. Use the table on the next page to rank these items from one to ten (one representing the most important item). If you add items to the list, you may include them in your ranking.

Rank	Behavior or Quality	Why You Ranked It This Way
1		
2		
3		
4		
5		
6		
7		
8		
9		
10		
Other		

Be prepared to discuss your reactions to the items and your rationale for the rankings you have given to these items

Developing Trust Inventory Sheet (Self)

Consider each of the components of establishing trust in relationships. Give yourself a score, based on the following rating scale, that best describes your behavior to most people, most of the time, at this time in your life.

Points *Meaning*

1   The behavior is exhibited consistently (most of the time)

2   The behavior is exhibited frequently (much of the time)

3   The behavior is inconsistent (sometimes yes, sometimes no)

4   The behavior is exhibited infrequently (sometimes)

5   The behavior is seldom exhibited (very little)

Component	Your Rating
Sharing	
Vulnerability	
Loyalty	
Accepting others	
Involving others	
Valuing	
Awareness	
Communicating	
Openness	
Honesty	
Other	

Developing Trust Inventory Sheet (Other)

Consider each of the components of establishing trust in relationships. Give yourself a score, based on the way you believe others perceive your behavior to most people, most of the time, at this time in your life.

Points	Meaning
1	The behavior is exhibited consistently (most of the time)
2	The behavior is exhibited frequently (much of the time)
3	The behavior is inconsistent (sometimes yes, sometimes no)
4	The behavior is exhibited infrequently (sometimes)
5	The behavior is seldom exhibited (very little)

Component	Perceptions of Others
Sharing	
Vulnerability	
Loyalty	
Accepting others	
Involving others	
Valuing	
Awareness	
Communicating	
Openness	
Honesty	
Other	

EXERCISE
Prisoner's Dilemma: An Intergroup Competition

Adapted from Marcic, 1992.

Purpose To explore trust and the consequences of its betrayal between group members. To demonstrate effects of interpersonal competition. In this exercise, you will work as part of a team in competition with two other teams. Your objective is to devise a strategy that will allow you to score as many points as possible. In some rounds, your team works autonomously to direct your leader how to vote. In other rounds, your team leader negotiates on your behalf with other team leaders to decide how your team will vote.

You Will Need
Pen or pencil

Seven ballots (distributed by your facilitator)

Payoff schedule (below)

Tally Sheet

Activity Form teams as directed and select a team representative. Your facilitator will explain the procedure for each round. Listen carefully. When you have completed the exercise, be prepared to discuss the questions your facilitator will ask.

Instructions

For seven successive rounds, each team will choose either an X or a Y. The score each team receives in a round is determined by the pattern made by the choices of all teams, according to the schedule below.

At the end of each round, record scores for each team on the Tally Sheet.

Payoff Schedule

XXX—All teams win 3 points.
XYY—Team choosing X loses 6 points; remaining teams win 6 points.
YXX—Team choosing Y wins 6 points; remaining teams lose 6 points.
YYY—All teams lose 3 points.

Prisoner's Dilemma Tally Sheet

Round	Minutes	Team 1	Team 2	Team 3	Total
1	3				
2	3				
3+	3 (reps) 3 (teams)				
4	3				
5	3				
6++	3 (reps) 5 (teams)				
7++	3 (reps) 5 (teams)				

+Payoff points are doubled for this round.

++Payoff points are squared for this round (retain the minus sign).

FURTHER ACTIVITY

Journal Writing

1. In your journal, write your own definition of trust. Then, in a paragraph, write a short description of the most trustworthy individual you know personally. What descriptors that you wrote about this individual help you consider him or her trustworthy?

2. Reflect on the ten elements of trust. Take each element, one at a time, and address your strengths and weaknesses within each element. Then, write one strategy for improving at least one of the weaknesses in each of the elements.

3. Observe and write, each day for one week, the daily interactions between roommates, particularly noting evidence or lack of evidence of the characteristics that are known to build trust.

4. Describe an event in your life when you felt your trust was betrayed. Which of the ten elements of trust were missing?

5. Likewise, describe a personal event when you betrayed someone's trust. What would you now do differently?

LEARNING POINTS

✓ Trust is a firm reliance on the integrity, ability, or character of another.

✓ Elements of trust that have been identified and observed in relationships include sharing, vulnerability, loyalty, accepting others, involving others, valuing, awareness, communicating, openness, and honesty.

✓ Trust is the foundation component in establishing oneself as a leader.

✓ Building trust is not complex—in fact, the simpler the better.

✓ Regaining trust in a relationship involves understanding others, showing respect, being fair and honest, and demonstrating patience.

✓ Trust can be destroyed in one word, one glance, one careless thought. Patience must be exercised in caring wisely for the trust that has been placed in us.

REFERENCES

American Heritage Dictionary, college ed., S. V. "trust."

Coleman, J. (1988). Social capital in the creation of human capital. *American Journal of Sociology. 94,* Supplement: S95-S120.

Ellis, A., and Harper, R. A. (1961). *A guide to rational living.* N. Hollywood, CA: Wilshire Book Co.

Fukuyama, F. (1996). *Trust: The social virtues and the creation of prosperity.* New York: The Free Press.

Giffin, K., and Patton, B. R. (1976). *Fundamentals of interpersonal communication.* Lanham, MD: University Press of America.

Magenau, J. (1976). The impact of trust on information exchange in bargaining. Paper presented at the annual meeting of Eastern Psychological Association. ERIC document #130 196.

Marcic, D. (1992). *Organizational behavior: Experiences and cases* (3rd ed.). St.Paul: West Publishing.

Pfeiffer, J. W., and Jones, J. E. (Eds.) (1981). Developing Trust Analysis Sheet. *A handbook of structured experiences for human relations training.* San Diego: University Associates.

Pheasant, M. (1985). Theory Z bargaining works: Teachers and administrators in two school districts replace hostility with trust. *OSSC Bulletin, 28* (7). ERIC document #254 937.

Rohnke, K. (1984). *Silver bullets: A guide to initiative problems, adventure games, stunts and trust activities.* Hamilton, MA: Project Adventure, Inc.

Rothberg, R. A. (1984). Trust development: The forgotten leadership skill. *NASSP Bulletin, 68* (476), 18–22.

Schmuck, R. A., Runkel, P. J., Arends, J. H., and Arends, R. I. (1977). *The second handbook of organization development in schools.* Palo Alto: Mayfield Publishing Co.

Chapter **12**

RESOLVING CONFLICT

A sense of humor enables us not so much to laugh at the people who provoke us as to laugh at ourselves for being so easily provoked.
—Robert Power

ADVANCE PLANNER: RESOLVING CONFLICT AND CONFLICT MANAGEMENT

When you complete this chapter, you will be able to:

✓ Define conflict.

✓ Recognize the benefits of the nominal decision-making technique.

✓ Identify how attitude affects individual behavior and group effectiveness.

✓ Demonstrate interference in communication and the problems it causes.

✓ Illustrate conflict management and the leader's role.

✓ Compare effectively the purposes and objectives of various conflict management theories.

✓ Appraise similarities and differences in group values, ideas, and beliefs.

✓ Develop a procedure for managing conflict in your life.

To accomplish these objectives, you will complete some or all of these activities:

1. Read and discuss the theoretical introduction to conflict management and compose a definition of conflict.

2. Discuss and summarize the nature of conflict and its implications for groups, teams, and organizations.

3. Examine a case study and identify the early warning signs of conflict and the levels of conflict in the situation.

4. Participate in a group activity in conflict negotiation using the concepts of conflict management presented in the chapter.

A CASE STUDY IN CONFLICT MANAGEMENT

He Said, She Said . . .

Shirley and Abdul both work for a software development company. The manager of the new product division was originally the leader of a project team

208

for which she interviewed and hired Abdul. Shirley, another project team member, also interviewed Abdul but strongly opposed hiring him for the project because she thought he was not competent to do the job.

Seven months after Abdul was hired, the manager left the project to start her own company and recommended that Abdul and Shirley serve as joint project leaders. Shirley agreed reluctantly—with the stipulation that it be made clear she was not working for Abdul. The General Manager consented; Shirley and Abdul were to share the project leadership.

Within a month Shirley was angry because Abdul was representing himself to others as the leader of the entire project and giving the impression that Shirley was working for him. Now Shirley and Abdul are meeting with you to see if you can help them resolve the conflict between them.

Shirley says: "Right after the joint leadership arrangement was reached with the General Manager, Abdul called a meeting of the project team without even consulting me about the time or content. He just told me when it was being held and said I should be there. At the meeting, Abdul reviewed everyone's duties line by line, including mine, treating me as just another team member working for him. He sends out letters and signs himself as project director, which obviously implies to others that I am working for him."

Abdul says: "Shirley is all hung up with feelings of power and titles. Just because I sign myself as project director doesn't mean that she is working for me. I don't see anything to get excited about. What difference does it make? She is too sensitive about everything. I call a meeting and right away she thinks I'm trying to run everything. Shirley has other things to do—other projects to run—so she doesn't pay too much attention to this one. She mostly lets things slide. But when I take the initiative to set up a meeting, she starts jumping up and down about how I am trying to make her work for me."

Discussion Questions

A variety of strategies can be used to help resolve the conflict between Abdul and Shirley. As you explore and develop concepts on conflict management presented in this chapter, keep this situation in mind. At the conclusion of this chapter you should be able to recognize the warning signs and know how to prevent this type of conflict from becoming a reality. But before reading the chapter, put yourself in the position of mediator between Abdul and Shirley and consider the following questions:

1. Abdul and Shirley seem to have several conflicts occurring simultaneously. Identify as many of these individual conflicts as possible.

2. Are there any general statements you can make about the overall nature of the conflict between Abdul and Shirley?

3. What are the possible ways to deal with the conflict between Abdul and Shirley (not just the ones that you would recommend, but *all* of the options)?

4. Given the choices identified in item three, what is the *best* way for Abdul and Shirley to deal with the conflict between them?

5. Given all the benefits of retrospection, what could or should have been done to avoid this conflict in the first place?

INTRODUCTION TO THEORIES OF CONFLICT RESOLUTION

What is conflict? Is it the same as a disagreement or an argument? Typically, conflict is characterized by three elements: 1) interdependence, 2) interaction, and 3) incompatible goals. We can define conflict as the interaction of interdependent people who perceive a disagreement about goals, aims, and values, and who see the other party as potentially interfering with the realization of these goals. Conflict is a social phenomenon that is woven into the fabric of human relationships; therefore, it can only be expressed and manifested through communication. We can only come into conflict with people with whom we are interdependent; that is, only when we become dependent on one another to meet our needs or goals does conflict emerge.

Conflicts are differentiated in a number of ways. One method of distinguishing among conflict situations is based on the context in which the conflict occurs. Barge (1994) indicates that traditionally conflict is viewed as occurring in the following three contexts:

Interpersonal conflict exists between two individuals within a group.

Intergroup conflict occurs between two groups within the larger social system.

Interorganizational conflict occurs between two organizations.

Understanding Conflict

Most authorities claim some conflict is inevitable in human relationships when people and groups are interdependent. Clashes occur more often over perceived differences than over real ones. People anticipate blocks to achieving their goals that may or may not be there. Thus conflict can be defined as two or more people independently perceiving that what each one wants is incompatible with what the other one wants.

There is a normal process of development in any conflict and this process tends to be cyclical, repeating itself over and over. At each stage of the cycle, the potential for conflict grows stronger. The table on the next page describes each stage of the conflict development process in terms of the thoughts or actions an individual experiences as the conflict develops.

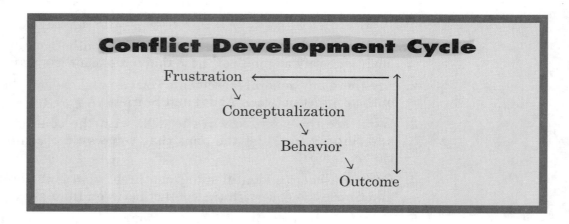

Conflict Development Cycle

Frustration →
↘ Conceptualization
↘ Behavior
↘ Outcome

Stage	Individual Thought or Action
Frustration	I am blocked from satisfying a goal or concern.
Conceptualization	I begin to determine in my mind what the problem is. I begin to attribute motives and blame based on my perceptions.
Behavior	I act on the perceptions above. (There is a cycle of reinforcement between conceptualization and behavior. How I act is determined by what I believe about the other party. How I act determines how the other perceives my motives and how he or she consequently acts.)
Outcome	The conflict is resolved in one of three ways: win/lose, lose/lose, or win/win, depending on the behavior of both parties.

Conflict often results when we fail to check our perceptions and assumptions about the other party's attitudes and motives. Our subsequent behavior and the outcome of the conflict are directly determined by the conceptualization phase.

We act on our beliefs about the other party. For example, we may decide that the person rejected our idea because he or she is threatened by or does not like us when, in fact, we did not communicate clearly or give enough information. We will respond quite differently depending on which case we believe to be true.

Rees (1991) suggests that conflict, like power, is neither good nor bad. It is what we do with it that makes the difference. Although conflict is generally viewed in a negative way and as something to avoid, when appropriately managed it can generate beneficial results. Conflict management theorists distinguish between constructive and destructive conflict. Constructive conflict is functional because it helps members accomplish goals and generate new insights into old problems. Destructive conflict is dysfunctional because it negatively affects group members by disrupting their activity. Bennis (1989) lists several characteristics that distinguish constructive and destructive conflict.

Constructive Conflict

✓ Allows constructive change and growth to occur within a system or group.

✓ Provides the opportunity for resolving problems associated with diversity of opinion.

✓ Provides a forum for unifying the group.

✓ Enhances group productivity.

✓ Enhances group commitment.

Destructive Conflict

✓ Develops when lack of common agreement leads to negativism.

✓ Leads to hardening of respective positions and diminished likelihood of a resolution.

✓ Causes the group to divide into camps, each supporting a different position.

✓ Results in a decrease in group productivity, satisfaction, and commitment.

Misconceptions about Conflict

Smith and Andrews (1989) suggest that people still hold negative opinions about the advisability of conflict resolution because of the following misconceptions:

1. *Harmony is normal and conflict is abnormal.* This belief is erroneous. Conflict is normal; in fact, it is inevitable. Whenever two people must interact in order to achieve goals, their subjective views and opinions about how to best achieve those goals will lead to conflict of some degree. Harmony occurs only when conflict is acknowledged and resolved.

2. *Conflicts and disagreements are the same.* Disagreement is usually temporary and limited, stemming from misunderstanding or differing views about a specific issue rather than a situation's underlying values and goals. Conflicts are more serious and usually are rooted in incompatible goals.

3. *Conflict is the result of personality problems.* Personalities themselves are not cause for conflict. While people of different personality types may approach situations differently, true conflict develops from and is reflected in behavior, not personality.

4. *Conflict and anger are the same thing.* While conflict and anger are closely merged in most people's minds, they don't necessarily go hand in hand. Conflict involves both issues and emotions—the issue and the participants determine what emotions will be generated. Serious conflicts can develop that do not necessarily result in anger. Other emotions are just as likely to surface: fear, excitement, sadness, frustration, and others.

Getting beyond the misconceptions described above is crucial to effective conflict resolution.

Levels of Conflict

One thing that determines the depth and complexity of conflict is the type of basic issue at stake. Most experts identify four levels of issues that may be the bases for conflict. Conflicts that escalate to higher levels become more complex and thus more difficult to resolve. See the table on the next page for a description of the four levels of conflict.

Warning Signs

Being aware of conflict warning signs can minimize conflict situations. The following social relationship characteristics should alert us to the potential for conflict.

1. *Ambiguous Jurisdictions.* If divisions of responsibility and authority are unclear, the possibility of conflict increases.

2. *Conflict of Interest.* Competition for perceived scarce resources (or rewards) escalates conflict possibilities.

3. *Communication Barriers.* Lack of communication, misunderstanding in terminology, unwillingness to listen to another person, etc., increase conflict possibilities.

4. *Overdependency of One Party.* If one person depends too heavily on another for information or assistance, conflict is more apt to occur.

Level Number	Type of Issue	Description
I	*Facts or Data*	The parties simply have different information. Conflict at this level is often a basic communication problem; when all pertinent information is shared with those concerned, differences usually disappear.
II	*Process or Methods*	The parties disagree over the best way to achieve a goal or solve a problem. Conflicts at this level are somewhat more difficult to resolve, but by using sound problem solving techniques they can usually be settled.
III	*Goals or Purpose*	The parties cannot agree on what the group's basic purpose or mission is. Negotiating goals takes patience and skill, but it is vital if collaboration is ever to be achieved.
IV	*Values*	The parties disagree about the basic meanings of the situation and things they hold dear. The bases for the conflict are highly subjective and at this level, conflicts are extremely difficult to resolve. In such cases, an expert third party may be needed to help resolve the conflict.

5. *Differentiation in Organization.* The greater the degree of differentiation in a group (e.g., levels of authority, types, and numbers of specific tasks), the greater the potential for conflict.

6. *Association of the Parties.* The more individuals interact, both informally and in decision making situations, the greater the opportunity for conflict. However, major incidents of conflict decrease as interaction increases.

7. *Need for Consensus.* When all parties must agree on the outcome, disagreements tend to escalate.

8. *Behavior Regulations.* Conflicts are greater when controls like rules, regulations, and formal policies are imposed.

9. *Unresolved Prior Conflicts.* As the number of past unresolved conflicts increases, so does the possibility for more conflicts in the future. (This underlines the importance of managing conflicts at their earliest stages, since they do not go away!)

Phases of Conflict Management

When parties in conflict agree that conflict resolution is needed, they are more likely to succeed if they move through prescribed phases to reach resolution (Johnson & Johnson, 1994).

1. *Collect data.* Know exactly what the conflict is about and objectively analyze the behavior of parties involved.

2. *Probe.* Ask open-ended, involved questions; actively listen; facilitate communication.

3. *Save face.* Work toward a win/win resolution; avoid embarrassing either party; maintain an objective (not emotional) level.

4. *Discover common interests*. This will help individuals redefine dimensions of the conflict and perhaps bring about a compromise.

5. *Reinforce*. Give additional support to common ideas of both parties and know when to use the data collected.

6. *Negotiate*. Suggest partial solutions or compromises identified by both parties. Continue to emphasize common goals of both parties involved.

7. *Solidify adjustments*. Review, summarize, and confirm areas of agreement. Resolution involves compromise.

Strategies for Coping with Conflict

There are a variety of strategies available for dealing with conflict. Some of us are more comfortable with some of these strategies than with others, but we all can be better conflict managers if we develop skills to implement several strategies and adapt resolution strategies to suit the particular conflict situation. Johnson and Johnson (1994) describe five possible approaches to conflict management: avoidance, accommodation, compromise, competition, and collaboration.

Avoidance

Avoidance occurs when an individual fails to address the conflict, but rather sidesteps, postpones, or simply withdraws. Some people attempt to avoid conflict by postponing it, hiding their feelings, changing the subject, leaving the room, or quitting the project.

Use avoidance when:

1. The stakes aren't that high and you don't have anything to lose.
2. You don't have time to deal with it.
3. The context isn't suitable to address the conflict—it isn't the right time or place.
4. More important issues are pressing.
5. You see no chance of getting your concerns met.
6. You would have to deal with an angry, hotheaded person.
7. You are totally unprepared, taken by surprise, and you need time to think and collect information.
8. You are too emotionally involved and the others around you can solve the conflict more successfully.

Avoidance may not be appropriate when the issue is very important and postponing resolution will only make matters worse. Avoiding conflict is generally not satisfying to the individuals involved in a conflict, nor does it help the group resolve a problem.

Accommodation

Accommodation is the opposite of competition and contains an element of self-sacrifice. An accommodating person neglects his or her own concerns to satisfy the concerns of the other person.

Use accomodation when:

1. The issue is more important to the other person than it is to you.
2. You discover that you are wrong.
3. Continued competition would be detrimental and you know you can't win.

4. Preserving harmony without disruption is the most important consideration.

Accommodation should **not** be used if an important issue is at stake that needs to be addressed immediately.

Compromise

The objective of compromise is to find an expedient, mutually acceptable solution that partially satisfies both parties. It falls in the middle between competition and accommodation. Compromise gives up more than competition does, but less than accommodation. Compromise is appropriate when all parties are satisfied with getting part of what they want and are willing to be flexible. Compromise is mutual. All parties should receive something, and all parties should give something up.

Use compromise when:

1. The goals are moderately important but not worth the use of more assertive strategies.
2. People of equal status are equally committed.
3. You want to reach temporary settlement on complex issues.
4. You want to reach expedient solutions on important issues.
5. You need a backup mode when competition or collaboration don't work.

Compromise doesn't work when initial demands are too great from the beginning and there is no commitment to honor the compromise.

Competition

An individual who employs the competition strategy pursues his or her own concerns at the other person's expense. This is a power-oriented strategy used in situations in which eventually someone wins and someone loses. Competition enables one party to win. Before using competition as a conflict resolution strategy, you must decide whether or not winning this conflict is beneficial to individuals or the group.

Use competition when:

1. You know you are right.
2. You need a quick decision.
3. You meet a steamroller type of person and you need to stand up for your own rights.

Competition will not enhance a group's ability to work together. It reduces cooperation.

Collaboration

Collaboration is the opposite of avoidance. It is characterized by an attempt to work with the other person to find some solution that fully satisfies the concerns of both. This strategy requires you to identify the underlying concerns of the two individuals in conflict and find an alternative that meets both sets of concerns. This strategy encourages teamwork and cooperation within a group. Collaboration does not create winners and losers and does not presuppose power over others. The best decisions are made by collaboration.

Use collaboration when:

1. Others' lives are involved.

2. You don't want to have full responsibility.

3. There is a high level of trust.

4. You want to gain commitment from others.

5. You need to work through hard feelings, animosity, etc.

Collaboration may not be the best strategy to use if time is limited and people must act before they can work through their conflict, or there is not enough trust, respect, or communication among the group for collaboration to occur.

Creative Ways to Manage Conflict

Conflict of some degree is inevitable when individuals or groups work together. Before conflict evolves, decide to take positive steps to manage it. When it does occur, discuss it openly with the group. Here are some useful guidelines to follow when managing conflict:

1. Deal with one issue at a time. More than one issue may be involved in the conflict, but someone in the group needs to provide leadership to identify the issues involved. Then address one issue at a time to make the problem manageable.

2. If there is a past problem blocking current communication, list it as one of the issues in this conflict. It may have to be dealt with before the current conflict can be resolved.

3. Choose the right time for conflict resolution. Individuals have to be willing to address the conflict. We are likely to resist if we feel we are being forced into negotiations.

4. Avoid reacting to unintentional remarks. Words like *always* and *never* may be said in the heat of battle and do not necessarily convey what the speaker means. Anger will increase the conflict rather than bring it closer to resolution.

5. Avoid resolutions that come too soon or too easily. People need time to think about all possible solutions and the impact of each. Quick answers may disguise the real problem. All parties need to feel some satisfaction with the resolution if they are to accept it. Conflict resolutions should not be rushed.

6. Avoid name-calling and threatening behavior. Don't corner the opponent. All parties need to preserve their dignity and self-respect. Threats usually increase the conflict and payback can occur some time in the future when we least expect it.

7. Agree to disagree. In spite of your differences, if you maintain respect for one another and value your relationship, you will keep disagreements from interfering with the group.

8. Don't insist on being right. There are usually several right solutions to every problem.

Humor and Conflict

Laughter can effectively relieve tension in conflict situations. A well-timed joke can refocus conflict negotiations in a positive direction. Laughter gives people time to rethink their positions and see alternatives that may not have been obvious before (Westcott, 1988).

A leader can read a humorous story at the beginning of a meeting to set the tone or be prepared with a humorous example to use in case conflict occurs. Laughing together helps individuals accept differences and still enjoy one another as group members.

Humor is most effective when it relates to the situation at hand. The best source of humor is personal experience and it's usually safe to use oneself as the target of the humor. However, humor should never belittle or insult anyone. Use humor to support talent within the group rather than as a way to cover lack of skill.

Summary

Leaders should learn how to manage and use conflict creatively for the betterment of communities, organizations, and personal relationships. We don't need to be devastated by conflict when we can learn to manage it and use the energy it produces. Leaders confront a variety of relational problems as groups and teams develop over time. Some problems may include defining roles, motivating followers, and managing conflict. Such problems can be overcome by leadership that recognizes them and takes appropriate action to resolve them. All leaders can facilitate resolving relational issues through conflict management, bargaining, and feedback.

EXERCISE
Setting the Stage for Conflict

Purpose Role-playing a conflict situation will help you see how competing objectives can lead to conflict.

You Will Need Pen or pencil and paper for observers

Role cards for seven characters:

- ✓ **ID** Sees the arrangement of chairs as an issue. Has analyzed the issue and is proposing the chairs be arranged in a circle.

- ✓ **Z** Believes that the present seating arrangement is the only possible seating arrangement.

- ✓ **VY** Wants the nomination for Person of the Year in Yorktown. Does not want to risk getting involved in an unpopular decision.

- ✓ **PU** Doesn't like the plan because of a dislike of the person proposing it—ID.

- ✓ **BX** Busy running in and out of the room—only catches part of the conversation, but tries to join in the decision.

- ✓ **NV** Leader of the group. Resists the plan because he or she was not consulted prior to the meeting.

- ✓ **OK** Always sides with NV, the leader.

Seven chairs at the front of the room, arranged in two unequal rows facing each other

Activity The seven players should sit in the chairs so everyone can see the others. You are members of a multidisciplinary scholarship selection committee and are meeting to name this year's scholarship winner.

Each person should take one role card from the instructor. Read the role you are to play, but don't let any of the other players see your card. The character named ID should start the role play whenever he or she is ready. Observers should take notes about what they see. Continue the role play for 7–8 minutes, as long as you can continue building the case of the characters you are playing. Stop when you run out of steam or the instructor calls a halt.

Observers should break into small groups and discuss what took place. Assign a recorder for your small group, who should take notes and summarize your comments for the class as a whole. When you have finished your discussion, return to the large group.

Discussion

1. What caused the conflict?
2. How are these conflicts similar to ones you have experienced in groups?
3. How did you feel in these situations?
4. What steps could be taken to reduce or resolve the conflict?

EXERCISE
Conflict Negotiation

Adapted from Pfeiffer & Co., 1994.

Purpose This exercise is designed to help two individuals resolve a particular disagreement or conflict. In order for it to work, both individuals must have either a real or realistic disagreement and wish to have some sort of resolution to the situation.

Process

1. Person A completes a sequence of four statements (as follows) from his or her point of view.

   a) Description of the current situation
   "The conflict I'm having with you is. . . . The problem as I see it is. . . ."

   b) Description of the ideal situation
   "What I'd like to see is. . . ."

   c) Description of current feelings
   "The way I feel about this situation is. . . ."

   d) Description of self-intention
   "What I'm willing to do to create what I want is. . . ."

2. Person B then paraphrases what Person A has said. If the paraphrase is accepted as accurate by Person A, Person B then moves through the same sequence of statements and Person A paraphrases.

3. Person A then asks, "Do we have a resolution?" If the answer is "no," Person A begins the sequence again. If the answer is "yes," both parties review their agreements.

   Note: It may be helpful to have a third person present to facilitate the statement sequence and paraphrasing process.

FURTHER ACTIVITY

Independent Practice

Learning is more complete when you begin to apply and experience what you have just learned. Here are some activities to do on your own or with a friend to learn more about coping with conflict.

✓ Identify someone with whom you have had a recent conflict. List the reason(s) that conflict occurred.

✓ Was the conflict resolved the same day? Why or why not?

✓ If the same situation happened again, what would you do differently?

LEARNING POINTS

✓ Typically, conflict is characterized by three elements: 1) interdependence, 2) interaction, and 3) incompatible goals.

✓ Conflict is the interaction of interdependent people who perceive a disagreement about goals, aims, and values, and who see the other party as potentially interfering with the realization of these goals.

✓ Conflict is viewed as occurring at the levels of: facts or data; process or methods; goals or purpose; and values.

✓ The warning signs of conflict include: 1) ambiguous jurisdictions; 2) conflict of interest; 3) communication barriers; 4) overdependency of one party; 5) differentiation in organization; 6) association of the parties; 7) need for consensus; 8) behavior regulations; 9) unresolved prior conflicts.

✓ The phases of conflict management include: 1) collecting data; 2) probing; 3) saving face; 4) discovering common interests; 5) reinforcing; 6) negotiating; 7) solidifying adjustments.

✓ There are five possible approaches to conflict management, each with specific advantages and disadvantages given a specific set of circumstances: avoidance, accommodation, compromise, competition, and collaboration.

✓ Some suggestions for dealing with conflict creatively include: 1) deal with one issue at a time; 2) if there is a past problem blocking current communication, list it as one of the issues in this conflict; 3) choose the right time for conflict resolution; 4) avoid reacting to unintentional remarks; 5) avoid resolutions that come too soon or too easily; 6) avoid name-calling and threatening behavior; 7) agree to disagree; 8) don't insist on being right. There are usually several right solutions to every problem.

REFERENCES

Barge, J. K. (1994). *Leadership communication skills for organizations and groups.* New York: St. Martin's Press.

Bennis, W. (1989). *Why leaders can't lead.* San Francisco: Jossey-Bass.

Johnson, D. W., and Johnson, F. P. (1994). *Joining together group theory and group skills.* Boston: Allyn and Bacon.

Pfeiffer & Company. (1994). *1994 Annual: Developing human resources.* San Diego: Pfeiffer & Company.

Rees, F. (1991). *How to lead work teams.* San Diego: Pfeiffer & Company.

Smith, W. F., and Andrews, R. L. (1989). *Instructional leadership: How principals make a difference.* Alexandria, VA: ASCD.

Westcott, J. M. (1988). Humor and the effective work group. In *1988 Annual: Developing human resources.* San Diego: Pfeiffer & Company.

Chapter **13**

The Nature of Power, Influence, and Leadership

We must not confuse leadership with power. Leaders always have some measure of power, rooted in their capacity to persuade, but many people with formal power are without leadership gifts. Their power derives from money, or from the capacity to inflict harm, or from control of some piece of institutional machinery, or from access to the media. A military dictator has power. The thug who sticks a gun in your ribs has power. Leadership is something else.

—John Gardner, *On Leadership* (1990)

ADVANCE PLANNER: THE NATURE OF POWER, INFLUENCE, AND LEADERSHIP

When you complete this chapter, you will be able to:

✓ Illustrate the relationship between leadership and influence.

✓ Differentiate between leadership and management.

✓ Describe the characteristics of transformational leaders.

✓ Identify and illustrate the appropriate use of each of nine influence tactics in a practical situation.

✓ Given a practical situation, devise the best option for dealing with an adverse influence attempt.

✓ Interpret the relationship between organizational and personal sources of power, influence tactics, and responses to adverse influence attempts.

To accomplish these objectives, you will complete some or all of these activities:

1. Read a short case study and discuss the sources and uses of power in the case.

2. Read and discuss an introduction to the nature of power, influence, and leadership.

3. Hear a brief lecture on the nature of power, influence, and leadership.

4. Observe and participate in role plays that offer opportunities to use and experience various forms of power and influence.

5. Create drawings that represent your positive and negative feelings about power and influence.

6. Complete a self-evaluation of your own uses of and responses to power and influence attempts.

7. Make entries in your journal examining your responses to power and influence attempts.

A CASE STUDY ON THE USE OF POWER AND INFLUENCE

Hey, Get to Work

After graduating from college with honors in horticulture, Eduardo continued on in graduate school and has just about completed his master's degree. Eduardo's professors consider him a brilliant student and have encouraged him to pursue a Ph.D. He works part-time as a supervisor of the outdoor retail sales area at a large nursery. Eduardo needs this job to keep his head above water financially, and so far he has just about been breaking even.

At the nursery Eduardo reports to Janette, the nursery manager, who also supervises the cashiers, the landscape crew supervisor, and the greenhouse and showroom sales staff. Janette is incredibly busy but always tries to make time for Eduardo when he has a question. Eduardo knows there is a good bit of pressure on her to increase the profitability of the nursery and that she is in line for a promotion if she can be successful at her current job. When she gets too busy, she has a reputation for being short-tempered and she sometimes interprets complaints by subordinates or suggestions for improving procedures as personal insults. (A worker who dared to complain once too often was permanently reassigned to the crew that hand-digs and plants large, field-grown trees.) In general, Eduardo's strategy for success has been to keep Janette happy by working hard, keeping customer complaints from his area to a minimum, and occasionally offering to assist with jobs that are not really part of his responsibility, but that he knows need to be done. Eduardo and Janette have a generally good relationship, and he respects her for both her hard work and her knowledge of the nursery business. Although everything has been strictly professional in their relationship, Eduardo finds Janette attractive and has thought about asking her for a date. Eduardo is not at all sure how she would react and so far has not found the right moment (or the courage) to bring up the idea.

Eduardo's work consists of supervising two or three other workers, keeping the nursery stock and outdoor sales area in good condition, unloading new shipments, answering customer questions, and helping load plants and materials into customer vehicles. In general he enjoys his work; however, he sometimes feels that customers have an unrealistic expectation of his ability to identify and solve every lawn or garden problem. For example, recently a customer brought in a small portion of a dead branch from an unidentified garden plant and asked, "Why did this die?" Eduardo didn't have a clue as to what the plant might be and knew it could have died from just about anything. He told the customer he wasn't really sure and started to list some of the more obvious possibilities, like improper watering, pests, and parasites. The customer interrupted brusquely and in a voice loud enough to be heard all over the sales area: "Where do I have to go to get a straight answer? It used to be that the people who worked here knew something about gardening! Now all we get is a bunch of kids who don't know squat about anything." Surprised and startled, Eduardo mumbled something about being sorry he couldn't help him and slunk away; thankfully, the customer soon left the grounds. Fortunately, incidents like this are relatively rare and most of Eduardo's interactions with customers are quite satisfying.

Recently Eduardo became aware that one of his workers on the afternoon shift, Jason—an undergraduate college student—is repeatedly absent or late and sometimes gives customers incorrect advice about plants they wish to buy. Jason seems to be satisfied with his poor performance, but Eduardo would like him to be more reliable and knowledgeable. Based on some conversations Eduardo has had with him, he knows Jason is interested in a career in landscape design, something that pleased Eduardo when he first heard about it. Eduardo is generally respected and liked by his workers and it truly irritates him that Jason does such a poor job. Eduardo wants Jason to start coming to work on time and to be more helpful to customers. Eduardo checked with Janette and she confirmed that he has the authority to fire Jason if he wishes to.

Discussion Questions

1. Why does Jason behave the way he does? What are all the possible reasons you can imagine? Based just on the information you presently have, what do you think is the most plausible reason?

2. What are some examples of the use of power in this case? What are the sources of power for Eduardo (the outdoor sales supervisor) in the case? What are Janette's sources of power?

3. If you are Eduardo, what are *all* of your possible choices in terms of how to deal with Jason? Which do you recommend and why?

4. Where do power and influence come from?

5. How well did Eduardo deal with the irate customer? What recommendations would you offer as to how he might behave next time?

6. In terms of Eduardo's relationship with Janette, the nursery manager, what are some things he can do to be influential in his relationship (both personal and professional) with her? How can he sustain or increase his influence with his nursery crew?

INTRODUCTION TO THEORIES OF POWER, INFLUENCE, AND LEADERSHIP

In the late 1960s, the Supreme Court was grappling with its proper role in regard to the regulation of pornography. At one point the Court considered the possibility of establishing some national standard for what was and was not obscene. For reasons of both legal philosophy and the inherent difficulty of the task, they eventually sent the responsibility for deciding those matters back to the states and local communities. However, during the period in which they were still attempting to define a standard, the justices were required to view large numbers of films, photographs, and other materials about which there was a claim that those items might be obscene. At the height of this debate someone asked Justice Potter Stewart if he could define pornography, and he replied: *"No, but I know it when I see it!"* (Woodward & Armstrong, 1970). Sometimes it seems we have a similar attitude about leadership. It is a variously defined concept, and although we all remain sure of its existence and importance, we sometimes have difficulty defining exactly what it is or is not; yet, like Justice Stewart, "we know it when we see it."

Definition of Leadership

Ralph Stogdill, scholar and chronicler of the research on leadership, says "there are as many different definitions of leadership as there are persons who have attempted to define the concept" (Stogdill, 1974). Although attempts to achieve universal agreement on a definition of leadership have been generally unsuccessful, a consensus is growing that it is useful to think about and describe leadership as an intentional social *influence* process exerted by one person to sway the behavior or attitudes of one or more others in regard to a goal (Yukl, 1994). So, every time we attempt to persuade a friend to accompany us to a certain place for lunch, or encourage someone to adopt a certain style of clothing, or persuade a fellow student to take a certain course, we are in fact exerting influence and therefore attempting to exercise leadership.

Sometimes we tend to think of leadership as the province only of elected officials, presidents of companies, politicians, generals, and other persons who hold positions of power. In fact these people may be exerting leadership; however, as suggested by the quotation from John Gardner that appears at the beginning of this chapter, we actually need to know more about how they use their authority before we can conclude whether they are really leading. To be sure, generals and presidents have considerable power at their disposal and certainly can cause people to spring into action; however, we may ask ourselves if this is really leadership. When followers comply with the requests or demands of the boss, are they necessarily responding to leadership or simply meeting the terms of their employment contracts?

There is a continuing debate about the difference between leadership and management (Zalenick, 1977), which occasionally degenerates into a tiresome exchange about the mere meanings of words; however, at least a part of that discourse may be useful to us in understanding the true nature of the relationships among power, influence, and leadership. One way we differentiate between leadership and management is to look at the sources of the influence that cause followers to accede to the efforts of others to guide their behavior. Another way we can differentiate between the exercise of leadership influence and other forms of power is in terms of the effect on followers (Kouzes & Posner, 1990). People who are being managed comply with the instructions because they must, and people who are being led do so because they want to. Leadership typically elicits a voluntary, enthusiastic response from followers, whereas other forms of power tend to extract compliance from followers out of a sense of obligation or duty, or a fear of the consequences of failure to comply.

Transactional vs. Transformational Leadership

Do the concepts of leadership and management, power and influence overlap each other? Absolutely! Is it possible to be a good manager and get a lot of things done, yet not be a very good leader? Absolutely, it happens all the time! Is it possible to be a good leader, yet be a poor manager? Yes, it is! One of the newest and most promising ways to describe leadership has come from the work of those describing the concepts of *transactional* and *transformational* leadership.

Bass and Avolio (1994) describe *transactional leaders* as those persons who emphasize the transaction or exchange that takes place between leaders, colleagues, and followers. In this exchange, the leader specifies what is expected and helps followers to clearly understand what they will receive, or avoid, if they fulfill those expectations. *Transformational leaders,* on the other hand, do more than set up simple exchanges or agreements. By virtue of the nature of their relationships with followers, they motivate others to do more than they originally intended and even more than they thought possible. Transformational leaders engage followers by employing one or more of the Four I's (see box) to stimulate voluntary and enthusiastic responses to their influence attempts.

One way of considering the differences between the two is to associate transactional influence primarily with management, and transformational influence with leadership. However, the concepts of transaction ("you do this

The Four I's of Transformational Leadership

Individualized Consideration: The leader gives personal attention to others, making each individual feel uniquely valued.

Intellectual Stimulation: The leader actively encourages a new look at old methods, stimulates creativity, encourages others to look at problems and issues in a new way.

Inspirational Motivation: The leader increases optimism and enthusiasm, communicates high expectations, points out possibilities not previously considered.

Idealized Influence: The leader provides vision and a sense of purpose; elicits respect, trust, and confidence from followers.

(Bass, 1990)

and I'll make sure you receive that") and transformation (intellectual stimulation, individualized consideration, inspiration, and idealized influence) are generally not thought to be independent of one another (Bass, 1985). In fact, a study of military officers and industrial managers (Waldman et al., 1986) showed that although the effects of transformational leadership were generally much stronger than those of transactional leadership, leaders who had both transactional and transformational characteristics were much more successful than those who had only one. The bottom line on leadership often comes down to the combined ability to both "rally the troops" and "make the trains run on time." Both these skills are important, but each is most effective in an appropriate combination with the other.

Often courses like this one emphasize the need to make logical, rational decisions and to array the reward structures of the organization to make things pay off for people who help us accomplish our goals. At work, these rewards take the form of pay, promotions, work assignments, etc.; in less formal situations, rewards often take the form of affection, approval, personal assistance, favors, or other interpersonal exchanges. While this capacity is important and needs to be developed, the skills described as the Four I's of Transformational Leadership are often overlooked. If you are seeking ways to be more influential, whether in an on-the-job situation, in a student work group, or in your relationships with others in general, you should consider increasing the frequency with which you engage in the behaviors that characterize transformational leaders. In most cases, you won't need to do something entirely new, but simply do more of an already learned behavior. Although insincere attempts to influence followers by using these behaviors in a manipulative manner are unlikely to succeed, those who can use the Four I's effectively and authentically are likely to increase their personal sources of power and influence.

The Sources of Power

An unfortunate mistake many people make when placed in positions of authority over others is to rely heavily, or in some cases exclusively, upon the power inherent in the position: "Because I'm the boss, you have to do what I say." It is an axiom of human nature that if you have a big enough club you can make people do just about anything.

Many of us can recall jobs we have had in which we were so desperate for a paycheck we swallowed our pride and anger and tolerated an officious or even occasionally abusive boss. However, if you reflect upon the best leaders and most influential people you have known or worked for, it is likely that their ability to influence you emanated from sources other than the titles they held or the positions they occupied.

One of the most widely known typologies of the sources of power (see box) is provided by French and Raven (1959). Understanding and identifying sources of power can be an important first step in becoming more influential in our own lives. It is important to understand that the use of any of these sources is neither good nor bad. The most effective leaders understand where their power comes from and how to effectively develop and use it. Some of these sources of power can be vested upon individuals by virtue of their positions; others are vested upon leaders by followers because of the followers' perceptions of the personal characteristics of the leader. Some of these sources of power can be earned by hard work and organizational success, in the form of promotions or appointments to positions of power. Still others re-

Sources of Power

Reward Power: The target person complies in order to obtain rewards he or she believes are controlled by the agent.

Coercive Power: The target person complies in order to avoid punishments he or she believes are controlled by the agent.

Legitimate Power: The target person complies because he or she believes the agent has the right to make the request and the target person has the obligation to comply.

Expert Power: The target person complies because he or she believes the agent has special knowledge about the best way to do something.

Referent Power: The target person complies because he or she admires or identifies with the agent and wants to gain the agent's approval.

(French & Raven, 1959)

sult from lifelong self-development and relate to the less obvious, but extraordinarily important, qualities of our relationships with others.

Reward, coercive, and legitimate sources of power are most often associated with organizational situations and are generally derived from the office or position a person holds. Expert and referent power are most often thought of as personal sources of power and belong to a person regardless of any position he or she occupies. However, it is sometimes possible for two or more sources of power to overlap, particularly in the case of reward or coercive power; just think about a time you may have been snubbed in a social situation or felt compelled to do something you preferred not to do just so you could fit in with a valued social group.

Both organizational and personal sources of power require effort to develop. In general, organizational power will flow to those who are particularly good at meeting the needs of an organization and helping it to achieve goals. Doing your job well, having good relationships with peers and superiors, being in a visible position, doing important work, expending extra effort, and understanding what it takes to succeed are good ways to increase your sources of organizational power. Developing expertise, being the kind of person people like and respect, showing regard for others, stimulating others to aspire to high goals, and activating one or more of the Four I's of transformational leadership are some ways you can increase the sources of personal power. Developing organizational power is generally something you do at work or in formal organizations; developing personal power is a lifelong process.

Influence Tactics

The presence or absence of power sources does not tell the whole story of how influence affects the behavior and attitudes of others. Simply because we have either the expertise or the power to adjust rewards or coerce doesn't mean we are obliged to use these power sources. Depending on the situation and our own personality, we may use a variety of tactics to try to influence others. A study of the ways in which individuals in organizations attempt to use influence (Yukl, 1994) revealed the nine tactics described in the box. One

Influence Tactics

Rational Persuasion:	The agent uses logical arguments to persuade the target that a proposal or request is viable and likely to result in attainment of task objectives.
Inspirational Appeals:	The agent makes a request or proposal that arouses the target's enthusiasm by appealing to the target's values, ideals, and aspirations, or by increasing the target's self-confidence.
Consultation:	The agent seeks the target's participation in planning a strategy, activity, or change for which the target's support and assistance are desired, or is willing to modify a proposal to deal with the target's concerns and suggestions.
Ingratiation:	The agent uses praise, flattery, friendly behavior, or helpful behavior to get the target in a good mood or to think favorably of his or her request for something.
Personal Appeal:	The agent appeals to the target's feelings of loyalty and friendship when asking for something.
Exchange:	The agent offers an exchange of favors, indicates a willingness to reciprocate at a later time, or promises a share of the benefits if the target helps accomplish the task.
Coalition Tactics:	The agent seeks the aid of others to persuade the target to do something, or uses the support of others as a reason for the target to agree also.
Legitimating Tactics:	The agent seeks to establish the legitimacy of a request by claiming the authority or right to make it, or by verifying that it is consistent with organizational politics, rules, practices, or traditions.
Pressure:	The agent uses demands, threats, frequent checking, or persistent reminders to influence the target to do what he or she wants.

(Yukl, 1994, p. 225)

of the most important life skills we can develop is the ability to understand our sources of power, identify which sources to call upon in a given situation, and choose appropriate influence tactics.

> # Resistance to Influence Attempts
>
> *Resistance to your influence attempts occurs when persons you are trying to influence:*
>
> 1. Refuse outright to accede to your attempts to influence them.
> 2. Ignore your efforts at influence.
> 3. Make excuses why they cannot do what you want.
> 4. Ask higher authorities to overrule your request.
> 5. Attempt to persuade you to withdraw your attempt at influence.
> 6. Delay acting on your influence efforts.
> 7. Make a pretense of complying while actively attempting to sabotage your efforts.

Outcomes of Influence Attempts

Clearly the nature of the influence process and the sources of power combine to influence the responses of followers. The success of any influence attempt is defined in terms of the response of the follower or object of the influence effort. Yukl (1994) describes three possible outcomes of influence attempts:

Resistance: The person you are trying to influence resists your efforts to influence his or her behavior and either avoids, ignores, or actively resists your efforts at influence. This resistance can take several forms, as noted in the box.

Compliance: The person you are trying to influence accedes to your influence attempt, but apathetically or unenthusiastically. When the response to your influence attempt can be described as compliance, it is likely you have been successful in influencing the behavior but not the attitudes of your influence target.

Commitment: The object of your influence attempt agrees with your decision or influence effort and makes an enthusiastic, voluntary effort to do what you have asked. The response comes not because the person has to but because he or she wants to.

Personal Responses to Inappropriate Uses of Power

When someone tries to influence us and we are either disinterested or mildly to moderately opposed, we typically resist. But what about those influence attempts in which the stakes are much higher and we are confronted with a situation that involves our dignity, safety, or important personal values and issues? According to Verderber and Verderber (1995), we typically have three choices: to respond passively, to respond aggressively, or to respond assertively.

Passive Behavior: Even though we may care deeply about the outcome of the influence attempt, we sometimes become passive in the face of overwhelming force or the consequences of the influence attempt.

Aggressive Behavior: When we lash out at the source of the influence attempt, either physically or verbally, we are engaging in aggressive behavior. We sometimes confuse aggressive behavior with assertive behavior when, in fact, they are quite different. Aggressive behavior is judgmental, fault find-

Characteristics of Assertive Behavior

Own your feelings: Acknowledge how you are feeling, but in a way that does not put down the other person.

Avoid confrontational language: Refrain from using threats, put-downs, or challenges.

Use specific behaviors appropriate for the situation at hand: Make your response appropriate to the situation; do not make unnecessary references to unrelated situations.

Maintain eye contact and a firm body position: you need to be seen as firm (even if you are frightened or unsure), but not confrontational. These are good skills to develop and practice in advance of the need to use them.

Maintain a firm but pleasant tone of voice; speak clearly; avoid hemming and hawing: Aggression is accompanied by yelling; passivity by extreme quietness. To be assertive you must remember that more of your message is transmitted in the way you deliver it than in the words themselves.

(Verderber & Verderber, 1995)

ing, dominating, pressuring, and often involves the overt expression of anger and hostility.

Assertive Behavior: Even though we may be hurt, frightened, or profoundly angry, the ability to respond to adverse attempts to influence us is one of the most important interpersonal skills we can develop. The ability to respond assertively in stressful or significant situations is generally considered a characteristic of emotional maturity. Assertive behavior is simply standing up for your own best interests, but in a way that is interpersonally effective and does not require that there be a winner and a loser. Assertive behavior usually leaves both the object and agent of the influence attempt emotionally intact and does not create a legacy likely to leave one party scheming about getting even for what is perceived as unfair treatment. Verderber and Verderber (1995) suggest the strategies listed in the box as practical ways to behave assertively.

Personal Strategies for Building Influence

To better understand the many ways power and influence are exerted in our lives and to be in a position to increase our own interpersonal power and influence, we need to bring together the concepts that have been previously discussed. As suggested in the Personal Influence Model (see diagram), the degree to which we are influential with others depends to a large extent on:

1. Our personal or organizational sources of power.
2. Our awareness of our sources of power.
3. Our ability to select a personal influence tactic appropriate to a given situation.

The Nature of Power, Influence, and Leadership   **231**

Personal Influence Model

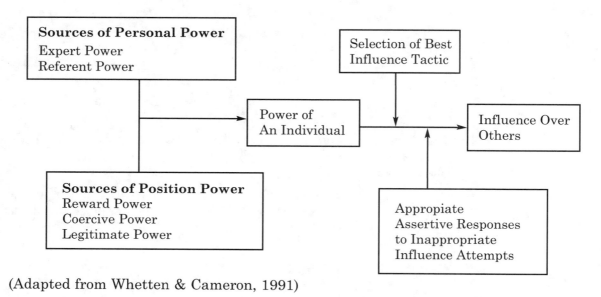

(Adapted from Whetten & Cameron, 1991)

4. Our ability to respond assertively when faced with inappropriate or adverse influence attempts.

The true measure of our ability to be influential arises from our awareness of our sources of power and our choices of influence tactics, as well as from the ability to consistently match an appropriate tactic to the demands of a situation while increasing and improving our repertoire of effective responses.

LARGE GROUP ACTIVITY
Practice Using Influence, Power, and Assertive Behavior

Purpose Role-playing using fictitious scenarios can help you identify and practice influence skills. The key is to select an influence tactic that is most likely to work in the given situation.

Activity Follow your instructor's directions about how to set up the role playing. These exercises can be done in small groups or dyads, with or without an observer. They also work quite well when members of the class are chosen to play the various roles and do so in front of the entire class. There are enough roles so everyone should have an opportunity to play at least one role. The key role is the one played by the person exerting the influence; however, it is important that each person stay fairly close to his or her role in order for the exercise to work. You are encouraged to really "act," but try to make your presentation as realistic as possible.

When you have finished each scenario, be prepared to discuss the questions that follow.

Discussion

1. What sources of power does the person trying to exert the influence have?
2. What sources of power do others in the role play have?
3. What influence tactic(s) did you identify?
4. How effective was the influencer?
5. What other influence tactics might have been appropriate and what advice do you have for the influencer?

Scenario #1: You Want to Go Where? With Who?

All your friends are going to spend spring break at Padre Island, Texas. They plan to drive there in a caravan and stay at a really great-sounding hotel which has advertised in the campus newspaper offering fantastic rates just for students from your school. Your parents haven't said no, but they haven't said yes either, and you need both their permission and some money before you can go.

Roles
The student needing permission and funding: Choose several influence tactics that might work and use them in the order of your preference. Even though it may not be realistic for you to need money or permission from your parents, treat this role as enthusiastically and realistically as possible.

Parents (one or two): This is a good role for a nontraditional undergraduate or the instructor. Don't make an outright denial of the request from your "child," but listen to each element of the request and bring up as many objections as you can (for example, you're too young, you need to work over spring break, we want you to stay with the family, something bad may happen, a lot of irresponsible people may be going, you need to study, the family budget is tight, etc.). It is critical that you play this role seriously; be as parent-like as you can.

Scenario #2: You're in a Heap of Trouble

You do get permission to make the trip. While you are driving through a neighboring state on the way to spring break in a car with five other undergraduates, you are stopped by a state trooper who informs you that you were timed traveling at 72 mph in a 65 mph zone and that you are about to receive a ticket. All of a sudden the trooper gets much more serious when an empty beer can rolls out from under the back seat. The trooper now informs you that it is highly likely you and all your companions will go to jail for underage drinking (two of you are 19; the other three are 20) and your car will be impounded, requiring your parents to personally come and pay a large fine to retrieve the car.

Roles

Driver: You and your friends have *definitely not been drinking* or intentionally transporting any alcoholic beverages. The beer can does not belong to any of you. You need to try a combination of various influence tactics and assertive behavior. (What are the most likely outcomes if you are either passive or aggressive with the officer?) Try to get in touch with how you would be feeling if this really happened to you.

Passengers: If you think you can help the driver in the attempt to influence the trooper do so, but be careful not to make things any worse than they might be if you just stayed quiet. (Assume that the trooper frequently goes back to the patrol car to make radio checks on your license and registration. When that happens you can give advice to the driver about how best to handle the situation.)

State Trooper: In order for this exercise to work you need to be firm, serious, and believable. Try not to be too aggressive with your role, but adopt an attitude of extreme cynicism and skepticism about everything the students tell you. Make occasional reference to the horrible consequences of drinking and driving you have personally witnessed as a state trooper. If the driver and passengers get aggressive with you, indicate that they are going straight to jail. Try not to get forced into making any final decision.

Scenario # 3: It Must Be in There Somewhere

You finally get to Padre Island. You have never seen so many people—you see T-shirts from just about every college and university in the world. The traffic is so bad it takes over an hour to get from the highway to your hotel, and when you finally arrive, the hotel has no record of your reservation. The desk clerk informs you that the whole town is booked solid and that the closest available accommodations are in a small town over 250 miles away. You and your friends leave the hotel, but decide it can't hurt to give it one more try. You are elected to go in and talk to the desk clerk one more time.

Roles

Person Elected to Talk to the Clerk One More Time: You need to be thinking in terms of both effective influence tactics and appropriately assertive behavior. You are absolutely sure that you made a reservation; however, you do not have any proof or confirmation of that.

Hotel Clerk: You need to play the role of a harassed, somewhat frustrated person. You would like to help these students, but you have no record of their reservation and no extra rooms available. Listen as well as you can, given that numerous persons are clamoring for your attention.

Other Hotel Guests (6–10): You should be huddled around the desk clerk asking for things like a spare key, to have your room stay extended for ten days, perhaps to report on some damage you have discovered in your bathroom—issues like that. Don't become so rowdy that the person with the reservation problem can't be heard at all; just provide a fairly continuous series of interruptions and distractions.

Scenario # 4: Never Eat Anyplace Without a Drive-Through

While on spring break you make friends with a number of students from other colleges and universities. One night you all decide to forego the usual fast food and splurge on a really good seafood dinner. Although it promises to be expensive, you agree to join the group for dinner that evening at a fancy seafood restaurant. You order the fried shrimp platter, and when it finally comes, the first shrimp you try tastes like it was fried in crude oil; so does the second one. The restaurant is quite busy and you haven't seen your server since the entrees arrived 15 minutes ago. Finally your server approaches the table. Your seat is against the wall with several people between you and the aisle.

Roles

Disgruntled Diner: You are determined not to pay a big bill for inedible food. Think about influence tactics that are likely to work and appropriately assertive behavior.

Dining Companions (5–8): Engage in a lot of friendly banter about vacations, school, movies, colleges, majors, music, etc. Sympathize with your friend who got the lousy meal, but point out that your food was great. When the server comes, make a lot of requests for more food and refills.

Server: You are a harassed college student and wish you could take off for spring break like all these kids you have to wait on. You are anxious to do a good job, but if you take food back to the kitchen, it's likely the chef will yell at you about it. Pay attention to the disgruntled diner as best you can, but without just ignoring her or his request, do everything you can to dissuade her or him from complaining or insisting on returning the food.

Scenario #5: What's the Problem? All You Have to Do Is Jump

About 1 a.m., you are headed back from a party with your friends, one of whom you know has had a few beers. Somehow you wind up on the bridge to the island and your friend signs up for a night bungee jump. The characters offering the jump are working out of a really shabby van with no license plates, stopped at the highest point on the bridge. You can see several frayed marks on the bungee cord and really don't want your friend to try this.

Roles

The Persuader: Think about your sources of power, the various influence tactics you intend to use, appropriately assertive behavior, and to what lengths you are prepared to go to prevent a bungee jump.

The Potential Jumper: Taking a bungee jump is something you have always wanted to do. Listen to your friend, but generally dismiss his or her arguments with the point of view that he or she is over-reacting; you just want to have a good time, and, after all, you're the one taking the risk here and you ought to be the one to make the decision.

Scenario #6: I Don't Want a Stinking Bachelor's Degree

The last night of spring break, your best friend joins you on the beach and tells you that she or he doesn't plan to go to school next semester, and, in fact, is seriously considering not finishing the current semester. This spring break trip has convinced your friend that school is for the birds and that even though graduation is only a year away, he or she just wants to stay here on the beach where it is warm all the time. Your friend tells you of plans to get a job in one of the local bars or perhaps on one of the shrimp boats in the harbor. You think this is a terrible mistake and feel a great need to convince your friend to return to school.

Roles

The Influencer: Think about your sources of power, the various influence tactics you intend to use, appropriately assertive behavior, and to what lengths you are prepared to go to influence your friend to return to school.

The Potential Bartender/Deckhand: Listen to your friend's influence efforts, but respond with arguments about how happy you have been since you have been on break, how you always wanted to work on a boat, how sick you are of school and tests, and how you feel your youth may be slipping away from you.

Some Ways to Diagnose and Talk about Our Uses of Power and Influence

Purpose Sometimes a visual representation of an idea can help us identify and talk about feelings that we can't always articulate in words.

You Will Need Two sheets of paper

A pen or pencil

Activity On one sheet of paper, draw a picture or an image of the kind of power you are afraid of, intimidated by, or feel most threatened by.

On the second sheet of paper, create a symbol that represents the kind of power you would most like to project or communicate.

When you have finished, share your drawings with others in a small discussion group and try to answer the discussion questions.

Discussion

1. What type of power threatens you the most? Why? What are some ways in which you have experienced this type of power? What were the outcomes of the influence attempt?

2. What type of power would you most like to project? Why? What are some situations in which you have exerted (or expect to exert) this type of power? What outcomes are likely?

EXERCISE
Analyzing Personal Responses to Power and Influence

Purpose This exercise will help you think about the ways in which you personally respond to the attempts of others to influence your actions and attitudes.

You Will Need *My Responses to Influence Attempts* table, on which you will find a short description of each of the sources of power discussed earlier in this chapter, and three columns headed with the three possible responses to influence attempts: Commitment, Compliance, and Resistance.

Personal Reflections on Influence Attempts table, which also identifies sources of power, but provides space for you to record reasons for your responses and ideas about how you might have responded differently under different circumstances.

Activity Complete the first table in this way:

1. Go down column one and try to recall a time when someone attempted to use each of these types of influence with you. The person attempting to influence you may have been someone at work, one of your university instructors, a coach, or simply an acquaintance.

2. Make a note or two about the circumstances of that influence attempt.

3. Look at the three possible outcomes (how you responded)—Commitment, Compliance, or Resistance—and make a note about your response in the appropriate section.

4. After you have completed the first table, look back and reflect a bit on your responses.

Complete the second table in this way:

1. For each influence attempt you recorded in the first table, explain why you responded as you did (with Commitment, Compliance, or Resistance).

2. In each case, make notes about how you might have responded if circumstances were different.

Discussion

1. Do you see any patterns in the way in which you respond? If someone was completing this worksheet in regard to the way you attempt to influence them, how would they have responded? Would you be pleased or displeased?

2. Be prepared to discuss incidents of your own response to influence attempts from others with the members of your small group. After everyone has had an opportunity to respond, see if there are any similarities in the way people respond to power and influence.

3. What, if anything, can we learn from all of this?

My Responses to Influence Attempts

When Someone Uses This Type of Influence Attempt	I Respond With		
	Commitment	**Compliance**	**Resistance**
Use of Power: *Legitimate/Position Power* (power that stems from a formal management position in an organization and the authority granted to it.)			
Reward Power (power that results from authority to reward others.)			
Coercive Power (power that stems from authority to punish or recommend punishment of others.)			
Expert Power (power that stems from special knowledge or skill in the tasks performed.)			
Referent Power (power that results from characteristics of the leader/manager that result in others' admiration, identification with, and desire to be like the manager/leader.)			

Reflections on My Responses to Influence Attempts

When Someone Used This Type of Influence Attempt	I responded the way I did because:	I would have responded differently if:
Use of Power: *Legitimate/Position Power* (power that stems from a formal management position in an organization and the authority granted to it.)		
Reward Power (power that results from authority to reward others.)		
Coercive Power (power that stems from authority to punish or recommend punishment of others.)		
Expert Power (power that stems from special knowledge or skill in the tasks performed.)		
Referent Power (power that results from characteristics of the leader/manager that result in others' admiration, identification with, and desire to be like the manager/leader.)		

EXERCISE
The Best Leader I Have Ever Known

Purpose To help you identify the characteristics of effective leaders by thinking of someone who has influenced you directly through his or her leadership.

Activity Please think about the best leader you have personally known, interacted with, and been influenced by. This should be someone in your past or present: a boss, a teacher, a coach, a friend, perhaps even a family member, but preferably someone who has had a profound positive effect or influence on your development. On a separate piece of paper, briefly give an overview of the leader, a short description of the context of your relationship, and specific behavioral examples of what this person actually did, that in your view made him or her so effective. List such things as how you became acquainted, the duration of your relationship, any relevant history that would be helpful to your classmates in understanding the leader's orientation toward leadership, and what you feel were the greatest advantages of having known this person.

After the general overview, please go into a bit of detail regarding the context in which you interacted with your ideal leader. The context may vary extensively depending on the particular leader you have chosen. Please describe the roles you and your ideal leader fulfilled, the nature of your interactions (e.g., were they all job or school related or did you interact socially?), the time period in your life when you had the greatest number of interactions, your current relationship with the leader, and so forth. Include in your discussion of the context any significant characteristics that affected your relationship (e.g., demands, challenges, crises, etc.).

After you have described the context, please identify the specific behaviors that would characterize this leader. For example, if you were describing this leader to a colleague, what sort of behaviors would you use to describe the leader?

Discussion

Once you have completed your description of the best leader you have known, your instructor will explain further how to proceed.

FURTHER ACTIVITY

Journal Writing

Reflecting on your readings, the class discussions, and your small group activity, consider the following matters as you write in your journal:

1. What patterns do you see in your response to power and influence attempts?

2. What patterns do you see in the way in which you attempt to influence others?

3. What types of influence are most and least effective in getting you to do things?

4. As you continue your education, what issues do you need to be aware of, in terms of the ways you respond to the influence attempts others make on you and the ways you attempt to use power and influence to shape the behavior and attitudes of others?

5. Over the next week make a special effort to be aware of the influence processes that go on around you. As you observe and experience influence and power attempts, try to classify them according to the categories you discussed in class.

6. Reflect on a significant event in your life when you were influenced by others. Think about the processes that occurred and the outcome. What, if anything, would you do differently now?

LEARNING POINTS

✓ Power and influence are omnipresent in our lives. We are almost constantly being influenced by others, or trying to influence the attitudes and behaviors of others.

✓ Although power has a negative connotation, it is neither good nor bad. The morality of power comes from the ways in which it is obtained, and most of all, *how it is used.*

✓ There are five basic sources of power. Two of these, expert and referent power, are personal in nature; the other three, coercive, reward, and legitimate power, generally come from the position one holds.

✓ Leadership is an influence process that is most closely associated with the personal sources of power. Management is traditionally associated with the organizational sources of power.

✓ Management and leadership can be highly complementary, and organizations usually require persons skilled in both.

✓ Transformational leaders are those persons who have a profound, changing effect on followers and organizations, typically through the use of the Four I's: Individualized Consideration, Intellectual Stimulation, Inspirational Motivation, and Idealized Influence.

✓ Nine commonly used influence tactics are: 1) rational persuasion, 2) inspirational appeals, 3) consultation, 4) ingratiation, 5) personal appeals, 6) exchange, 7) coalition tactics, 8) legitimating tactics, and 9) pressure.

✓ Being aware of your sources of power and matching an appropriate influence tactic to the demands of the situation are the keys to being personally influential.

✓ There are three possible responses to influence attempts: 1) compliance, 2) commitment, and 3) resistance.

✓ Inappropriate or adverse influence attempts generally require an assertive response. An appropriately assertive response is almost always more effective than a passive or aggressive response.

REFERENCES

Bass, B. M., and Avolio, B. J. (1994). Executive summary. In Bass, B. M., and Avolio, B. J. (Eds.). *Improving organizational effectiveness through transformational leadership.* Thousand Oaks, California: Sage.

Bass, B. M. (1990). From transactional to transformational leadership: Learning to share the vision. *Organizational Dynamics, 18* (3), 19–36.

Bass, B. M. (1985). *Leadership and performance beyond expectations.* New York: Free Press.

French, J. P. R., and Raven, B. (1959). The bases of social power. In Cartwright, D. (Ed.). *Studies in social power* (7th ed.). Ann Arbor: University of Michigan, Institute for Social Research.

Gardner, J. W. (1990). *On leadership.* New York: Free Press.

Kouzes, J. M., and Posner, B. Z. (1990). *The leadership challenge.* San Francisco: Jossey-Bass.

Stogdill, R. M. (1974). *Handbook of leadership: A survey of theory and research.* New York: Free Press.

Verderber, R. F., and Verderber, K. S. (1995). *Inter-act: Using interpersonal communications skills* (7th ed.). Belmont, CA: Wadsworth.

Whetten, D. A., and Cameron, K. S. (1991). *Developing management skills.* New York: Harper Collins.

Waldman, D. A., Bass, B. M., and Einstein, W. O. (1986). Effort, performance, and transformational leadership in industrial and military settings (Working paper 84–78). Binghamton State University of New York, School of Management.

Woodward, B., and Armstrong, S. (1970). *The brethren.* New York: Simon & Schuster.

Yukl, G. A. (1994). *Leadership in organizations* (3rd ed.). Englewood Cliffs, NJ: Prentice Hall.

Zalenick, A. (1977). Managers and leaders: Are they different? *Harvard Business Review, 55:3,* 67–78.

Chapter **14**

RESPONDING WITH EMPATHY

> *Empathic listening is so powerful because it gives you accurate data to work with. Instead of projecting your own autobiography and assuming thoughts, feelings, motives and interpretation, you're dealing with the reality inside another person's head and heart. You're listening to understand. You're focused on receiving the deep communication of another soul.*
>
> —Stephen R. Covey, *The Seven Habits of Highly Effective People* (1989)

ADVANCE PLANNER: RESPONDING WITH EMPATHY

When you complete this chapter, you will be able to:

✓ Define empathy, give its characteristics, and cite examples of it.
✓ Differentiate between empathy and sympathy and tell why the difference is important.
✓ Identify the skills and attitudes you need to respond with empathy.
✓ Employ empathic listening skills successfully in your daily life.

    To accomplish these objectives, you will complete some or all of these activities:

1. Analyze a case to help you recognize when skills in responding with empathy are needed.
2. Read and discuss theories about empathy and its applications.
3. Practice responding with empathy, in groups of three.
4. Practice the Friend-to-Friend Process.
5. Write a plan to improve a relationship in your life by practicing empathy.

CASE STUDY IN RESPONDING WITH EMPATHY

The Troubled Roommate

"I hate this place!" Olga shouted, hurling her physiology textbook across the room. It landed at Maria's feet. Maria, who was standing by the closet shaking January snow from her coat, could not have been more startled by her roommate's outburst. "Wh-what's the matter?" she stammered, picking up the book and placing it on Olga's bed.

Maria and Olga had been roommates since the beginning of fall semester. They met as first-year students at a large university when they were assigned to room with each other. Although the residence hall program had supposedly matched them for compatibility, they did not seem to be much alike, except that both were pre-veterinary science majors.

Since she was a child, Maria wanted to be a vet and treat small pets and horses. She was delighted to tell you about her menagerie—a dog, a turtle, a parrot, and a horse she kept at a stable near the edge of town. Olga's interest in veterinary science was not as well defined. Her parents owned a modest swine operation, which her brothers were already taking over. Beyond usual chores, she had not been much involved with the animals as she grew up, but she thought being a vet was one way she could earn a good living in her rural community.

Even after six months of sharing a room and attending some of the same classes, Maria and Olga had not become close. Maria was becoming more and more involved in a growing circle of friends and social activities. On the other hand, Olga seemed only to go through the motions of being a student, and apart from making numerous long-distance telephone calls home, she rarely did anything but go to classes and the cafeteria. She had been especially silent since returning from winter break. Her sudden outburst, therefore, came as a complete surprise to Maria.

"Hey, what's the problem?" Maria tried again, glancing at her watch as she spoke.

Olga's angry face crumpled and tears were close to the surface. "Oh, I'm sorry; I hope the book didn't hit you. I just have to let off steam."

"What about?" was Maria's crisp response.

Everything tumbled out at once for Olga. "You know my grades were awful—mostly C's—last semester; you can't get into vet school with that kind of record. When my grades came before I left home last week, Mom and Dad really blew up; they are going to cut me off if I don't do better this semester. I can't afford college by myself and anyway, nothing is happening here, this place is so unfriendly." The last words came out as a sob.

"Yeah, this place is hard to take lots of the time," Maria said, busily unzipping her boots. "I think I'm going to quit," Olga said in a broken voice.

Maria drew a quick breath. "I know how you feel!" she answered. "Maybe you should call your parents. You know my parents don't always get my check deposited in my account at the first of the month, so I just call them up and tell them I need the cash **now.** They grumble but I get the funds right away, usually."

There was a pause. Olga stared at the top of her desk. "You're probably right," she sniffed.

Maria walked to her desk and flipped on her computer switch. "Our writing class is starting an e-mail network. Some of the comments are just so funny! One guy accidentally sent all of us a hot message he meant for just one girl in the class!"

Olga did not respond.

Discussion Questions

1. How well does Maria understand Olga's problems?

2. How would you rate Maria's skills as an effective listener?

3. To what extent was Olga justified in drawing Maria into her personal problems?

4. What seems to be missing in this exchange between roommates?

5. Put yourself in Maria's place and tell how you would have acted and what you would have said to Olga.

INTRODUCTION TO THEORIES OF EMPATHY AND RESPONDING WITH EMPATHY

What do you do when a friend or acquaintance opens up and begins to share her troubles, as Olga did in the *Case of the Troubled Roommate*? Often the toughest situations we find ourselves in are those that call for responding with empathy. An understanding of empathy as a concept, its importance, and how to apply it in daily life will prepare you to be a better friend, family member, co-worker, leader, and citizen.

Understanding Empathy

Empathy is the capacity to enter into the thoughts and feelings of others. It is the ability to set aside one's own life experiences, or "autobiography" (Covey's word, 1989), and profoundly understand another person's feelings, thoughts, and point of view. In explaining empathy, we often use such expressions as "seeing through someone else's eyes," "walking in another's shoes," or "getting inside another's head or skin." Ordinarily, it is difficult to think of getting outside oneself. We always filter experience through our own consciousness. Empathy, however, is a concentrated effort to get beyond who we are and experience someone else's thoughts, feelings, and emotions as if they were our own (Rogers as cited in Stotland et al., 1978; Smith, 1989; Goleman, 1995).

Characteristics of Empathy

Responding with empathy involves two seemingly opposite concepts: thinking and feeling. There appears to be a contradiction between the purely emotional or feeling (affective) and rational or thinking (cognitive) qualities that enter into the meaning of empathy (Smith, 1989; Sharma, 1993). These two concepts give rise to another pair of contrasting concepts also found within the meaning of empathy: we practice listening skills we have learned cognitively, while simultaneously displaying a caring or feeling attitude toward the other person. As Covey (1989) points out, you cannot practice empathic listening skills alone: "You have to build the skills of empathic listening on a base of character that inspires openness and trust" (p. 239). These conflicts in meaning and difficulties in practice can be resolved, however, as illustrated in the remainder of this chapter; we can use both feeling and thinking, both learned skills and a caring attitude, in responding with empathy in our relationships.

Empathy: History and Contexts

Empathy as a concept did not come from disciplines and studies in human behavior. Rather it was a term first applied in aesthetics in the late nineteenth century. The German word *Einfühlung,* as used in the early twentieth century, meant the ability to enter into the total meaning of a painting. It also meant to appreciate fully a piece of literature or a musical composition (Smith, 1989; Sharma, 1993). The term *empathy,* which first appeared in an English dictionary in 1904, comes from a Greek word (*empatheia*) that literally means *in feeling.* The Greek roots of the word *empathy* include *passion, suffering,* and *what one has experienced or felt* (Woodruff, 1995, personal communication).

Empathy, Not Sympathy

We differentiate empathy from the more familiar term, *sympathy*. The etymology of *sympathy* suggests the primary contrast with empathy. *Sym* means *with,* as opposed to *em,* which means *in.* That is, *sympathy* suggests we feel with someone, whereas *empathy* suggests we enter in someone else's feelings. Sympathy comes from one's own perspective; it takes the form of pity or condolence (Sharma, 1993). For example, when Pat's grandfather died unexpectedly, Sam's family sent flowers. Although this gift expressed the feeling of shared sorrow, the gesture, as thoughtful as it was, did not express an empathic understanding of Pat's grief. Why? The answer lies in the unique loss each of us feels on the death of someone who has been important and significant in our lives; others can express their own concern for our sorrow (sympathy), but can rarely share fully in that sorrow (empathy).

Sympathy may also be viewed as simply agreeing with someone (Covey, 1989). While agreement is soothing, it may not encompass true understanding. In many cases, sympathy is all that is required and is a sufficient response. Responding with empathy, however, goes beyond mere agreement and is needed to build trust. It leads to more open communication, confidence in one's own ability to solve problems, and feelings of self-worth.

Empathy Empowers

In the early twentieth century, the potential for using the idea of empathy in studying human behavior was recognized. Empathy is not associated with any one field of study, and both the concept and means to measure its practice are still being developed. In the last forty years, however, scholars in various disciplines have been able to demonstrate through empirical studies both meaning and application of empathy in human interaction and communication.

It is fairly easy to see how empathy can be employed in the helping professions—counseling, psychiatry, teaching, ministry, child development, and the like. But empathy as the path to understanding others is important in many other fields, as well. For example, studies of empathy are found in philosophy, anthropology, medicine, journalism, the law, marketing and sales, supervision, and multicultural education. As a prime ingredient in healthy behavior and as an antidote to violence (Richardson et al., 1994), empathy plays an important role in positive social interactions.

When empathy is withheld, low self-esteem and poor social skills can result. Studies have demonstrated, for example, that those who rape and commit other violent crimes lack the capacity for empathy (Rice et al., 1994). Practicing empathy is important with family, friends, partners, classmates, teachers, co-workers, customers, and others we encounter in our daily lives, making us less likely to stereotype those who differ from us (Stotland et al., 1978).

Empathy is especially important in motivating altruistic behavior (Kohn, 1990; Goleman, 1995). That is, if we feel how someone else feels, we are more likely to want to help that person. Therefore, understanding and responding with empathy are useful for anyone engaged in a service or volunteer project. We empower others when we seek to understand them, and we empower ourselves when we see others without the blinders of our own motives and self-interest.

Empathy and Joy

So far, we have talked about empathy in cases when there is sadness or difficulty. Empathy, however, can serve us equally well to help celebrate someone's successes and joy. We are taught from childhood that we should be modest about our accomplishments. Therefore, it is difficult to accept a compliment, or to share with others our successes without feeling—or being labeled—boastful. To illustrate, read the following and think about how each of Dad's possible responses might affect Charlie:

Charlie says, "Guess what, Dad? Our science club advisor chose my essay on ground water pollution to enter into the state contest! She says it is the best one she has ever read by any student!"

Dad might respond in one of several ways:

a. Quick nod

b. Silence

c. "I thought you were going to rake the yard for me today!"

d. "Don't boast."

e. "Ground water pollution!? Did your teacher put you up to that? Next thing I know you'll be a tree-hugger."

f. "You must feel really pleased, Charlie. I know how hard you worked on that project!"

Of course, Dad's response "f" would have the most positive effect on Charlie. In this case, he clearly feels Charlie's pride and sense of accomplishment and responds with true understanding and empathy. Children and adults need praise and affirmation as feedback. Rationally, we know that without positive understanding and support, one does not learn or grow in positive directions. In fact, if a child has not experienced empathy, he or she may become socially isolated, falling prey to socially deviant behaviors.

Sometimes we cannot bring ourselves to feel the joy of others. Some people apparently are pleased when others suffer and are glum when others experience joy (Stotland et al., 1978). Those are extremes of behavior, of course, but to be honest, sometimes it is difficult to respond to another person's joy. We may feel the blow when someone else gets the promotion we had hoped for, or the honor we thought we were equally qualified to receive. It takes an extraordinarily sunny personality never to feel the pangs of jealousy. We can practice swallowing our own disappointment, however, and congratulate the winner, with at least an attempt at genuine empathy.

Empathy in Daily Life

In addition to responding with empathy when friends share difficulties or experience joy, we can practice empathy in many encounters in our daily life. Friends, family, and strangers, as well, will benefit if we take a moment to see a situation from another's perspective. For example, a supermarket clerk may make a mistake on your order on a busy Friday. If you take a moment to imagine yourself behind the counter and read the exhaustion and frustration in the clerk's face, your own feelings of frustration may be lessened, your response more open to solving the problem. If you are the clerk behind the counter, if you understand why a customer may be impatient, you are more likely to respond with positive behavior.

Every day we experience dozens of similar episodes in which understanding how others feel leads to positive results. Empathic response averts unnecessary conflict, improves personal relationships, prevents stereotyping, and even de-escalates the potential for violence (Richardson et al., 1994).

Applying Empathic Response Skills

Who Can Learn to Practice Empathy?

Studies reveal that empathy is most frequently associated with feeling, which is perceived as a predominantly female trait, as opposed to logic and rationality, which are perceived as male traits (Sharma, 1993). While studies have demonstrated that females frequently test higher than males on components of empathy (Zahn-Waxler et al., 1992), individuals of either sex can develop the capacity for empathy and responding with empathy. A study of high school and college students demonstrated that empathy and the ability to respond with empathy increases for both males and females after participating in training in interpersonal skills (Hatcher et al., 1994). You might not have been born with the empathic ability of Deanna Troi, Star Trek's counselor, but you still can improve your capacity to respond with empathy.

You also may feel reluctant and uncomfortable about getting to know others "up close and personal." You are not alone. Responding with empathy takes investment of who you are; it is risk-taking behavior, because as you enter into someone else's life, you must let yourself become more open and vulnerable. Many people resist being empathic because they know once they start to understand others, their compassion will force them to take action that could be costly in time or resources (Shaw et al., 1994). A human form lying on the sidewalk in a big city may ask too much of the passerby. We excuse ourselves for not helping if we can avoid thinking that what we see is a person suffering pain. "Just a drunk," we conclude. We are more likely to act, however, if our compassions are aroused. The risk of feeling and responding with empathy is balanced by the benefits we gain in better understanding others and the differences among individuals (Stotland et al., 1978).

Feeling and Thinking in Practice

To respond with empathy, you need to feel what another feels. To do so, you must rely on your own experience, perceptions, knowledge, and observations of verbal and nonverbal behavior. For example, if your roommate fails a test, you observe his pale face and wrinkled frown and hear discouragement in his voice. You can sense, almost intuitively, what a setback this low grade is for him. His facial expression, tone of voice, and verbal messages are strong enough to stir you to feel empathy.

Feeling alone, however, may not be sufficient in responding to your roommate's state of mind. You also bring some thought or reason to the process—the thinking or cognitive part of empathy. Your knowledge of the details of your roommate's life might help enrich your sense of empathy. Perhaps, for example, you know that this test meant the difference between getting into graduate school or having to choose a different major.

Another kind of cognitive activity relates to the conscious choices you make in your response. While you feel your roommate's disappointment, it would not be helpful to enter totally into his despair. To blurt out, "That's horrible! You won't get into grad school!" will probably only increase his pain. Your responses instead should help him express his frustration, disappointment, or anger, and identify some way of handling the situation. Skills required for responding with empathy (see the next section) can be learned. They are an extension of active listening skills, but they take you more specifically into the mind and heart of the other person. The Friend-to-Friend Process (Stone & Keefauver, 1987), described in one of the exercises at the end of this chapter, demonstrates both the feeling and the thinking side of the empathic response.

Empathic Response Skills

Although skills or techniques alone may be inadequate to help you develop a fully empathic response, reviewing and adding to your effective listening skills is a comfortable and useful place to start. Some especially important active listening skills are:

1. *Positive nonverbal behavior.* As you know, such behavior includes expression, body language, proxemics, voice tone, and the like. To respond to another person with empathy, you will need to use eye contact, sit at a comfortable distance (preferably across from each other), nod and use facial expressions to convey hearing, understanding, and acceptance. It will take some concentration to appear relaxed and focused on what the other person is saying.

2. *Paraphrasing.* When we engage in active listening, we put someone else's words into our own words to reflect understanding. In responding with empathy, paraphrasing for feeling may be more important than paraphrasing for content. In this case you put into words what you think someone else feels. Take the following exchange, for example:

Joe says, "My truck had a flat tire, I was late to work, the supervisor wouldn't let me clock in, and now I'm out a day's pay. I am teeeeeed off!"

Jim replies (paraphrasing for content), "You're saying because you were late, you weren't allowed to work." Or he replies (paraphrasing for feeling), "You sound boiling mad!"

If Jim merely paraphrases the content of Joe's message, Joe may become irritated with what he perceives as a superficial summary. Jim's paraphrase of the feeling he hears beneath Joe's words is better because Joe hears validation of his feelings and perceives Jim as a supportive friend. Paraphrases of content are important when clarification of information is actually needed; they should not be used to merely repeat information. Paraphrasing feelings is an empathic response skill because it shows an understanding and acceptance (not necessarily approval) of feelings.

3. *Perception checking.* Perception checking is similar to paraphrasing for feelings, but the purpose is different. This time you want to be sure that you have correctly identified the feeling. Otherwise a misconception becomes miscommunication, which in turn leads to misunderstanding. In the previous example, if Joe's words suggest anger, but he says them in a light, ironic tone, Jim's perception check might be, "Are you really angry—or are you just going to blow it off?" Joe's answer might explain the ironic tone, if he said, "Well, I guess I had it coming—it was the third time I was late this week."

4. *Questioning.* Questioning not only clarifies your own understanding, but also provides direction and structure to the conversation. For example, if Jim isn't sure whether Joe wants his help in making a better impression on the supervisor, avoiding chronic tardiness, or buying a new set of tires, he might eventually ask Joe the question: "What are you going to do about it?" This question, asked after there has been some acceptance and understanding of feelings, will help Joe reflect on where he wants to go next. On the whole, when responding with empathy you should use questioning sparingly. Your empathic response should not turn into an interview or interrogation. If Jim keeps probing Joe about the condition of his truck, his dislike of his supervisor, and his tendency to be tardy, or if he exacts an account of what everyone said, Joe may become even more impatient. Jim can never know all the facts, and empathy does not require him to diagnose Joe's problem; focusing on facts alone may remove Jim too far from Joe's feelings.

Caring

You can always practice response skills with classmates, friends, or even alone in front of the bathroom mirror. But how do you practice caring?

As an editorial writer in *America* observed, "global empathy" is "noble" but not realistic ("How close," 1995). Global empathy appears to be an abstraction, but the empathic response can be expanded. Caring, which develops from infancy, usually happens gradually, over time, with acquaintances, friends, family, and significant others, and especially with those whose welfare concerns us (Batson et al., 1995).

At the core of forming a caring attitude toward someone is awareness that each individual you meet is very much a human being who feels both pleasure and pain, as you have felt both pleasure and pain (Smith, 1989). Following are some levels of relationships that can serve as benchmarks as you expand your ability to develop a caring attitude.

1. *Family and friends.* Caring comes more easily with someone who shares your lifestyle and values. You may have many arguments with your brother, but you have grown up with him and you share your love of Thanksgiving dinner, the outdoors, sports, and Western humor. You were proud when your brother won in cross-country racing, and suffered with him when he received a failing grade on his first college composition. Even if your relationship with someone close to you has not been smooth, the many experiences and values you share will reinforce your caring response.

2. *Support groups.* The kind of caring in which you identify with someone else is found at the heart of various support and helping groups. Individuals who suffer losses in a national disaster (like the Oklahoma City bombing), suffer an illness (like cancer), or share causes (like the civil rights movement) have a starting point for empathy. Disclosure and sharing of feelings arising out of overwhelming life experiences can help individuals form strong bonds.

3. *Cross-cultural caring.* How do you care for someone who is a stranger? How do you practice empathy with someone from a different cultural background, someone who appears as an outsider in your community? Practicing cross-cultural empathy is complicated, but even if it is difficult, all of us need to educate ourselves and learn about others. You might start with small first steps. Finding out something about another person is one way to start. Listening for dreams, hopes, joys, and sorrows of others makes bridges to your own mind and heart. Chapter 15, Cross-Cultural Communication, helps you build an awareness of how to understand those from another culture.

What to Avoid

Before we turn concepts into the steps of responding with empathy, we need to consider some cautions and what to avoid.

1. *Handling serious problems.* If a friend comes to you with serious problems—depression, thoughts of suicide, drugs, alcohol, abusive behavior, irrational behavior—you should not try to tackle them yourself. Such difficulties are not for amateurs to handle. Because these problems are often first evident to family and friends, however, you should know what to do. Both in your college life and in your professional career, you need to know what your resources are. Many large organizations and agencies have access to employee assistance programs where qualified counselors can be found. A college or university health center is another place to find help. Residence hall counselors, local helping organizations and shelters, religious organizations, and local mental health clinics are other places.

You may have to be proactive in calling agencies and persuading your friend to seek help. If your friend starts to share problems beyond your scope, you need to be ready with a response. Such a response might be, "I care very much what happens to you. As much as I wish I could, I can't help you handle these problems. Let's find a way to get you some help." Follow through as completely as possible. You cannot, however, "save" someone else. Guiding that person to professional assistance may be the best and only way to help.

2. *Offering unwanted help.* Even if a friend's problem is of the ordinary everyday variety, you need to wait for him or her to ask you to listen. You should not wade into someone else's difficulties unasked. A clear-cut invitation to listen occurs when your friend says, "I have a problem. Do you think you could listen and help me reach a decision?" Other situations are less clear-cut. If your friend starts to share a problem or difficulty, however, you may use a perception check to find out whether he or she really wants your help to work on a solution.

3. *Using self-referencing.* You empathize with feelings of others because you are a human being and have suffered yourself. However, if a friend starts to tell you her problems, and you switch the focus of the conversation to what happened to you last week, you are no longer responding with empathy. This is not the time to practice turn-taking. When responding with empathy, keep the focus on the other's needs, not your own.

4. *Being judgmental.* Don't evaluate your friend's experience or decisions for her, either the ones she has made or those she intends to make. She does not need to hear you say, for instance, "Going on a date with that loser was a really stupid thing to do."

5. *Harmonizing.* Don't attempt to diffuse the emotions expressed or diminish the problem. Be ready to support your friend in negative feelings, without necessarily agreeing. For instance, Seth labels his mother "a domineering, shallow skinflint" because she won't pay for Seth's travels to Europe next summer. As Seth's listener, you may be tempted to say, "Your mom's not that bad, Seth, I know you love her." While Seth's perception is distorted by disappointment, now is not the time to point that out. Rather, responding with empathy would lead you to say something like this: "Seth, you *are* disappointed! I know how much you wanted to make that trip."

6. *Disagreeing, arguing, defending, contradicting.* Empathy will cease if you engage in any of these behaviors, since they come out of your experience and don't further your attempt to understand your friend's perspective and feelings.

7. *Advice-giving.* Perhaps the hardest behavior to avoid is advice-giving. Friends come to us for advice, and we give it. As a kind of pseudo-empathic response, we may even say, "If I were you. . . ." Giving advice is a poor response for a number of reasons. You may try to offer it before the situation is clear. It may not be appropriate, since each situation is unique. It may be bad advice. Your friend may not take your advice and it could then create a barrier of guilt and resentment. Your friend may take it, but with poor results, and you will either be blamed, feel guilty, or both. It may be successful and you may take credit for it to the eternal annoyance of your friend. And so forth.

It's hard not to respond immediately when your friend's life is in shambles and he or she demands, "Tell me what to do!" A preferred alternative to quick advice, however, is to ask the friend to list some solutions; you may add to the list, point out alternatives, or help examine the pluses and minuses. Even this participation needs to be limited. Often those asking for help really do have the solution within themselves and it only takes an empathic listener to help discover it.

Steps in Responding with Empathy

We can employ empathy in our daily lives in either episodic or small instances, by allowing others to express joy, and by listening to their difficulties. If you develop some of the active listening skills described earlier and follow previous suggestions about developing a caring attitude and dangers to avoid, you're ready to apply the concepts of empathic response and put your skills into action. (Some of these steps are synthesized from ideas presented by Verderber & Verderber, 1992; Dodge, 1986.)

Imagine that a friend has come to you with a problem. The following steps give you a basic plan of action for responding with empathy:

1. Find a quiet place where you can talk uninterrupted. You may agree on how long you can spend in conversation.

2. Remind yourself that you *care* about this person. You do not wish to see her or him suffer pain. You can sense that pain, unhappiness, anger, confusion, or whatever emotion it is as the person talks.

3. Concentrate on what the person says, listening to words and tone of voice; observe the person's nonverbal behavior.

4. Use the response skills identified above, as appropriate and sparingly. Let the individual have most of the "air time." Keep your nonverbal behavior open and inviting.

5. Help the person evaluate the situation. Are there alternative explanations for an event? Do perceptions seem too narrow? Check for possible distortions of the situation.

6. End with a decision, not necessarily a solution. Having an empathic listener may be sufficient in itself. The friend who brought the problem, not the listener, makes the decision, which may be as simple as an agreement to meet again.

As you go through the steps, your concentration, intentional caring, and effort to imagine how things look through the other's eyes will help you empathize and respond with empathy. As you open yourself to caring for others, you, too, will develop your skill and capacity to be empathic.

EXERCISE
Trios

Purpose   To practice listening and responding with empathy. In this exercise you have the opportunity to apply concepts of empathic listening by playing one of three roles:

   a. *Friend.* The friend goes to the listener to ask for assistance in solving a problem. (The problem may be one of your own, or it may be a role play; see problem description in the Activity Section.)

   b. *Listener.* The listener practices listening and responding with empathy, using both skills and concepts. (See observation sheet.)

   c. *Observer.* Keeps time; records observations on the observation sheet; facilitates discussion.

You Will Need

Pen or pencil

Observation Sheet

Activity

1. In groups of three, as assigned or selected, determine which of three roles—friend, listener, observer—each will play.

2. Prepare for your role: friend chooses a problem; listener and observer review empathic response skills (5 min.). The student playing the friend role has two choices of problems:

   An Issue of Your Own. Select some issue from your life you would like to talk to someone about. Choose a real but not overwhelming problem, something that is current in your life and can be described in a short space of time. To start the conversation, describe the issue to your listener.

   Friend Role Play. You have started to date someone you recently met. One thing you have in common is that both of you recently broke off longtime relationships. While you have had many conversations about your "ex"es, you thought the two of you were on track for romance. However, last evening, sitting in a booth in a popular restaurant, your new friend tells you that he or she is thinking of seeing his or her former love. The next day, you decide to talk over this situation with another acquaintance (the listener). Start by describing the situation and your feelings to the listener.

3. Friend describes situation to listener, who responds by using empathic listening skills. Observer, who remains silent, records listener's empathic listening behavior on the observation sheet (10 min.).

4. Observer facilitates discussion, tallies data on observation sheet, and gives feedback, also practicing listening skills (10 min.).

Discussion

1. How did the listener feel in attempting to practice empathic listening skills? What was easiest to do? Hardest? Did you find yourself using any of the less useful behaviors (i.e., self-referencing, being judgmental, harmonizing, advice giving, etc.)?

2. How did the friend feel during the conversation? What was most helpful? Least helpful?

3. What listening skills are used most often?

4. Which empathic listening skills are most difficult to use?

5. How was caring expressed?

Observation Sheet: Responding with Empathy

Instructions to the observer: Observe the conversation between friend and listener, and put a check mark by the concept, behavior, or skill every time you observe or hear the *Listener* performing this skill. Jot a note about one or two specific words or examples you can share with the other two at the end of the conversation.

Skill, Concept	Check Marks	Comments
Nonverbal Behavior		
Paraphrasing: Content		
Paraphrasing: Feeling		
Perception Checking		
Questioning: Clarifying		
Questioning: Directional		
Caring		

The Friend-to-Friend Process

Adapted by C. Blake from Stone and Keefauver, 1987.

Purpose The Friend-to-Friend Process is a model for helping a friend address a problem. The empathic response skills, as described in this chapter, apply here.

Description

In this model, the listener should not ask for a large amount of background or recounting of events. The key is to focus on what the friend wants. Another feature of Friend-to-Friend is that questions are repeated, but different answers to the same question are required each time the question is asked. The questions and repetitions are necessary because, according to the creators of this process, it takes time and hard work for the friend to delve deep enough to get at the real problem.

You Will Need

The list of questions in the five-step Friend-to-Friend Process.

The Friend-to-Friend Process

Step one: Explain the Friend-to-Friend Process.
Step two: Ask the first three questions in order:

1. What do you want for you? (thoughts)
2. What are you feeling? (feelings)
3. What are you doing about it (to get what you want)? (actions)

(Repeat the three questions in order, as necessary, usually three times.)

Step three: Ask the big question: What do you need to do?
Step four: Ask follow-up questions:

1. Will you do it?
2. When will you do it?
3. How will you do it?
4. Will you let me know how it goes?

Step five: Close the conversation with encouragement.

Activity

Form pairs as your instructor directs.

1. Decide who is the listening friend (the Listener) and who is the friend bringing the subject for discussion (the Friend).

2. The Listener describes the Friend-to-Friend Process to the other, and they agree to proceed.

3. The Friend briefly describes the situation or problem. (Since this is practice, choose a real, but not overwhelming problem. You also may use the role-play situation described in the Trios Exercise.)

4. The Listener asks the first three questions in order, using empathic responses while listening to the Friend. Repeat the questions in order three times, or until the Friend's feelings are clear.

5. In step three the Friend identifies a specific action to take to solve the problem. The Listener should encourage the Friend to list alternatives and select the best one. The Listener should not intervene, unless an alternative may be harmful.

6. When the Friend is ready, ask the questions in step four to help determine what will be done and to come to a conclusion (step five).

7. When you finish the Friend-to-Friend Process, step out of your roles and talk about the process. Use the questions below as a guide to your discussion. Be prepared to report your answers in a large group discussion.

Additional Hints for the Friend-to-Friend Listener

1. Proceed at the Friend's pace, not your own. If the Friend is not ready to do something about the situation, do not force the issue. You may stop the process at any time.

2. Stick to the questions in the process, especially at the beginning. Explain that a lot of background and detail are not needed. The three questions in step two and their repetition are intended to get at feelings and the real problem.

3. As you work through the steps, confront the "cons" (as in a con game)— the Friend's excuses for not taking action, or attempts to con both of you by reporting superficial actions. (For example, "What are you doing about it?" may be answered by the con: "I am thinking about it a lot.")

4. Do not ask the big question in step three—What do you need to do?— until you are both sure the real problem has been identified.

5. End with encouragement. Perhaps a pat on the elbow or a hug may be appropriate. Although you have expressed willingness to listen again, the Friend has no obligation to report back and the Listener should refrain from checking up.

Discussion

1. Was the process comfortable?

2. Did it work for you?

3. What empathic listening skills were used?

4. What was most useful? Least useful?

EXERCISE
Setting an Empathy Goal (Small Group)

Purpose   This exercise, which takes place in a small group setting, is designed to help you improve an important relationship in your life by using your empathic response skills.

Activity   You will first work alone, then in pairs; finally you will share your feelings and observations with the others in your group.

1. Begin by selecting a person you already know. He or she may be a teacher, a co-worker, a parent or grandparent, a sibling, a partner, or someone else within your circle of acquaintances whom you see frequently. Your goal is to improve your relationship with this person.

2. Answer the questions on the planning guide below, writing in the space provided, to plan how you will achieve your empathy goal.

3. After you have finished your answers, share them with one other person in your small group. Make a contract with this person to report what happened to your empathy goal.

4. In the entire small group, complete the exercise by sharing something you learned about yourself and empathy. You may tell how you plan to improve your communication through empathy and what skills you will try.

Empathy Goal Planning Guide

1. Who is the person in this relationship you wish to improve (use first or fictional name) and what is this person's connection to you (family, co-worker, etc.)?

2. What is the current state of your relationship (friends, close, family but not close, etc.)?

3. What do you need to do to improve this relationship? Identify at least two empathic response skills you will use.

FURTHER ACTIVITIES

Independent Practice

1. Follow through on the Empathy Goal Setting exercise with the person you identified. Reflect on the results and be prepared to share what happened with others in your small group.

2. Practice empathy by imagining yourself in another's shoes. For example: your mother, father, spouse, or child as he or she experiences a particular difficulty; the cashier in a fast-food restaurant you enter; a classmate giving a speech in a communications class; an elderly person you visit in a nursing home; a person you hear interviewed in a television broadcast from one of the globe's war zones. Can you care for someone remote from yourself?

3. Practice your empathic listening skills with a friend. Together evaluate the process. Use the Friend-to-Friend Process if you feel comfortable with it.

4. Sharpen your understanding of effective or empathic listening skills. Using the observation sheet from the Trios Exercise, watch a television drama (taping the show would be useful, or rent a video movie), select a scene, and record examples of individuals using empathic listening skills. You might also try this with a talk-show program. What are the results? Do you find empathic responses in both fictional and nonfictional programs?

Journal Writing

1. Write about your reflections and the results of any or all of the above activities in your journal. Evaluate these experiences, telling what you learned and what you need to improve.

2. Evaluate yourself as an empathic listener. Start with who you are—your personality and preferences. Write about the response skills you were able to practice. Discuss your ability to be caring. Speculate on how you will develop further as an empathic listener.

3. Write a personality sketch or profile of the "most empathic person I know." What behavior does this person exhibit to earn this title from you?

LEARNING POINTS

✓ Empathy is the capacity to enter into the thoughts and feelings of others. It includes both feeling (affective) and thinking (cognitive) sides of mental activity.

✓ To respond with empathy requires an understanding of the concept of empathy, competency in empathic response skills, and, most important, a caring attitude.

✓ The concept of empathy came from a German term signifying an in-depth appreciation of art. The word comes from the Greek word *empatheia* meaning "in feeling."

✓ Sympathy is an expression of feelings from our own viewpoint and does not represent an understanding of the feelings of others.

✓ Empathy is studied in a broad range of disciplines; it is associated with altruism, but is often missing in those who exhibit violent behavior toward others.

✓ Empathy can be learned, practiced, and improved by anyone—male or female—on various levels, from close family and friends to strangers. Responding with empathy is appropriate in helping others with difficulty or problems, in affirming accomplishments, and in interactions with others in daily life.

✓ Sometimes people avoid practicing empathy because of the personal emotional investment involved.

✓ Active listening skills important in making an empathic response include paraphrasing (especially for feeling), perception checking, and questioning, as well as positive nonverbal behavior.

✓ You are not responding with empathy when you engage in self-reference, judging, harmonizing, advice-giving, and other responses from your own point of view. Avoid trying to handle problems requiring professional assistance or attempting to help when it is not requested.

✓ Steps in practicing empathy include: positive nonverbal behavior, a caring attitude, concentration, response skills, consideration of alternatives, and closure.

REFERENCES

Batson, C. D., Turk, C. L., Shaw, L. L., and Klein, T. (1995). Information function of the empathic emotion: Learning that we value the other's welfare. *Journal of Personality and Social Psychology, 68*(2), 300–313.

Covey, S. R. (1989). *The seven habits of highly effective people.* New York: Simon & Schuster.

Dodge, G. W. (1986). *Priceless people* (2nd ed.). Lincoln, NE: Nebraska Human Resources Research Foundation.

Goleman, D. (1995). *Emotional intelligence.* New York: Bantam Books.

Hatcher, S. L., Nadeau, M. S., Walsh, L. K., Reynolds, M., Galen, J., and Mart, K. (1994). The teaching of empathy for high school and college students: Testing Rogerian methods with the interpersonal reactivity index. *Adolescence, 29*(116), 961–975.

How close are we, anyway? (Empathy and foreign aid) [Editorial]. (1995). *America, 172*(2), 31.

Kohn, A. (1990). *The brighter side of human nature: Altruism and empathy in everyday life.* New York: Basic Books.

Rice, M., Chaplin, T. C., Harris, G. T., and Courts, J. (1994). Empathy for the victim and sexual arousal among rapists and nonrapists. *Journal of Interpersonal Violence, 9*(4), 435–450.

Richardson, D., Hammock, G. S., Smith, S. M., Gardner, W., and Signo, M. (1994). Empathy as a cognitive inhibitor of interpersonal aggression. *Aggressive Behavior, 20*(4), 275–290.

Sharma, R. M. (1993). *Understanding the concept of empathy and its foundations in psychoanalysis.* Lewiston, NY: The Edwin Mellen Press.

Shaw, L. L., Batson, C. D., and Todd, R. M. (1994). Empathy avoidance forestalling feeling for another in order to escape the motivational consequences. *Journal of Personality and Social Psychology, 67*(5), 879–888.

Smith, D. W. (1989). The circle acquaintance: Perception, consciousness, and empathy. In *Studies in epistemology, logic, methodology, and philosophy of science,* Vol. 205. Dordrecht, Boston, London: Kluwer Academic Publishers.

Stone, J. D., and Keefauver, L. (1987). How to help your friend: The friend-to-friend process. *Insights,* 2–15.

Stotland, E., Mathewes, K. E., Sherman, S. E., Hannson, R. O., and Richardson, B. Z. (1978). *Empathy, fantasy and helping.* Sage Library of Social Research. Beverly Hills, CA: Sage Publications.

Verderber, R. F., and Verderber, K. S. (1992). *Inter-act: Using interpersonal skills* (6th ed.). Belmont, CA: Wadsworth Publishing.

Zahn-Waxler, C., Robinson, J. L., and Emde, R. N. (1992). The development of empathy in twins. *Developmental Psychology, 28* (6), 1038–1048.

CROSS-CULTURAL COMMUNICATION

If we are to achieve a richer culture, rich in contrasting values, we must recognize the whole gamut of human potentialities, . . . in which each diverse human gift will find a fitting place.
—Margaret Mead

ADVANCE PLANNER: CROSS-CULTURAL COMMUNICATION

When you complete this chapter, you will be able to:

✓ Identify demographic realities and projections.

✓ Define culture and characteristics of culture.

✓ Describe the basic functions of culture.

✓ Define ethnocentrism.

✓ Classify cultural patterns.

✓ Describe the relationship between culture and communication.

✓ Apply the cross-cultural learning model.

To accomplish these objectives, you will complete some or all of these activities:

1. Discuss a case study related to cross-cultural communication.

2. Read and discuss some theories about cross-cultural communication and understanding.

3. Analyze a personal experience where you felt different from those around you.

4. Participate in small group activities that will increase your understanding about culture and cultural empathy.

5. Become acquainted with a class visitor whose cultural background may be different from yours and test the degree of empathy you establish with him or her.

A CASE STUDY IN CROSS-CULTURAL COMMUNICATION

Off to a Bad Start

Mark Sullivan, recently hired in a multi-county social agency in South Florida, decided to contact the leaders of a large ethnic community in one of the counties where he was to expand an established youth program. Having set up three appointments in two days, he arrived for the first two scheduled meetings at the appointed times but was kept waiting for more than half an hour in each instance. Mark then assumed that people in this ethnic community in South Florida, like the Mexican and other Latino groups he had worked with, were very "mañana" oriented and had a very relaxed concept of time and punctuality. The next day, not as concerned about being on time as he had been the previous day, Mark assumed his early afternoon appointment would not start on time, so he decided to stop at his office on his way. Mark took his time, arriving almost forty-five minutes late for his meeting. Dr. Gonzalez, an older and well-known local personality in the community, greeted him politely but coldly. Mark immediately sensed that Dr. Gonzalez was quite displeased with his tardiness. "I suppose," said Dr. Gonzalez, "that you assumed I was taking my after-lunch siesta and I would arrive late to our meeting as is customary with all Latinos." Mark was quite lost for words, and although he did apologize, he felt the meeting with this important contact person had not started on the right foot.

Discussion Questions

1. What happened? Answer this question from the perspective of both Mark and Dr. Gonzalez.

2. What is the problem? Would Mark and Dr. Gonzalez see the problem differently? How does the problem involve values, practices, stereotypes, and expectations?

3. Which cultural factors (age, social status, purpose of visit, etc.) played a role in this situation? Explain each.

4. How can the situation be resolved? Consider as many courses of action as possible.

5. What are the probable results or repercussions of each solution?

INTRODUCTION TO THEORIES AND APPLICATIONS OF CROSS-CULTURAL COMMUNICATION

A multi-cultural organization is one whose members with nontraditional backgrounds are respected and supported so that they can contribute to their fullest potential.—Milkovich and Boudreau, 1994.

Demographic Realities

The need to understand the role of culture in interpersonal communication is growing not only domestically but internationally. The old boundaries of national economics and markets have given way to a borderless system, with the globalization of economic activity perhaps being the most significant defining trend. The political relationship of the United States with other nations is matched by the global interdependence that characterizes U.S. economic connections. Diplomatic and economic links are reinforced by the radical transformation in the mass media and the exchange of technology. Individual and collective abilities to communicate competently with people from other cultures are fundamental to the political and economic effectiveness of the United States in the global arena. Robert Shuter (1990) has declared that "culture is the single most important global communication issue in the 1990s."

The United States is a pluralistic nation that was built upon the acceptance and alliance of individuals from different ethnic and cultural origins. Given this unique characteristic of our country, a multitude of distinctly different cultural populations are located in all parts of the United States, each with its own unique lifestyle and sets of values and beliefs.

The composition of this nation's workforce is also changing. By the end of the year 2000, the profile of new hires will dramatically change, with only 15 percent being Anglo-American males (Kennedy and Everest, 1991). The remaining 85 percent will be females, African Americans, Hispanics or Latinos, Asians, and Native Americans. Kennedy and Everest (1991) contend that industries can remain competitive only if employers recognize diversity and accept cultural differences while using strategies to maximize employees' talents and abilities.

Ethical Considerations

As individuals of different cultures interact at an increasingly frequent rate, it is imperative to account for and respect differences. Confucius noted that "Human beings draw close to one another by their common nature, but habits and customs keep them apart." Rather than focusing on differences between cultures, we should appreciate the similarities that all cultures share. For example, if you are in a class with individuals from different cultures and the topic of women's rights arises, you need to be aware of and sensitive to cultural differences related to roles based on gender and age.

Socioeconomic Justification

Industrial development is no longer confined within the borders of the country of origin. Not only are North American industries relocating plants and companies in other countries, foreign companies are developing or relocating industries in the United States. These international business operations require individuals to adapt to cultural differences. Adaptations may take the form of revised marketing strategies and promotional campaigns to include different employee incentives and hiring criteria. It is important to realize that these issues reach beyond internal changes and modifications, for not only will the majority of new *hires* be female and non-white, but *consumers* of tomorrow also will reflect the demographic changes in the population. A manager's inability to cope with cultural differences may compromise the efficiency and competitiveness of an organization.

A society that employs all segments of its population will have a richer and more varied perspective on issues. More and more societal and global issues will require individuals to develop multidimensional perspectives toward culture. The ability of a country to recognize, accept, and support diversity is associated with the culture and mores of that country. In countries with relatively homogeneous populations and in countries where the society has not expanded its views and definitions of rights, very different standards of workplace actions may exist (Milkovich & Boudreau, 1994). As we move toward an increasingly global economy, those companies that turn workforce diversity into a competitive advantage are more likely to succeed (Milkovich & Boudreau, 1994).

What Is Culture?

Culture is the medium evolved by humans to survive. Nothing in our lives is free from cultural influence. It is the keystone in civilization's arch and is the medium through which all life's events must flow (Hall, 1976). Culture is a system of shared beliefs, values, customs, behaviors, and artifacts that members of a society use to cope with their world and with one another (Bates & Plog, 1990).

Characteristics of Culture

Culture is fundamentally instilled in people from birth. A child is formally and informally taught the acceptable behaviors, actions, and expectations of his or her cultural group. These behaviors offer the child—and later the adult—an unconscious pattern of acceptable behaviors and actions. The content of culture is transferred from generation to generation. For the most part, this process occurs unconsciously.

Cultures are integrated, dynamic systems that may need to change to survive. For example, within the last few hundred years, the Jewish culture has experienced traumatic events and persecution. However, that culture has adapted and survived.

As we view the cultural practices and beliefs of others, we unconsciously measure them against our own cultural beliefs. This practice is called ethnocentrism. Often the visceral belief that "we are right" and "they are wrong" pervades every aspect of a culture's existence and leads to detachment and division (Samovar & Porter, 1995). You may be aware of or have attended campuswide events at which cultural differences are celebrated. How did you react or feel when you observed some new cultural practices or traditions?

Basic Functions of Culture

Culture teaches us how to act in a manner that is expected, accepted, and predicted by members of our cultural group. It helps individuals fit into their "world" and reduces the amount of uncertainty and energy that would be spent anticipating or selecting the appropriate behavior or action for a given situation.

Not only does culture allow individuals to effectively assimilate into their world and its norms, it also assists individuals in meeting their basic needs. While means of meeting these needs may vary among cultural groups, the basic tenet is the same for all cultures: an individual's culture allows individuals to exist in an emotionally, socially, and physically secure world. Social patterns vary from culture to culture. Some family units, for example, are matriarchal, some are nuclear, some are extended; the role and status of the members of each type of family unit are culturally determined.

Elements of Cultural Differences

Culture influences our subjective reality, which is associated with behavior. Behaviors result from how we perceive events and issues. Our reaction, or how we behave, is largely a result of cultural conditioning (Samovar & Porter, 1995). Norms reflect the principles of appropriate actions for a group or culture. They guide, control, or regulate proper and acceptable behavior within a specific culture or group. Cultural beliefs, values, and norms affect an individual's perception and behavior. Understanding and acknowledging cultural beliefs, values, and norms increases an individual's ability to interact effectively with people from different cultures, at both a professional and a personal level.

Classifications of Cultural Patterns

Cultural patterns are shared beliefs, values, and norms that have persisted over time and that lead to similar behaviors across comparable situations. They affect perception, the way a people views the world (a *people,* as the term is used here, is a collection of individuals who share the same culture). Cultural patterns determine an individual's orientation toward the world. They represent a mental framework from which a people approaches life.

Orientation

Cultural anthropologists have identified five areas in which a people orients itself: activities, social relations, time, the self, and the world (Stewart & Bennett 1991; Kluckhohn & Strodtbeck, 1960).

An *activity orientation* explains how a culture views human actions and their value. Cultures oriented to "being" activity, such as the African American and the Greek cultures, value embracing life just as it is; they are characterized by an unwillingness to alter the present condition. The "doing" orientation, on the other hand, is exemplified by the American culture. Individuals in this culture identify themselves in terms of their activities, professions, or occupations. Activities that reflect "doing" are highly valued. What one wants to be or do is a significant preoccupation of members of a "doing" culture. Cultures that view humans in search of self-discovery or fulfillment are said to have a "being-in-becoming" orientation. In Buddhist cultures, for example, the main purpose of life is the inner or spiritual development.

The *social relations orientation* refers to how people relate to one another and how they organize themselves socially. Asian cultures, for example, highly value harmony in interpersonal relations. Members of these cultures have a collective view of themselves—that is, they see themselves as part of the group. On the other hand, cultures that value the individual tend to regard equality and personal choice of primary importance in society. The

American culture epitomizes the individualistic orientation. Americans believe all people should have equal rights. This concept of social relations may make it necessary to extend the length of a scheduled meeting or event to ensure participation by individuals of different cultural groups. Another example of the effect of the social relations orientation is reflected in cultural perceptions about invitations. Some cultures consider the entire extended family invited if an invitation is extended to a family.

The basis for a people's *time orientation* involves the concept and perception of time by different cultures (Hall, 1983; Hall & Hall, 1990). Cultures in countries like India and those in the Far East, as well as the culture of the Asian-American community in the United States, are past-oriented. Traditions and ancestry play major roles in these cultures. Future-oriented cultures, like the dominant American culture, emphasize what is to come. People in these cultures place great importance on planning ahead, being ready for the future. Other cultures, such as the Hispanic or Latino culture, perceive the present as the most important segment of the time frame. It is the here and now that should matter, not what has already happened or the uncertainty of things to come.

The *human nature orientation* of a culture reflects the manner in which we perceive ourselves. The meaning of self, the sense of who we are and what we want to or should be, is culturally determined. Some cultures believe that human nature is basically evil, while others hold human nature as being naturally good. These orientations have great significance in terms of the individual's responsibilities to others and the characteristics that are valued and cherished.

The way people view themselves and the spiritual—the *world orientation*—is closely allied to their view of nature and their relationship with the world. The Latino culture holds a fatalistic view of the person: humans are viewed as being subjugated to nature with very little power to control their destiny. The Native American culture strives for a harmonious relationship between people and nature. Still other cultures, such as the European Americans, regard themselves as in control of nature, masters of nature. The environment is perceived as something to be manipulated to make human life better.

Communication Context

Edward T. Hall, a cultural anthropologist who has written extensively about the intrinsic relationship between culture and communication, organizes cultures by the degree of importance placed on the setting of the communication process. Hall has classified cultures as being "high-context" or "low-context." In high-context cultures, the most important information to be derived from an interaction comes from its setting or context and from the individuals who are part of it. In low-context cultures, the most important information derives solely from the verbal message, the explicit code itself. Hall classifies Asians, African Americans, and Latinos as being high-context; while European Americans, Germans, Swiss, Scandinavians, and other Europeans are low-context (Hall, 1976; Hall & Hall, 1990). The illustration on the next page depicts a continuum of cultures by context, as described by Samovar and Porter (1995).

Low-context people tend to compartmentalize their personal relationships; consequently, each time they interact with each other, they need more background information. High-context people, on the other hand, have very strong interpersonal bonds and highly extensive information networks with

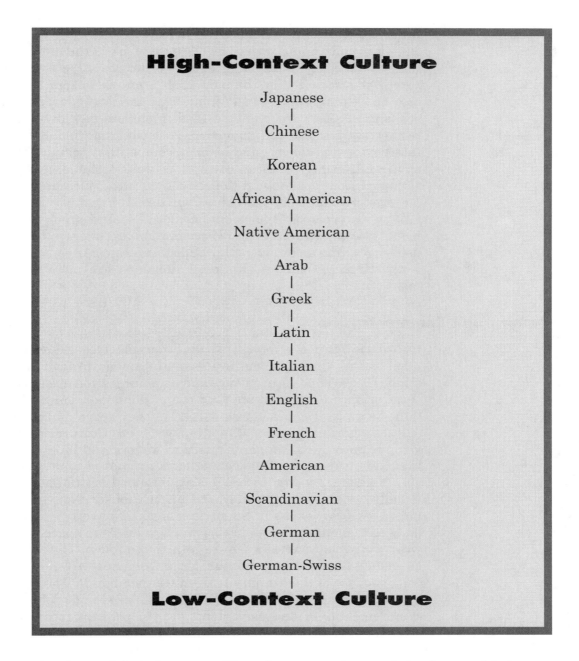

High-Context Culture
|
Japanese
|
Chinese
|
Korean
|
African American
|
Native American
|
Arab
|
Greek
|
Latin
|
Italian
|
English
|
French
|
American
|
Scandinavian
|
German
|
German-Swiss
|
Low-Context Culture

members of their in-group. They do not require much background information when they interact. Meanings are internalized in high-context cultures, and emphasis is placed on nonverbal codes. In low-context cultures, the meaning of another's behavior is expressed in the message itself. In this type of culture, therefore, it is imperative for the message to be expressed in precise and specific verbal codes when trying to communicate with others. The verbal message carries most of the information and very little is embedded in the context of the communication process.

Another characteristic of high- and low-context cultures is their orientation to time. In low-context cultures, time is highly organized and compartmentalized. Time commitments are taken seriously; the culture emphasizes promptness, and people are used to doing one thing at a time. Commitments to people and human relationships are characteristic of high-context cultures. Time commitments are considered an objective to be achieved, if possible, and people feel comfortable doing many things at once.

Individual vs. Collective Dimensions

One final cultural pattern to be discussed here is the individualism vs. collectivism dimension displayed by cultures (Hofstede, 1980). An individualist culture is characterized by the individual's concerns about his or her own interests and the interests of the immediate family. Independence, privacy, and self-actualization are highly valued. Members of individualist cultures are trained to speak out, ask questions, use confrontational strategies in solving interpersonal problems, and be more competitive. Individualist cultures, such as the European American culture, are task-oriented, and job life is sharply set apart from private life. Collectivist cultures, such as the Latino and Middle Eastern cultures, are defined in terms of groups, family, and close in-groups. Interpersonal harmony, conformity, and group solidarity are paramount. People with a collective orientation are likely to be cooperative and to use face-saving techniques, third-party intermediaries, and avoidance. In collectivistic organizations, work relationships are more important than the tasks.

Culture and Communication

Culture is learned primarily at an unconscious level rather than through explicit instruction, but culture is maintained through human interaction (Hall, 1959). Therefore, culture and communication are inseparable. The cultural orientations, contexts, and dimensions mentioned above are invisible differences that characterize cultures. They serve as lenses through which cultures can be understood and appreciated. Cultural patterns help us develop frameworks that can be used to understand intercultural communication so we can achieve the competencies required to practice it effectively.

Nonverbal communication is a subtle and multidimensional process that usually occurs spontaneously and unconsciously. Nonverbal communication messages function as a "silent language." Nonverbal code systems include body movements, how people orient themselves in space and time, what they wear, voice characteristics, eye contact, and touch. The rules and norms that govern most nonverbal communication behaviors are culture-specific.

The face is the primary transmitter of emotional cues. Some body movements, such as shifts of the body and the head nod, help control the flow of communication. Hand movements are the primary means of showing intensity. The way we move our bodies, our posture, the manner in which we walk and sit tell others something about us. Touch is perhaps the most fundamental part of the human experience, and cultures differ in the amount of touching they prefer, who touches whom, and where and when touching is acceptable. Touch behaviors include hugging, kissing, slapping, hitting, stroking, shaking hands, and clasping shoulders. In high-context cultures, such as the Middle Eastern and Latino cultures, touching is an intrinsic part of social conversations, and people, therefore, are much more tactile. But in other cultures, such as low-context Northern European cultures, touch is not an intrinsic part of the communication process.

Use of space functions as an important communication system in all cultures. Space distances differ considerably from one culture to another (Hall, 1982). Low-context, individualist cultures, such as the European American, prefer large physical distances when they communicate, whereas high-context, collectivist cultures prefer close distances. In the process of intercultural communication, space is one of the most important but difficult codes to learn and use. For example, if an individual from a high-context culture, such as a Hispanic female, violated the low-context cultural codes for space, her actions could be misunderstood by a low-context individual.

Perceptions and use of time are part of nonverbal code systems. Cultures differ in their time orientations and in the time systems they use to order their experiences (Hall, 1983). There are implicit rules in each culture concerning the use of formal and informal time systems. Units of time are perceived differently among cultures. How time should be used or experienced also varies cross-culturally. People in the United States are time-driven. Time is viewed as a commodity; it is scheduled, managed, and arranged. People are very punctual and they adhere to schedules. However, among Native American cultures, for instance, the concept of time is quite different from that of the European American. "Late" and "waiting" are terms that do not exist in the language of some Native American cultures.

It is imperative to understand, learn, and respect the nonverbal code system of another culture to be able to communicate effectively with members of that culture.

Cross-Cultural Competence

A preference for communication and interaction with individuals like ourselves is a predictable human trait. We are more at ease communicating with those who share similar experiences, lifestyles, and cultural values. However, to successfully communicate with others of a different culture, it is important to recognize and appreciate differences, while seeking shared issues that transcend all cultures.

When we are placed into experiences, situations, and locations that are different from our culture, we can experience some degree of culture shock. The severity of culture shock can be reduced through a culture-specific or culture-general educational approach. A culture-specific orientation would require study of the particular culture to which you will be exposed. For example, if you were going to Japan on business, you would learn about the Japanese culture. A culture-general approach, on the other hand, would expose you to a multitude of traits and behaviors common to many cultures.

As you interact with individuals from a different culture, remember that they may not recognize or understand your behaviors, attitudes, or actions. Reflect on cultural interpretations and differences, such as time and verbal or nonverbal communication, before you judge or act.

In order to appreciate, learn from, and communicate with others in a different culture, you must be motivated to gain new knowledge and skills. In many instances this motivation must begin with an introspective look at your own culture, values, and perceptions. Once you can identify your personal beliefs, attitudes, and biases, you can begin to accept and appreciate those of another culture. The acquisition of knowledge about other cultures can be specific or general in nature. But remember: although learning about cultural values, norms, and communication patterns can help you develop cultural understanding, it is valueless without empathy, which allows you to recognize and accept differences among individuals and cultures.

Samovar and Porter (1995) suggest a list of skills we can develop to improve intercultural communication competence:

1. Know yourself and your own cultural makeup.
2. Consider the physical and human settings.
3. Seek to understand diverse message systems.

4. Develop and display empathy.

5. Encourage and provide feedback.

6. Develop communication flexibility.

7. Avoid stereotyping and prejudice.

8. Be aware of consequences.

9. Seek commonalities.

10. Recognize the validity of differences.

11. Communicate respect.

12. Be nonjudgmental.

13. Tolerate ambiguity.

14. Be aware of individual differences.

Conclusion

Through education, empathy, appreciation of cultural differences, and recognition of cultural similarities, we can begin to better understand ourselves and our world. Changing demographics, increased technology, a global economy, and industrial expansion have changed how we interact and communicate with others. This increased and sometimes abrupt exposure to and interaction with individuals from different cultures may sometimes cause us to feel threatened or uneasy. The ability to appreciate diversity, communicate effectively, and interact with individuals from different cultures are valuable skills in today's world.

EXERCISE
On Being Different

Adapted from Kolb et al., 1995.

Purpose   Most of us at one time or another have experienced the feeling of being different when we have been in a group—at school, work, professional meetings, or social occasions. This feeling of difference may range from mild awareness of being an outsider to perceptions of being isolated, misunderstood, or not valued. In any case, such experiences leave one feeling alienated and uncomfortable. This exercise is intended to help you think about instances in which you felt different and to explore some ways in which you can become more open to differences and uniqueness in both yourself and others.

Task   Recall a recent (within the last year or so) experience when you felt different from those around you. It could be an experience at school, at work, or in a social setting. When you have the experience in mind, give some thought to the questions that follow and before the next class meeting, write your responses to them.

1. Describe the situation (who, when, where, what happened).
2. What did you do? How did you feel? How did you act?
3. What did you observe others doing? How did they react to you?
4. How did the situation end?

To help you think further about differences, your instructor will give you a questionnaire to complete about the experience you have described.

EXERCISE
The Visitor

Adapted from Dodge, 1988.

Purpose This exercise helps group members strengthen their communication skills with a person whom they have just met, by emphasizing skills to help you understand and empathize with a person who is a stranger to the group.

You Will Need Pen or pencil

Paper for taking notes

Activity

1. A person you have probably never met before will visit your class. This visitor may be someone of a culture or race different from the majority of the students in the class. Before the visitor enters, list some questions you might ask to learn something about the visitor. List polite questions that will help you reach a level of understanding of the person's thoughts and feelings. Brainstorm with others in the class and write down these questions to prompt your conversation.

2. You will play one of three roles:

   a. One or two persons will serve as host, greeting and talking briefly with the guest before he or she enters.

   b. Six persons will ask questions and carry on a conversation; these persons will be sitting at the front of the room with the guest.

   c. The remainder will serve as observers. Observers will be asked for their impressions at times after the first part of the visit. They should also take notes during the conversation to aid in recall.

3. The six conversationalists—those who have volunteered—should take seats in a semicircle. After entering and being introduced by the host, the visitor will take a seat facing the semicircle and the class.

4. One of the conversationalists should begin the exercise by asking a question the class has generated. Other conversationalists respond and also may ask questions. The key is to get to know the visitor well enough in a short period of time so that a feeling of understanding and empathy can develop. (The conversation should run 15–20 minutes.)

5. After all the conversationalists have addressed the visitor, he or she will leave the room. Based on what you have heard and observed, together predict how the visitor will answer some additional questions. (Your instructor will provide those questions after the visitor leaves the room.)

6. The visitor will then return, and together you will discover how your predictions compare with the visitor's answers. The visitor should give his or her answers to the questions before the group's predictions are shared.

7. At the conclusion, hosts should invite the visitor to ask some questions of the group. Thank the visitor for his or her contribution to your learning. (Note: Follow up with a thank-you note.)

8. After the visitor leaves, discuss the questions below.

Discussion

1. How does the exercise help you understand how to empathize?

2. Could you empathize with the visitor? How did it feel?

3. What implications does this exercise have for putting more depth into communication with others?

FURTHER ACTIVITY

Journal Writing

1. Do you have a close friend of a different ethnic background or race? Describe this relationship and how it got started. Did you have to overcome any barriers? If your friends are all very much like you (ethnicity, race), explore why this might be so.

2. What family practices, beliefs, or values do you have that might be attributed to your cultural orientation? Describe several of them.

3. Observe your family and relatives during a holiday celebration. What customs do you observe?

Independent Practice

1. Select a foreign country you are interested in visiting (for pleasure or business). Investigate that country's culture in relation to your purpose. For example, if you are interested in developing agricultural business contacts, find out about the country's agriculture department or ministry, regulations involving imports and exports, resources in the country, etc.

2. Assemble 10 to 12 examples of American ethnocentrism in news or magazine articles, industry advertisements, marketing materials, etc. Bring them to class and discuss the issues and cultural beliefs. How do they portray American values?

3. Describe a typical day, recording all actions and corresponding cultural values that guide your actions (Samover & Porter, 1995). For example:

Action: Brush Teeth, take shower

Value: Personal hygiene is valued in American culture

LEARNING POINTS

✓ We live in an intercultural world that requires the ability to behave competently in intercultural encounters. Current socioeconomic trends accentuate the need to be able to communicate effectively cross-culturally.

✓ The two key concepts underlying the study of intercultural competence are culture and communication. Culture may be defined as a learned set of shared perceptions about values, beliefs, and practices that affect the behaviors of a relatively large group of people.

✓ Through its set of value orientations, a culture addresses common human issues with a preferred set of choices. Culture determines the manner in which people orient themselves to activities, social relations, the self, and the world.

✓ Cultural patterns such as value orientations, context, and dimensions provide multiple frames of reference that can be used to understand cultural differences.

✓ Nonverbal behavior is culturally determined and is an integral part of the communication process.

✓ Intercultural communication competence is an essential attribute for personal survival and professional success; it is imperative in this increasingly multicultural world.

REFERENCES

Bates, D. C., and Plog, F. (1990). *Cultural anthropology* (3rd ed.). New York: McGraw-Hill.

Dodge, G. W. (1988). *Handbook for teaching assistants.* Lincoln, NE: University of Nebraska, Department of Agricultural Education.

Hall, E. T. (1959). *The silent language.* Garden City, NY: Anchor Press/Doubleday.

Hall, E. T. (1976). *Beyond culture.* Garden City, NY: Anchor Press/Doubleday.

Hall, E. T. (1982). *The hidden dimension.* Garden City, NY: Anchor Press/Doubleday.

Hall, E. T. (1983). *The dance of life.* Garden City, NY: Anchor Press/Doubleday.

Hall, E. T., and Hall, M. R. (1990). *Understanding cultural differences: Germans, French and Americans.* Yarmouth, ME: Intercultural Press, Inc.

Hofstede, G. (1980). *Culture's consequences: International differences in work-related values.* Beverly Hills, CA: Sage.

Kennedy, J., and Everest, A. (1991). Put diversity in context. *Personnel Journal.* September, 50–54.

Kolb, D. A., Osland, J. S., and Rubin, M. (1995). *Organizational behavior: An experiential approach* (6th ed.). Englewood Cliffs, NJ: Prentice Hall.

Kluckhohn, F. R., and Strodtbeck, F. L. (1960). *Variations in value orientations.* New York: Row and Peterson.

Milkovich, G. T., and Boudreau, J. W. (1994). *Human resource management* (7th ed.). Boston: Irwin Press.

Samovar, L. A., and Porter, R. E. (1995). *Communication between cultures* (2nd ed.). Belmont, CA: Wadsworth Publishing.

Shuter, R. (1990). The centrality of culture. *Southern Communication Journal, 55,* 291.

Stewart, E. C., and Bennett, M. J. (1991). *American cultural patterns: A cross-cultural perspective* (revised ed.). Yarmouth, ME: Intercultural Press, Inc.

16

GENDER ISSUES

Perhaps the greatest progress, humanly speaking, in these past twenty years, for both women and men, is in the growth of consciousness. . . . A new consciousness of the dignity and rights of an individual, regardless of race, creed, class, or sex. A new consciousness and questioning of the materialistic values of the Western world.
—Anne Morrow Lindbergh, *Gifts from the Sea* (1983)

ADVANCE PLANNER: GENDER ISSUES

When you complete this chapter, you will be able to:

✓ Understand the necessity for learning about gender issues.

✓ Develop some appreciation of the historical and evolutionary processes that affect gender issues.

✓ Be sensitive to gender issues as they relate to communication and, specifically, to language.

✓ Discuss issues relating to the politics, law, and ethics of gender.

✓ Analyze relevant gender issues as they pertain to the future in the workplace and in your personal life.

To accomplish these objectives, you will complete some or all of these activities:

1. Identify careers or roles of men and women during the Agricultural, Industrial, and Information Ages.

2. Analyze the meaning of friendship for both genders.

3. Analyze ten statements related to gender communication differences and provide personal experiences that illustrate or challenge each statement.

CASE STUDIES IN GENDER ISSUES

Dividing the Work

George and Sally, co-workers who were on friendly terms with each other, were assigned to do a marketing survey together. When they got the assignment, George began by saying, "I'll do the airline and automobile industries, and you can do the housewares and direct-mail markets." Sally was taken aback. "Hey," she said, "it sounds like you've got it all figured out. As a matter of fact, I'd like to do airlines and autos. I've already got a lot of contacts in those areas." "Oh," George said, a little chagrined and a lot surprised. Sally continued, "I wish you wouldn't come on so strong." "Well, how would you have started?" George asked. She said, "I wouldn't have just said what I wanted to do. I would have asked, 'What parts do you want to do?'" This made no sense to George. "Then what are you complaining about? If you had asked me what parts I wanted to do, I would have said, 'I'll do the airlines and autos.' We would have ended up in the same place anyway" (Tannen, 1994, p. 29).

Discussion Questions

1. What basic assumptions have George and Sally made here? How often do we make the kinds of assumptions that George has made? Do you agree that he has "come on too strong"?

2. Does this case describe an innocent mistake, or does it describe a situation we need to become more aware of and sensitive about in our society?

3. How would you have started this assignment? Offer an alternative scenario to this case that would reflect greater gender awareness.

4. Can you think of any situations that are similar to this case?

Gender Equity

You are a student at a major university with a comprehensive NCAA athletic program. The football team is one of the best in the nation, has set records for sell-out crowds, and generates millions of dollars in revenue every year, which supports many of the other non-revenue-generating sports on campus. You have been elected a student representative to the Athletic Council, which oversees and advises on matters of policy and procedure. You also have become aware of the importance of Title IX, the U.S. Government rules and regulations that apply to gender equity. You are now aware that your university is out of compliance with the mandated requirements. The athletic department clearly tends to favor and reward men's athletic programs over women's athletic programs. This is seen in terms of total number of scholarships offered to athletes, the number of sponsored programs, the salaries offered to coaches, and so on.

As a student representative, you have to form a clear opinion on the problem and achieve a clear understanding of the issues. You also realize that in all likelihood if greater equity is to be achieved in the overall program, it will probably mean reducing the number of football scholarships and shifting greater revenues to other sports, particularly women's sports. You can anticipate that any decisions made will be controversial and will meet with some hostility from those who would see the football program endangered. Reducing football scholarships from, let us say, 85 per year to 75 or 70 would significantly impact the program in terms of its ability to compete with other Division 1 schools.

Discussion Questions

1. What criteria do you think are necessary in order to help you arrive at a fair understanding of this case?

2. What additional factual information might you need in order to effectively address the main issues of this case? Where would you find such information?

3. Does "fairness" mean a 50–50 arrangement, or are there other possible ways of defining a fair solution?

INTRODUCTION TO THEORIES ABOUT GENDER ISSUES

Unless you attended an all-male or all-female high school, you probably were not concerned about having members of the opposite sex in your college classes, but you may have been surprised by the experience of living on a mixed-gender floor in your housing unit. If you had been able to contrast this experience with the experience of living on an all-male or all-female floor, you might have noticed a difference in floor government and expectations for residents.

Mixed-gender classes and living arrangements mirror what you will likely find when you graduate and begin your professional career—men and women living and working together. To become as effective as possible in your personal life and career, therefore, it is critical to understand the changes and events related to gender that have gotten us to this point and to understand the kinds of things both genders can do to insure the likelihood of success.

It has been said that corporations as we have known them were created by men for men. "After World War II, America's fighting men exchanged their military uniforms for factory overalls and gray flannel suits." The authoritarian, military approach to organization—which had guided men so well in wartime—soon became the management model by which they would run their companies in peacetime. This management model actually worked quite well for about three decades (Naisbitt & Aburdene, 1990).

But dramatic change emerged in time. For example, in the legal profession, because more women are becoming lawyers, the rhetoric of the law has undergone significant evolutionary changes. As more female law clerks have become responsible for drafting new laws, a traditionally male-oriented rhetoric has been transforming itself gradually into a gender-neutral rhetoric.

This transformation is one of many examples of societal changes that have instilled the need for greater sensitivity to and inclusion of both genders. Those who contemplate careers in business or the professions and are not sensitive to issues of gender as they relate to the way we use language and behave jeopardize their chances for success.

Historical and Evolutionary Processes That Affect Gender Issues

As the U.S. matured as a nation, our economy moved from an agrarian base to an industrial base to what economists now call an information base. In an information-based economy, where people are well educated and are expected to think for and manage themselves, leadership can no longer be defined according to traditional models (for example, a military model based largely on issuing orders) (Naisbitt & Aburdene, 1990) nor in exclusively gender-specific terms, either.

The military model relied heavily on androcentrism, ". . . the privileging of male experience and the 'otherizing' of female experience; that is males and

> Androcentrism—the male experience is the norm by which all other behavior is measured; female experiences are considered gender-specific and less desirable than male experiences (de Beauvoir, 1952).

male experience are treated as a neutral standard norm for the culture or the species as a whole, and females and female experience are treated as a sex-specific deviation from that allegedly universal standard" (Bem, 1993, p. 41).

Over time, androcentrism, and consequently the employment patterns to which it gave rise, were challenged by several changes and advances. One of the most dramatic advances to change the patterns of gender employment was the availability of oral contraceptives in 1960. Prior to 1960, women and men had very few birth control options, and it was not uncommon for women to have many children during their childbearing years. (That is, if they lived through their childbearing years—one need only visit nineteenth-century cemeteries to see the telltale markers of women who died during childbirth.)

Today, 80 percent of women have used birth control pills at some point in their lives, making the pill the nation's most popular form of reversible contraception. As a result, fewer children have been born and couples can practice more effective family planning. Today, more women are delaying childbirth and taking advantage of opportunities to balance both career and parenthood.

The movement from the Industrial Age into the Information Age also has called androcentrism into question. At no time in history has the U.S. population had greater access to education. Such access has led to a population (male and female) that is better educated and able to respond to technological advances rapidly and efficiently.

Gender Issues and Language

If it is true that we are what we eat, then it is equally true that we are no less than what we speak! In both respects we should pay careful attention to what is "good" for us and avoid what is "bad." Perhaps nowhere more than in our speech and communication practices do we reveal ourselves to others. It is, therefore, crucial that we teach ourselves the appropriate forms of address as dictated by the social rules and avoid violations of the social rules through carelessness or ignorance. Such violations often leave the listener with the impression that the speaker is excluding the opposite gender, when, in fact, the speaker does not mean to be exclusive. Using an inclusive language—neither male nor female referenced—helps create an atmosphere of greater goodwill in which both sexes are treated equally and respectfully. Inclusive speech frequently means that we must make a greater effort to find a term that is gender neutral. So, for example, we should find more suitable terminology than *man-hours* or *manpower* or *salesman*. To the extent that police forces now include many women, the term *policeman* has become more exclusive than inclusive. Why not *police officer* instead? Or *flight attendant* rather than *stewardess*? And so on.

Gender-exclusive	Gender-neutral
Congressman	Representative
Chairman	Chair
Mailman	Mail Carrier
Fireman	Firefighter
Actress	Actor

Some people may argue that such distinctions are trivial and the work of politically correct "speech police." But a little reflection suggests that while inclusive speech is a political act, it also reveals how we think and act with respect to the dynamics of social change within our society. Do we resist change? Or do we see the larger purposes behind such changes in language and acknowledge that they reflect a society simply trying to become more democratic and free through language? We are constantly being challenged to grow and change and to become more inclusive in our thoughts about diversity. People who resist such challenges and changes fail to grow and mature; they fail to expand their own personal horizons and, in the end, fail to experience the successes, joys, and satisfaction of a life fully open to diversity.

One explanation of how we create meaning through language is through the *social construction theory* of language. The words themselves don't contain meaning; their meanings are not fixed, permanent, or unchangeable. Rather, meaning is an agreement between speaker and listener or writer and reader. Words on a page are only meaningful when we as readers construct meaning through our interpretation of what the author intended. Readers can never fully know what the author meant; we can only approximate such meaning based upon what we bring to the text from our own experiences, prior reading knowledge, etc.

Gender issues are also language issues; we make our meaning available to each other in the way we think of each other. The culture we live in is being remade continuously in the language we use to express ourselves. We are who we are by virtue of how we express to others what we mean. The wider we can construct our social agreements about what language means, the more harmonious and agreeable our relationships become. Men and women speaking a language of greater mutual understanding will obviously lead us toward a less divisive, more civil and respectful world.

Politics, Law, and Ethics of Gender

We cannot think about gender in a vacuum. It needs to be examined within other contexts and perspectives. For example, we can think about gender from political, social, legal, or ethical perspectives. Depending upon our perspective, our attitudes toward the other gender will take shape. There was a time not so long ago when women did not have the vote, could not be employed in certain professions, and were prohibited from behaving, participating, and even dressing in any number of ways. Dramatic changes—usually attributed to the consequences of World War II and its aftermath—have resulted in considerably more freedoms for women than they enjoyed previously.

Still, the politics of gender, as well as the legal, social, and ethical aspects of gender, remain controversial and sometimes divisive. The public debate over the equal rights amendment (ERA) revealed a wide variety of opinions within society and resulted in failure of the proposed amendment to become part of our constitution. Similarly, the *Roe v. Wade* ruling of the Supreme Court in 1973 has remained a controversial topic to the present time, and the controversy shows no signs of ending soon. Our nation remains critically divided over the issue of choice and probably no issue since slavery has so dominated moral and ethical discussion in America as has the abortion debate.

The important point, however, is that we can never return to the way things were. Our thinking about gender has changed, whether we are consciously aware of the fact or not, and there is no going back. Fortunately, the vast majority of people practice considerable tolerance for gender, religious, and ethnic diversity. Similarly, our tolerance for diversity within this society must be balanced against a clear intolerance for sexual violence and sexual harassment. Behaviors once winked at or dismissed as trivial can no longer be so treated. Just as society has imposed stricter standards of acceptable behavior with respect to alcohol and driving, so also does it impose stricter standards with respect to appropriate speech and behavior regarding matters of gender.

As a direct result of a more focused attention to gender issues, children's issues also will garner greater attention. Parental leave and flextime in the workplace will offer both men and women new opportunities to nurture their children and achieve better balance between home and work, family and career. Both parents, whether separated or not, now share responsibility for the proper nurturing and well-being of children. As our society becomes more insistent on shared parenting, we are moving into gender neutrality, not holding one gender more accountable than the other for rearing children.

Some Thoughts on Sexual Harassment

Sexual harassment is simultaneously one of the least understood and most frequent legal transgressions in our society. We need only list the accused *versus* the accusers to gain some sense of the problem: Supreme Court Justice *Clarence Thomas vs. Anita Hill*; Evangelist *Jim Baker vs. Jessica Hahn*; Former *Senator Robert Packwood vs. several female accusers*; President *Bill Clinton vs. Paula Jones*. And on it goes: the Navy Tailhook scandal, the ongoing Army scandals, the Mitsubishi Corporation exposés about its treatment of female employees—all serious cases of proven or asserted sexual harassment. And on and on.

What exactly is sexual harassment? The Equal Employment Opportunity Commission defines it as *unwelcome* sexual attention—whether verbal or physical—that affects an employee's job conditions or creates a *hostile* working environment. But what then constitutes *unwelcome* or *hostile* (Adler, 1991)? Attitudes about sex and sexuality are deeply embedded in the cultural practices of our society and create conditions of fundamental debate and disagreement among men and women.

Legal definitions and parameters of what constitutes legal harassment are in continuous flux, and final determinations often need to be adjudicated in the courts. There is still, obviously, much gray area—outside the obvious instances of clear harassment that are neither debatable nor defensible.

So the real question is: how do we behave in ways that charges of sexual harassment are avoidable? How should we relate to and treat men and women so harassment remains a non-issue of our behavior?

Harassment is not, finally, a gender issue at all; it is a *power* issue. It is most often a male issue only because males are more often in power positions in society. This point is underscored in the 1994 film *Disclosure*, in which Demi Moore plays a female sexual predator who uses her corporate power to harass a male subordinate (played by Michael Douglas) in a reversal of the usual plot situation.

The extent to which our society is in continuous debate about the appropriate behaviors of males and females suggests the greater need for each of us to bring a specialized sensitivity and awareness to the general problem. More than ever before, we need to exercise a special caution about our behavior and linguistic discourse.

Our society is changing its fundamental attitudes about relationships between the sexes. The goal—as is appropriate to a democratic republic—is proper: There should be maximum equality between the sexes, no distinctions about the opportunities available to men or to women. And the United States will help establish the standards across the world for how gender equity will be defined and managed well into the future. It is an obligation we must assume both as a nation and as individuals. The bottom line is that each of us needs to reflect most carefully upon our fundamental ways of relating to members of the opposite sex. Are our relationships premised upon power, control, or absolute authority—unquestionably oppressive and dangerous—or upon equality, consensus, and mutual respect? These are profoundly personal questions, but questions that have now assumed significant societal implications. We can no longer afford to hold personal attitudes about men or women without measuring or evaluating them against the larger expected standards of our evolving society and culture.

Both corporations and the courts are taking an increasingly stricter and more unequivocal stance on harassment. Harassment policies are being written in more precise language, and follow-up employee training sessions and grievance procedures are being put in place across the nation. The prevalence of overt harassment practices has been reduced considerably over the past decade, in spite of the high-visibility cases mentioned earlier. Given, however, that sociological research has shown fundamental differences between the sexes on the nature of sexual advances (75 percent of males said they would be flattered, while 75 percent of women said they would be offended), the dialogue toward a more harmonious understanding and agreement still has a long way to go (Lublin, 1991).

Communications Technology, Employability, and Gender

Randy, a regional sales executive with a major food company, lives in a rural community in Nebraska. He carries his morning cup of coffee from the kitchen into his den, where he will spend most of his work day interacting with co-workers and clients located in a ten-state area in the southeast United States. Randy is one of a growing number of people who use the Internet to conduct business from the comfort of home. His company no longer maintains regional headquarters, which of course saves considerable overhead costs, and instead provides executives with fax machines, computers, modems, and other technological support to get the work done.

Catherine works as a director for an organization based in Washington, D.C., but her office is located in her home in Lincoln, Nebraska. Like Randy, she is connected via fax and modem and computer to people at the main office, with whom she communicates several times a day; she also is linked to her staff members, who are located throughout the United States. In addition, she employs Glenda as her secretary on an independent contractor basis; Glenda (a mother of four) conducts her own secretarial business out of her home, as well, allowing her to balance her private role with her professional role in a way that gives her both maximum satisfaction and a generous annual income. Her knowledge of computer technology has helped make her indispensable to Catherine, as well as to her other clients.

The capability to work out of the home offers increasing benefits to both men and women. At a time when dual couple employment is becoming commonplace, the need for companies to become more flexible and sensitive to the living accommodations of partners is growing. When Lenora's husband

Ken, a cardiologist, finished his residency in New Jersey and returned to Pittsburgh to practice, her company, AT&T, recognizing her value as an excellent employee, changed its traditional practices and allowed her to continue working from her new home in Pennsylvania. The arrangement has proven highly beneficial for everyone, and Lenora continues to get promotions and new assignments and responsibilities.

Technological innovations are changing the landscape and gender composition of corporate America and will continue to have a profound effect on the way we work and do business in the future. They have diminished the importance of where we need to be physically located to do our work.

The Glass Ceiling

According to a 1991 Department of Labor report, progress of women into executive positions has been extremely slow. Between 1979 and 1989, the representation of women and minorities in top executive positions of the top 1000 corporations in America rose only from three percent to five percent. An independent 1991 random sampling of 94 Fortune 1000 Companies found that women, while comprising 37 percent of total employees (17 percent at management level), occupied only 6.5 percent of executive level positions.

These figures illustrate the glass ceiling syndrome, about which much has been said and written. In response to the glass ceiling phenomenon, however, women are now starting new businesses twice as fast as men. Reports indicate that in Canada one-third of small businesses are owned by women, and, in France, one-fifth. Given the increased flexibility in scheduling and workplace location, one can predict that future opportunities for both genders, but especially for women, are growing exponentially (Naisbitt & Aburdene, 1990).

Corporations and government increasingly recognize the need to ensure the wellness of their employees. The Family and Medical Leave Law of 1993, for example, requires employers with more than 50 employees to provide up to 12 weeks of unpaid leave per year for the serious illness of the employee or an immediate family member, or the birth or adoption of a child. While these benefits suggest an improving climate for gender issues, the fact remains that here in the United States we still lag considerably behind certain other countries. France, for example, provides a guaranteed national day care service for children of working mothers and, like other European nations, places an emphasis and priority on children and workers not yet fully realized in this country.

Stereotypical Careers

During their college years, students make a public commitment to a professional career area through their choice of college major. It is likely you have been influenced in your career choice by individuals who work in the career area, books you have read, or movies you have watched. Whether you realize it or not, you have been subtly influenced in your career choice ever since you were old enough to be aware of your surroundings.

Those who grew up in the 1950s can remember the Dick and Jane books used in the elementary schools to teach reading. Dick played ball and climbed trees and romped with his dog, Spot, while Jane enjoyed swings and tea parties and playing with her dolls. Such stereotypes were commonplace, as even a brief glimpse at the television programs of that era would show.

Father Knows Best, Leave It to Beaver, I Remember Mama, and *The Andy Griffith Show* all suggested a world of clearly defined duties and responsibilities for males and females. Looking at these shows today evokes, perhaps, a smile of nostalgia for a world that seemed simpler, more innocent, more friendly, and less frantic than our own. The worlds of those old television shows, we know, never really existed and were myths even then. But roles and duties did indeed seem clearer and, prior to the single-parent phenomenon of the 1980s and 1990s, the notion of family values seemed to be more easily definable and more generally acceptable.

There is no question that our world has become more complex, that traditional roles are less easily defined, and that the difficulties of parenting and career have become more complicated. At the same time, however, opportunities have increased considerably. An increased number of choices no doubt makes decision making more difficult. Women, for example, can enter professions they may not have formerly dreamed about; they can participate in any number of activities not available to their mothers. This range of choices has, indeed, made life more difficult for many modern women and they are experiencing the stresses and pressures of having to choose among many possibilities. It is clearly not an easy time and many young women (and young men also) suffer from multiple pressures inflicted by society. Learning to make good choices, however, and to live in terms of a well-defined purpose and plan is preferable to being forced to live within the very limited choices of more traditional and sexist societies.

Summary

"We can't know where we're going until we know where we have been" is certainly true about our understanding of gender. When we realize how separately men and women lived their lives just a few decades back, we have a sense of how far we have come today. While there is much optimism about the future, there can be no underestimating the difficulties that still need to be overcome. Men and women need to continue dialoguing with each other and to extend the boundaries of their own thinking about gender. In practical terms this means examining the premises upon which we make our daily judgments about what girls and boys and men and women should be. Should women be allowed admission to the Citadel, for example? Should gay couples or single persons be allowed to adopt children? Should women be allowed to become priests? Should priests be allowed to marry?

There are no easy answers to many of these questions; sometimes there are no right or wrong answers, either. But these are real human questions and concerns, and there is every reason to argue that we should be free to talk about them. To "agree to disagree" is a perfectly legitimate outcome. How we speak with each other is the important issue here; a conversation based upon mutual respect is always a good experience and is the hallmark of a civilized person—and society.

EXERCISE
Gender Role Playing

Purpose To demonstrate the stereotypes each gender harbors about the other's behavior.

You Will Need The Observation Matrix

Activity Members of your class will do some impromptu role playing as you switch your gender role (males will perform as females, females will perform as males). Act out these scenarios as assigned:

1. Two male friends (played by two females) meet each other on campus for the first time this year.
2. Two female friends (played by two males) meet each other on campus for the first time this year.
3. A group of males (played by five females) are together at a party.
4. A group of females (played by five males) are together at a party.
5. Two males (played by two females) are discussing one of the male's feelings about his girlfriend breaking up with him.
6. Two females (played by two males) are discussing one of the female's feelings about her boyfriend breaking up with her.

   If you are an observer, watch your peers role play, listen carefully to their conversations, and observe their behavior. On the matrix, record any accuracies, inaccuracies, and distortions you observe, and identify the sources (e.g. television, newspapers, books) you think your peers drew upon for their portrayal.

Discussion

1. How accurate was the role playing?
2. What were some inaccuracies in the role playing?
3. Were there some situations that seemed to have been magnified or distorted?
4. What do you think were the sources of the inaccuracies and distortions?
5. How did you feel about portraying your opposite gender?
6. What past experiences did you draw upon to help you in your portrayal?

Observation Matrix

Situation	Accuracy	Inaccuracy	Distortions	Sources
We "male" friends				
We "female" friends				
The "guys" at a party				
The "coeds" at a party				
Breaking up with "her"				
Breaking up with "him"				

EXERCISE
Gender and Friendship

Purpose To identify differences and commonalities genders share in regard to relationships, specifically in regard to friendship.

Activity In small groups by gender, address the following questions by brainstorming. (One person in each group should record responses.) When a group brainstorms, any answer is acceptable and is not subject to debate. Spend only a few minutes on each question.

   a. What is friendship?

   b. What do you think friendship is to the other gender group (male/female)?

   c. What do you expect of a friendship?

   d. What do you think the opposite gender expects of friendship?

   e. At what point do you classify a relationship as a friendship?

   f. At what point do you think the opposite gender classifies a relationship as a friendship?

   g. How do you react to the termination of a friendship?

   h. How do you think the opposite gender reacts to the termination of a friendship?

    When your group has finished its brainstorming, join the other group. The recorder from each group should summarize her or his group's responses item by item. Following the presentation, discuss the similarities and differences among the comments.

FURTHER ACTIVITY

Journal Writing

1. Imagine you are the victim of unwelcome verbal or physical sexual attention (or perhaps reflect back to a time when you have been in such a situation). Would (did) this attention affect the way you behave? If this were to happen (or were to happen again), what would you do (differently) and why?

2. Do you agree that harassment often is a power issue? Diagnose a court case in which sexual harassment has been the core issue. Who was affected and how? What were the associated risks for the accused and the accuser in formalizing the charges? Was power an issue (defend your position)? What was the outcome? Was it just? What questions would you like to ask the accused and the accuser?

3. Pick up a promotional brochure of a major corporation at the campus career planning and placement office. Analyze the brochure for the following: entry-level position descriptions, benefits offered, pictures of employees, and training or education opportunities. Does the corporation appear to be appealing to both genders? Do they have family-friendly policies (day care on site, flexible work schedules, family health insurance, etc.)? Why will this information be important in hiring the best graduates for the corporation?

Independent Practice

The following ten statements about gender communication differences are generally supported by gender theorists. Provide an illustration from your personal experiences that either supports or negates two of the following statements (summarized from Tannen, 1990):

1. Men communicate mostly for information, women communicate mostly for interaction.

2. Little girls' friendships are made by telling and sharing personal experiences. A little girl's social life revolves around her best friend.

3. Little boys' friendships are made by playing games, usually team or group games.

4. For all of their lives, women have had practice in verbalizing their thoughts and feelings in private conversations with people to whom they are close.

5. For all of their lives, men have had practice in dismissing their feelings and keeping their thoughts to themselves.

6. For girls, talk is the glue that holds relationships together.

7. For boys, relationships are held together primarily by activities: doing things together or talking about activities such as sports.

8. To most women, conflict is a threat to connection, to be avoided at all costs. Disputes are preferably settled without direct confrontation.

9. To most men, conflict is the necessary means by which status is negotiated, so it is to be accepted and may even be sought, embraced, and enjoyed. Men can create affiliation by opposition.

10. At every age, girls and women sit closer to each other and look at each other directly. At every age, boys and men sit at angles to each other, and never look directly into each other's faces.

LEARNING POINTS

✓ Gender equity is a goal for our democratic society. We have not arrived there yet but, with a joint commitment, the process should be made easier.

✓ Androcentrism needs to be replaced by gender neutrality.

✓ Our basic attitudes about gender are reflected in our use of language. We need to become particularly sensitized to our own uses of language as it reveals who we are.

✓ The meanings that words acquire can be thought of as socially constructed. The greater the degree of consensus about meaning, the more complete is our understanding and the more intimately are we involved in the conversation.

✓ The Information Age has hastened progress toward gender equity. New technologies are helping to liberate men and women from traditional structures and offer many new opportunities.

✓ Gender equity is not in conflict with notions of gender differences. We can maintain our differences without losing our equality.

REFERENCES

Adler, S. J. (1991). Suits over sexual harassment prove difficult due to issue of definition. *Wall Street Journal,* October 9, B4.

Bem, S. L. (1993). *The lenses of gender.* New Haven: Yale University Press.

de Beauvoir, S. (1952). *The second sex.* New York: Knopf.

Lindbergh, A. M. (1983). *Gifts from the sea.* New York: Vintage.

Lublin, J. (1991). Thomas battle spotlights harassment. *Wall Street Journal,* October 9, B1, B4.

Naisbitt, J., and Aburdene, P. (1990). *Megatrends 2000.* New York: Avon.

Tannen, D. (1990). *You just don't understand me.* New York: Ballantine.

Tannen, D. (1994). *Talking from 9 to 5.* New York: Morrow.

17

SERVANT LEADERSHIP

What is the use of living if not to strive for noble causes and to make this muddled world a better place for those who will live in it after we are gone?
—Winston Churchill

Let them remember that there is a meaning beyond absurdity. Let them be sure that every little deed counts, that every word has power, and that we can—every one—do our share to redeem the world in spite of all absurdities and all frustrations and all disappointments. And above all, remember that the meaning of life is to build a life as if it were a work of art.
—Rabbi Abraham Joshua Heschel

If there is a problem somewhere, this is what happens. Three people will try to do something concrete to settle the issue. Ten people will give a lecture analyzing what the three are doing. One hundred people will commend or condemn the ten for their lecture. One thousand people will argue about the problem. And one person—only one—will involve himself so deeply in the true solution that he is too busy to listen to any of it.
—Father Longere

ADVANCE PLANNER: SERVANT LEADERSHIP

When you complete this chapter, you will be able to:

✓ Define servant leadership.

✓ List and provide examples of the characteristics of the servant leader.

✓ Differentiate between the leader, follower, and bystander roles in your life.

✓ Identify your level of trust and practice strategies for increasing your level of trust, if necessary.

✓ Analyze the impact of your trust level on past, current, and future follower–leader relationships.

✓ Practice the characteristics of an effective servant leader.

To accomplish these objectives, you will complete some or all of these activities:

1. Discuss a case study to help identify characteristics of a servant leader.

2. Read and discuss a summary of literature, theories, and examples of servant leadership.

3. Identify roles you perform and their relationship to the functions of leader, follower, and bystander.

4. Determine your degree of interpersonal trust and its implications for your success as a leader and a follower.

5. Write in your journal about an individual you have encountered whom you would characterize as a servant leader and this individual's impact on followers and bystanders.

CASE STUDY IN SERVANT LEADERSHIP

The Josephson Institute of Ethics

Graduating as the valedictorian of his UCLA Law School class in 1967, Michael Josephson moved into a professorship at Wayne State University in Detroit. As a faculty member, he started a law-related publishing company. By 1985, his company had become so successful he was able to sell it for nearly $10 million.

Josephson had a passion, one that he nurtured as an undergraduate student, a graduate student, and eventually as a law school faculty member—educating others about ethical decision making. True to his passion, he invested the proceeds of the sale of his publishing company into the Joseph & Edna Josephson Institute of Ethics.

The Josephson Institute of Ethics' mission is to increase the ethical consciousness and commitment of America's leaders through intensive workshops, speeches, and publications. Josephson donates his time and talents, delivering over 100 workshops annually and writing on behalf of the Institute. His audiences include state and federal leaders and executives from some of the nation's largest corporations (3M, Bank of America, Goodyear Tire and Rubber, Levi-Strauss, Pacific Telesis, State Farm Insurance, and Union Pacific Railroad). Josephson's largest project to date has been providing programs for the 120,000 employees and leaders of the Internal Revenue Service.

In these programs, Josephson challenges participants to look beyond simply following the law to the application of principles of honor, fairness, honesty, and justice. Through education, he is trying to narrow what he sees as a widening gap "between society's emphasis on measures designed to prevent bad conduct and its incentives to promote good behavior" (Mitchell, 1991).

His most recent effort to influence ethical decision making has involved the organization of the Character Counts! Coalition. This national coalition brought together educators, youth leaders, and ethicists to develop a program that stresses development of character built on what Josephson refers to as the six pillars or core ethical values: trustworthiness, respect, responsibility, fairness, caring, and citizenship. The coalition seeks to combat youth violence, irresponsibility, and dishonesty by stressing the six pillars in an age-appropriate curriculum. The Character Counts! Coalition offers ethical decision-making education early in children's lives, positively influencing their character development. Character Counts! has been endorsed by the President of the United States, the U.S. House of Representatives, the U.S. Senate, over 40 states, and 450 cities, counties, school districts, and chambers of commerce (Mitchell, 1991; Josephson Institute of Ethics, 1996; Character Counts! Fact Sheet, 1997).

Discussion Questions

1. What characteristics or qualities has Josephson demonstrated that have been keys to the success of the Josephson Institute?

2. What are some national ethical dilemmas that encouraged Josephson to follow his passion for ethical decision-making education?

3. What obstacles has Josephson likely encountered in his crusade to educate others about ethical decision making?

4. After years of working exclusively with adults, Josephson felt compelled to lead the formation of the Character Counts! Coalition to educate youth about character. Discuss the logic behind Josephson's focusing some of the Institute's resources on educating young people.

5. Do you know people like Michael Josephson? What need (s) have they responded to and how have they made a difference for others?

INTRODUCTION TO THEORIES OF SERVANT LEADERSHIP

Perhaps you have seen or heard the phrase "Lead, follow, or get out of the way." It is enjoying much popularity and can be found almost everywhere, from bumper stickers to T-shirts. The phrase seems pretty straightforward—it categorizes people as performers of one of three functions in our society: leader, follower, and bystander.

These three functions are not exclusive of each other; each of us performs them simultaneously in the many different arenas in which we operate. But regardless of the mix of functions in our lives, we know the most successful leaders are also capable of being successful followers.

What are the attributes of successful leaders? You may be able to identify individuals you know who are successful leaders. They are always searching, listening to others, and expecting that a better mousetrap is just around the next bend. Above all, they make certain that meeting other people's needs is their highest priority. Because of their extreme dedication to the service of others before themselves, we call them *Servant Leaders.*

Characteristics of a Servant Leader

Self-Knowledge	Vision
Service to Others	Ability to Cope with Uncertainty
Motivation of Others	Realism
Active Listening	Future Orientation
Instigation of Change	Ownership of Problems
Trustworthiness	Followership

Self-Knowledge

Servant leaders know a great deal about themselves. They know about their skills, prejudices, talents, and shortcomings. This knowledge of self is at the heart of the development of their self confidence, and self-confidence is critical to successful leadership (Kouzes & Posner, 1990). Leaders know they are most successful when they lead with their strengths and work to manage their weaknesses.

Service to Others

Often we encounter people who seem to wander through life without purpose or a sense of direction, playing the third role: bystander. Such a malady was suffered for a time by Jane Addams, co-founder of the Hull House in Chicago, as she lamented

"Weary of myself and sick asking
What I am and what I ought to be" (Henderson, 1930, p. 126).

Jane Addams eventually moved beyond the bystander function to become a servant leader who is remembered for her "ruthless determination" for social betterment and humanistic living (Henderson, 1930). Many reform efforts in Chicago originated with Hull House, including cleaner streets, better housing, and laws to regulate child labor. Today, the Hull House Association carries on Addams' work through 25 community centers located around Chicago. Addams is an excellent example of a human being who found her purpose in life when losing herself in the total service of others (Covey, 1990). This service is other-directed, with no thought of personal gain for the servant leader.

Devoting one's energies through service not only assists in the development of another but also brings with it "a kind of psychological, emotional, spiritual reward in the form of internal security and peace" (Covey, 1990, p. 141). This reward is not necessarily felt immediately when the servant leader is focusing on the follower, but comes along in what Covey calls "the second mile." In reflecting on the impact he or she has had on the follower, the leader assesses his or her role in the other's development. This assessment includes consideration of the leader's talents that were instrumental in the follower's development; through this assessment, the servant leader bolsters his or her self-confidence.

Just how do servant leaders build one-to-one servant relationships? Servant leadership relationships progress through a series of five developmental levels (Dodge, 1988). It is important for the leader to be aware of each level so that gentle nudges can be given, when appropriate, to encourage the progress of the relationship.

Levels of Servant Leader Investment

Level 1—Observation-Entertainment
Level 2—Participation-Entertainment
Level 3—Learning-Participation
Level 4—Teaching-Organizing
Level 5—Investing in Others
(Dodge, 1988)

1. Observation-Entertainment

During this initial stage, the servant leader and the individual with whom the leader is building the relationship (or "investee") are getting to know one another. They begin to explore each other's likes and dislikes. Participation in spectator activities, watching television, or attending movies or athletic events gives both individuals opportunities to begin the process of discovery.

2. Participation-Entertainment

In this second stage, the relationship moves beyond the observation of others to an active role in joint activities.

3. Learning-Participation

At this level of involvement, the servant leader and the investee participate in some activity in which they are learning a new skill. (Examples would be learning to play tennis or chess, taking a class in photography, or participating in wilderness education hikes.) The strength of this type of activity lies in the sharing of both individuals growing together in the same skill at the same time. Because both individuals are trying to learn something new, they are taking risks. Their willingness to risk with one another builds trust in the relationship. This trust building is critical, making this one of the significant levels of interaction.

4. Teaching-Organizing

This level of activity occurs only after the relationship has successfully moved beyond the first three stages. The two individuals begin to help organize and plan events for others, confident of each other's skills and interests. The servant leader and investee begin to focus on using their common skills to help other individuals learn new skills and have meaningful experiences.

5. Investing in Others

At this level, the investee is able to identify personal strengths and, with the support and guidance of the servant leader, direct these strengths toward helping other individuals grow. Once the relationship successfully moves through this level, the investee is poised to begin his or her role as the servant leader in someone else's life.

Healthy relationships are easily recognized through the strong desire of both parties for mutual growth and development of the other's potential. The emotional bank accounts of the servant leader and the investee grow as both put the needs of the other before their own (Covey, 1990). This selflessness is born out of a genuine desire for what is best for the other, and that desire, coupled with trust building, will carry the relationship successfully through these five levels of servant leader investment.

Motivation of Others

A well-respected leader who had experienced success in both his professional career and his volunteer endeavors was asked, "How do you motivate your followers, the people you work with?" He replied that even though his followers appeared to be highly motivated, he didn't motivate them. He said he couldn't make them do what they didn't want to do. Therefore, to motivate followers, he said, "they gotta wanna."

How do leaders get to "wanna" with their followers? They start by getting to know their followers, taking the time to determine the individual strengths and interests of each. Using the knowledge of individual strengths and interests, leaders delegate tasks the followers are capable of *and* interested in doing.

As Senge (1990, p. 145) says, "Motivation then becomes what people generate for themselves when they experience growth." Companies are moving out of the old paradigm in which firms were in business to make a profit and serve their customers. Things were done for and to employees to get them to be productive. In the new paradigm, the leader's primary focus is the growth of those who do the work, the followers. In turn, the followers see to it that the customer is served, and as a result, the ink on the bottom line is black. Development and growth are the primary motivators, not profit (Juran, 1988).

Active Listening

Servant leaders have well-developed listening skills. They are able to focus all their attention on the speaker and to "seek first to understand then to be understood" (Covey, 1990, p. 272). Servant leaders do not merely wait for the speaker to finish so they may tell their stories, but analyze the speaker's message, preparing to ask questions and respond empathetically. Servant leaders recognize that little can be learned by speaking, but only by listening to the messages of others.

Instigation of Change

Servant leaders realize that things seldom remain as they are and that change is a way of life. In fact, most often servant leaders are the ones who instigate change. If asked to describe the change, servant leaders would focus on the change's impact on the followers and others who will be directly or indirectly affected or influenced by the change. Servant leaders apply a simple litmus test when contemplating change: *If I encourage this, do those served grow as persons? Do they, while being served, become healthier, wiser, freer, more autonomous, more likely themselves to become servants? And, what is the effect on the least privileged in society; will they benefit or, at least, not be further deprived?* (Greenleaf, 1977, p.13).

Trustworthiness

We often hear leaders say they would not ask others to do something they themselves wouldn't do. In involving others in the effort, the building of the vision community begins (Neal, 1990). The vision community is a group of individuals bound together by the same vision, shared values, and common goals. In the beginning, the servant leader and the followers are on a honeymoon, finding out about each other—their hopes, dreams, strengths, and weaknesses—and building a relationship. During this time of discovery, the followers are learning about the integrity of the leader. The followers will be sensitized to the leader's actions, ever vigilant to be sure that the leader's words are mirrored in his or her actions. The perceived integrity of the leader sets up a demonstrated expectation of the integrity of the follower. As a result, the quality of the leader's integrity will be reflected in the followers.

One important way in which servant leaders inspire the trust of followers is by freely sharing the key resource for solving problems: information. Therefore, servant leaders must skillfully communicate with their followers. They risk as they share because, along with information, they communicate their opinions, judgments, concerns, intentions, and feelings. This vulnerability of the servant leader builds trust with the followers as they begin to see themselves as equal partners in achieving the mutual vision. The mutual vision is supported by a mutually agreed-on strategy.

If an undercurrent of distrust is allowed to enter the process, followers will hold back. Their emotional stability will not allow them to be free to express themselves through creative endeavors. Mistrust causes followers to feel rejected or defensive. Those who do not trust others will conceal or distort information, and this distortion will lead to action on the basis of an incomplete portrayal of reality. Mistrust does not allow for development of a mutually agreed-on strategy between the servant leader and the follower.

Vision

When a young assistant of the inventor Thomas Edison concluded that several thousand experiments had brought no results, Edison exclaimed: "No results! Why, man, I've gotten a lot of results! I know several thousand things that won't work" (Henderson, 1930, p. 49).

Servant leaders, much like Edison, see failure as a means to success. The failure is an opportunity to learn about flawed strategies and personal strengths. Edison had tens of thousands of volumes in which he chronicled both his successful and failed experiments. Although servant leaders do not necessarily chronicle their successes and failures, their clarity of vision helps them refocus, adjust direction, and continue forward progress.

Ability to Cope with Uncertainty

As we moved through our early education, it may have seemed every question had a definite answer. As we grow older, we find this is not always the case. When we work with individuals, not equations, definite answers may not be readily available. There is no solution manual for all the problems we encounter as we move through life.

Servant leaders realize before embarking on the journey that all the preliminary questions may not have answers. In some cases, a perfect solution may not exist, and midstream adjustments may be needed along the way; but the journey is worth the energy the leader and followers give to it, for along the course of the journey exist opportunities to help others develop.

Realism

Although sometimes seen as dreamers, servant leaders are grounded in reality. They have an accurate, insightful view of current reality, and are able to understand and account for the limitations and possibilities in themselves and others (Senge, 1990). This realism is as important to the successful servant leader as are goal setting and clear vision. In place kicking in football, the kicker is encouraged to "keep an eye on the prize," mindful that the objective is to kick the ball squarely between the goal posts, while facing the rush of the opposing team. Similarly, servant leaders hold their vision in their mind's eye while remaining clearly in tune with what is happening around them.

Future-Orientation

Lee Iacocca believes in focusing on the future and his place in it (Iacocca, 1988). If, like Iacocca, you see yourself in the future in any way different than you are today, no doubt something will happen to cause change in your life. Inherent in any change process is the element of risk. Iacocca comments about risk: "Well, you're never going to get what you want out of life without taking some risks. Everything worthwhile carries the risk of failure. I have to take risks every day. I'd rather not, but the world doesn't give you or me that option" (Iacocca, 1988, p. 309). To servant leaders, taking risks for a better future is part of life. To soften the element of risk, servant leaders have their antennae out, ready to analyze situations and the implications of potential outcomes. Some would call this perceptiveness intuition, but regardless of what we call it, servant leaders are living for the future.

Ownership of Problems

Servant leaders see problems as situations whose solutions begin with them, and they assume ownership for finding and implementing solutions to problems. Those who assume the role of bystander may view themselves as "only one person," incapable of bringing about change, but servant leaders see themselves as compelled to act. This action is often grounded in the servant leader's personal responsibility to make a positive difference in the life of another and, ultimately, the world. The servant leader's quest is truly to leave the world a better place. This betterment translates into touching others in a positive manner, either directly or indirectly.

Followership

As human beings we participate in many arenas and, generally, we do not (indeed, cannot) each play the role of the servant leader in every arena. But the irony is that "the follower that is willing to speak out shows precisely the kind of initiative that leadership is made of (Bennis, 1993, p. 160). In essence, the very characteristics we see in servant leaders often are found in their followers. Followership with the support of a strong servant leader is rich training ground for future servant leaders.

Further, servant leaders are not necessarily the individuals found in the upper strata of organizations. Servant leaders know that leadership is action, not position, and often they can have a greater impact on others if they are *not* serving in the upper strata (Kelley, 1985).

Conclusion

In his inaugural address of January 20, 1961, John F. Kennedy immortalized the statement: "And so, my fellow Americans, ask not what your country can do for you—ask what you can do for your country." On a more personal level, servant leadership asks not what others can do for you, but what you can do for others. Servant leadership is an inherent responsibility borne out of a desire to help others. It is found in our colleges, factories, boardrooms, hospitals, civic centers, and any other place people are bound together in a successful vision community. Servant leadership makes a positive difference in the lives of the followers as well as the leader; most important, each of us has the capacity to be a successful servant leader.

EXERCISE
Identification of Leader, Follower, and Bystander Roles

Purpose   To help you associate the many roles you perform by identifying for each: the people with whom you interact; the function you perform (leader, follower, or bystander); and the skills that help you successfully perform the role.

You Will Need   Pen or pencil

The Identification of Role matrix

Activity   Complete the matrix by first listing in column one the types of roles you play in various relationships. Then fill in the next three columns by answering the questions at the column heads in relation to the role you listed in the corresponding box in column one.

   When your matrix is complete, in small groups, share the following with each other: a role; people with whom you interact while in that role; the function (leader, follower, or bystander) you perform while in the role; and the skills that help you successfully perform this role. Continue this sharing until all group members have exhausted their lists of roles. When you have finished, go on to the discussion questions below.

Discussion

1. Which roles were most prevalent in the group?
2. Which functions (leader, follower, bystander) were most prevalent in the group?
3. Which interpersonal skills did most people identify as important to help perform these roles successfully?
4. Do any of you see your function (leader, follower, bystander) evolving in your roles in the future?
5. What interpersonal skills do you anticipate will assist in changing your function so you may be successful?

Identification of Leader, Follower, and Bystander Roles

Role (brother, sister, officer, group member, mentoring partner, friend, etc.)	With whom do you interact in this role?	Which function do you perform—leader, follower, bystander?	What skills do you use to successfully perform this role?

EXERCISE
Interpersonal Trust Scale

Adapted from Christie, 1970.

Purpose Successful servant leaders and followers operate on a foundation built upon trust. Therefore, it is important as both leaders and followers to determine the degree to which you tend to trust people. The higher your score on the Interpersonal Trust Scale, the more you believe people to be decent and worthy of trust; the lower your score, the less you believe people to be decent and worthy of trust. Therefore, the higher your level of trust, the more easily you can lead or be led.

You Will Need Pen or pencil

The Interpersonal Trust Scale Survey

Activity The survey questions should be answered relying on your own experience and judgment in dealing with people. You may find yourself agreeing strongly with some of the statements, disagreeing with others, and perhaps feeling undecided about others. Whether you agree or disagree with any statement, you can be sure that many people feel the same as you do.

When you have completed the survey, calculate your score according to the self-scoring directions. Then move on to the discussion questions as a group.

Interpersonal Trust Scale Survey

Answer each statement by circling the response showing how much you agree or disagree.

1. The best way to handle people is to tell them what they want to hear.
   a. Strongly disagree
   b. Disagree
   c. Undecided
   d. Agree
   e. Strongly agree

2. It is hard to get ahead without cutting corners here and there (for example, doing just enough to get by).
   a. Strongly disagree
   b. Disagree
   c. Undecided
   d. Agree
   e. Strongly agree

3. Anyone who completely trusts someone else is asking for trouble.
   a. Strongly disagree
   b. Disagree
   c. Undecided
   d. Agree
   e. Strongly agree

4. When you ask someone to do something for you, it is best to give the real reasons for wanting it rather than giving reasons you think will influence the person regardless of whether they are real.
   a. Strongly disagree
   b. Disagree
   c. Undecided
   d. Agree
   e. Strongly agree

5. It is safest to assume that all people have a mean streak and it will come out when they are given a chance to express it.
   a. Strongly disagree
   b. Disagree
   c. Undecided
   d. Agree
   e. Strongly agree

6. One should take action only when sure it will not break the law or hurt someone.
   a. Strongly disagree
   b. Disagree
   c. Undecided
   d. Agree
   e. Strongly agree

7. Most people are basically good and kind.
   a. Strongly disagree
   b. Disagree
   c. Undecided
   d. Agree
   e. Strongly agree

8. There is no good reason for lying to someone else.
   a. Strongly disagree
   b. Disagree
   c. Undecided
   d. Agree
   e. Strongly agree

9. Generally speaking, people won't work hard unless they are forced to do so.
   a. Strongly disagree
   b. Disagree
   c. Undecided
   d. Agree
   e. Strongly agree

10. Most people forget more easily the death of a parent than the loss of their property.
    a. Strongly disagree
    b. Disagree
    c. Undecided
    d. Agree
    e. Strongly agree

Self-Scoring the Interpersonal Trust Scale

Using the following table, for each item from the questionnaire, find the column that corresponds to your answer (a, b, c, d, or e) and circle the number in that column. Record that number in the Points column. Add the points and divide the total by 10.

Question	Response	Points
	a b c d e	
1	1 2 3 4 5 *a*	1
2	1 2 3 4 5 *b*	2
3	1 2 3 4 5 *b*	2
4	5 4 3 2 1 *d*	2 ✱
5	1 2 3 4 5 *d*	4 ✖
6	5 4 3 2 1 *d*	2 ✱
7	5 4 3 2 1 *d*	2
8	5 4 3 2 1 *d*	2
9	1 2 3 4 5 *c*	3
10	1 2 3 4 5 *d*	4
	Total Points	24
	Divide by 10	2.4

Plot your score on the diagram below:

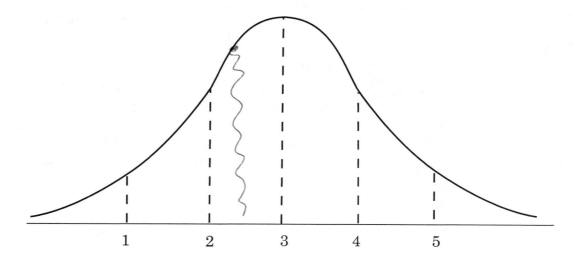

Discussion

In small groups, discuss your answers to the following questions about your Interpersonal Trust Scale score. Your group leader will facilitate the sharing of responses with the remainder of the group.

1. What is your tendency? Do you agree with it?

2. Are you suspicious of others and so would rather depend on your own skills? If yes, can you think of a time your hesitance to collaborate with others hindered your success?

3. Keeping your trust level in mind, are you difficult to lead? Why?

4. What things would a leader need to do to gain your trust?

EXERCISE
Strengths Bulls-Eye

Purpose To help you identify your strengths (skills, talents, and abilities) and areas that you would like to develop into strengths.

You Will Need The bulls-eye diagram

Pencil or pen

Activity List your strengths in the center of the bulls-eye. Along the perimeter of the bulls-eye, list those skills, talents, or abilities that you want to develop to enhance your leadership ability.

    Move into a small group (6–8). Identify strengths you have noted in each of your group's members throughout the semester. Pass your bulls-eye around the group (or put strengths on stickers for each group member) and write the strength you noted and your initials in the second circle of other members' bulls-eyes.

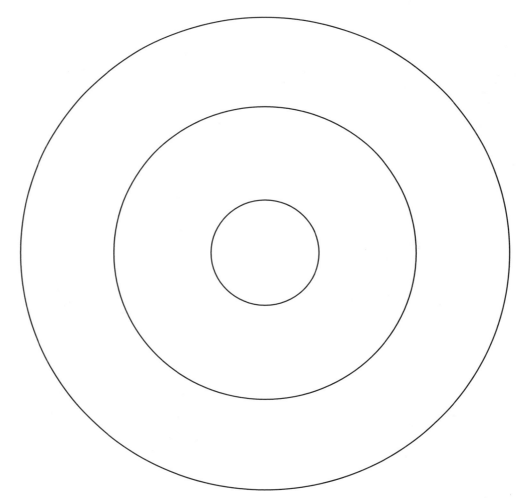

Discussion

Review the strengths others have listed and discuss the following:

1. How similar are the strengths group members listed to the strengths you listed?

2. Did group members list some strengths you are surprised about? Explore with the group member(s) their rationale for identifying those strengths in you. Do you agree with their observations?

3. Did group members note some strengths in you that you do not see as your current strengths but rather ones you wish to develop in the future? Have you been working on developing these strengths?

4. How do the strengths you identified, strengths group members identified, and strengths you wish to develop compare to the characteristics of a servant leader? Are there other strengths you would like to develop that are not on the list? Why do you want to develop them?

FURTHER ACTIVITY

Journal Writing

1. Think about individuals with whom you have interacted whom you would classify as servant leaders. Write about some of the situations in which you saw them display leadership skills and describe how they made a significant impact.

2. Imagine where you would like to be in five years. Write about some of the roles you see yourself performing and your function in each of these roles—leader, follower, and bystander. What skills do you need to improve upon today to help you be as effective as possible in the future? Do you see yourself as a servant leader in any of these roles? Why or why not?

3. Using the five levels of service to others, describe how you were able to help someone else develop and grow.

LEARNING POINTS

✓ We perform one of three functions (leader, follower, or bystander) in every role in our lives.

✓ Servant leaders place other people's needs ahead of their own, and, therefore, are extremely dedicated to the service of others.

✓ Servant leaders know themselves, have a sense of purpose, identify motivators in their followers, are active listeners, instigate change, are worthy of trusting, are directed by a vision that is supported by goals, cope with uncertainty, are realistic, are futuristic, and own the challenges they identify.

✓ The attributes of a successful servant leader are mirrored in the attributes of the followers surrounding the leader.

✓ Servant leadership is action, not position, and, consequently, can be found in all levels of organizations.

REFERENCES

Bennis, W. (1993). *An invented life: reflections on leadership and change.* Reading, MA: Addison-Wesley.

Character Counts! Fact Sheet (1997). Los Angeles: Josephson Institute of Ethics.

Covey, S. R. (1990). *Principle-centered leadership.* New York: Fireside.

Christie, R. (1970). The Machiavellians among us. *Psychology Today,* November, 82–83, 85–86.

Dodge, G. W. (1988). *Priceless People.* Lincoln, NE: Nebraska Human Resources Research Foundation.

Greenleaf, R. K. (1977). *Servant leadership: A journey into the nature of legitimate power and greatness.* New York: Paulist.

Henderson, A. (1930). *Contemporary immortals.* New York: Appleton.

Iacocca, L., with S. Kleinfield. (1988). *Talking straight.* New York: Bantam.

Josephson Institute of Ethics (1996). Michael S. Josephson.

Juran, J. M. (1988). *Juran on planning for quality.* Cambridge, MA: Productivity Press.

Kelley, R. E. (1985). *The gold-collar worker.* Reading, MA: Addison-Wesley.

Kouzes, J. M., and Posner, B. Z. (1990). *The leadership challenge.* San Francisco: Jossey-Bass.

Mitchell, E. (1991). Brushing up on right and wrong. *Time,* April 15, p. 63.

Neal, B. (Producer), and Christensen, R. D. (Director). (1990). *Power of vision* [Videotape]. Burnsville, MN: Charthouse International.

Senge, P. M. (1990). *The fifth discipline.* New York: Doubleday.

JOURNALING

Writing journals, diaries, or daybooks is a method of keeping track of what happened during your day, from mere facts (like what the thermometer at the airport read at noon) to details of personal psychological growth you perceived as a result of some encounter. Facts, events, and moments of insight are equally valid subjects of journal entries.

To get the most from this textbook and the course it accompanies, you need to actually apply the concepts it describes. Journaling is a basic tool to accomplish this goal. Two basic purposes are served in keeping written records and reflections drawn from daily life:

1. Your journal may contain observations, reflections, and evaluations of your growth in developing interpersonal skills needed for leadership.

2. If you are involved in a project at a social agency, you may record your plans, accounts of your work with individuals, observations of interactions, and evaluations.

Keeping a Journal

A journal is a personal record used to keep track of experience—whether that experience becomes the basis of a public history or science, or is a record of self, for the self only. The term *journal* had its origin in the French word *jour,* or *day*. A journal is a record, a daily record if one adheres carefully to the defined meaning. Like trying to do any chore once a week when it should be done daily, one cannot enter into a journal for a whole week by opening the journal just once. (You don't eat one big meal each week or try to read a week's worth of newspapers in one sitting—instead you engage in those activities daily.) The point is that you should make entries in your journal daily, or the minimum required by your instructor.

Finding Meaning in Experience

People use journals, daybooks, scientific journals, or memoirs for different purposes; but underlying them all is the daily-ness of entries. One journal-like writer, the memorist, deliberately selects and shapes material for entry. Historians viewing journals written by others may have a variety of purposes, but some may use journals to corroborate an era's weather conditions, dress, or common slang. Scientists and inventors use their journals very carefully, recording activities, results, and conditions under which activities took place; they conjecture as to cause, and, if necessary, introduce their journals in courts of law to defend their intellectual property.

Of course, journal-keepers may shape meaning deliberately by omitting certain kinds of activities of the day. Journal-keepers may be like scientists, interested in building knowledge, keeping track not only of experiences, but also of equipment, the time actions were performed, and processes used. They may record ideas they consider new, either theirs or another's, upon which their experiment is building. Inventors definitely use journals to answer questions about intellectual property. Writers of both fiction and nonfiction use journals in many ways; to jot down good lines, make notes about resources, and define plots. Some writers record their private lives, and some rewrite their journals for public consumption.

An example of the latter is Peter Barth, who "came to find it more agreeable and convenient to leave the novel-in-the-works back in Baltimore on those Thursday shiftings [a move across the Chesapeake Bay to a country retreat on Langford Creek], with its accumulating worknotes . . . and to spend the Friday mornings (in bad weather . . .), with what presently became my country muse, the muse of nonfiction" (Barth, 1995, p. xiii).

As a journal writer, like Barth, you can use the muse of nonfiction; that is you can find inspiration in moments and events of daily life. An example of the products of Barth's experiences is this entry from the second of his *Friday* books:

> . . . *I have eaten my breakfast, and scanned my morning newspaper; I have done certain stretching exercises both physical and mental, the latter of a Pavlovian character and the former too, come to that; a combined self-mesmerizing, self-priming, warm-up routine and invocation to Mnemosyne [muse or inspiration of writers] and her daughters that began with my waking automatically at 7 A.M. or so, eating breakfast, etc., and continues now with my going to my writing table and opening my ancient Johns Hopkins loose-leaf binder that I bought during freshman orientation week in September 1974 and have since first-drafted five thousand-plus pages of published fiction in, and regathering in my memory and muscles both the threads and the knitting-momentum of a certain complex narrative argyle-sock-in-progress: not only the peculiar narrative called* Once Upon a Time, *but the ongoing fabrications of the antecedent of all those mysteries.*
>
> *But how is that done? After forty-plus years of doing it . . . I find the process still mysterious and fascinating. I'm speaking not particularly of the 'material,' although its invention, discovery, or selection is mysterious enough* (Barth, 1995, p. 192).

In Barth's journal we see how one writer uses the journal for recording thoughts and reflections on Fridays, though he interweaves his past into the present, so it becomes foolish to say that the journal is only one day's record at a time, for it is more than only today's experiences. Whatever we enter in journals is obviously something we have been trained to consider important, or is something so outside our ken that we note it for its mysteriousness; we, as Barth says, discover, as well as uncover.

There are no hard rules if you are writing a journal as a record. Naturally, inventors and scientists have to follow some pretty stringent rules, because their notebooks become evidence of when they did what, and at what point they had intellectual ownership of what particular property.

In preparing to write your journal about course concepts and their applications, however, you have some choices. Writers use journals in a great variety of ways. You've seen that for Barth the journal is a respite from the demanding work in fiction of keeping the plot moving, of making characters say what they are supposed to say, of maintaining scenes for as long as the characters inhabit them. That's work, control, organization. In your journals, daily-ness dictates sequence, and teachers often give guidance. You will keep records of what happened both in and out of class. Your focus can vary from reporting your own or others' activities to reflecting the growth afforded you by certain experiences, as well as the growth you are responsible for having (or attempting to have) achieved.

Journal As Record

A journal record is easy to keep, but you must keep it regularly. You record what happened, even if you are sure you won't forget. You will forget. Test yourself, and try to remember exactly the way three people you saw yesterday were dressed. If you can remember that, then you are pretty good. But most of us don't see all and don't remember all of what we see.

What sort of book do you use for a journal? Whatever you wish, or what your instructor asks you to use, probably a notebook of a certain size. In some cases, a journal kept on your computer may be acceptable, with a copy produced on a printer for sharing with others.

What do you include in your journal entries? Consider:

✓ time
✓ date
✓ place
✓ activity
✓ title
✓ actors (self as actor or as observer)
✓ feelings
✓ attitudes (yours, as developed, and those you observed in others)
✓ time an activity took

Topics for journal entries are suggested in each chapter in the text. Typically, you will be asked to reflect on the day's lesson, practice a skill learned in class, and reflect on this experience. Note that you will wish to think about what you have recorded, and what you interpret and explain. You may need to meditate on your recorded experiences (the poet William Wordsworth called this activity "meditating in tranquillity"). At a later time, then, you may discover the personal growth you have experienced by rereading several entries in your journal and seeing what you recorded and considered important. Or you may try to hypothesize about meaning, or to examine your behavior and try to account for it.

Immediate vs. Reflective Experience

One way to better understand the journaling process is to read the published journals of people like Barth, or the theorist and naturalist Henry David Thoreau, or explorers like Lewis and Clark, Richard Burton, and Richard Speke. Compare those that were composed in meditative quiet with those you believe were composed while the author was in the thick of life as it happened. Raise questions about the differences you see and try to discern what accounts for those differences (perceptions, personality, setting, time, date). Below is a memory of an occurrence, composed after the fact, but most dramatic:

> *It was a funeral to which they all came. They gathered in the red brick chapel beside the cemetery gate. Six gray horses were hitched to the caisson that would carry the coffin to the grave. A marching band was ready. An honor guard from the Army's oldest regiment, the regiment whose rolls reached back to the Revolution, was also formed in ranks before the white Georgian portico of the chapel. The soldiers were in full dress, dark blue trimmed with gold, the colors of the Union Army, which had safeguarded the integrity of the nation. The uniform was unsuited to the warmth and humidity of this Friday morning in early summer of Washington, but his state funeral was worthy of the discomfort. John Paul Vann, the soldier of the war in Vietnam, was being buried at Arlington on June 16, 1972.*
>
> *The war had already lasted longer than any other in the nation's history and divided America more than any conflict since the Civil War. In this war without heroes, this man had been the one compelling figure. The intensity and distinctiveness of his character and the courage and drama of his life had seemed to sum up so many of the qualities Americans admired in themselves as a people. By an obsession, by an unyielding dedication to the war, he had come to personify the American endeavor in Vietnam. He had exemplified it in his illusions, in his good intentions gone awry, in his pride, in his will to win. Where others had been defeated or discouraged over the years, or had become disenchanted and had turned against the war, he had been undeterred in his crusade to find a way to redeem the unredeemable, to lay hold of victory in this doomed enterprise. At the end of a decade of struggling to prevail, he had been killed one night a week earlier when his helicopter had crashed and burned in rain and fog in the mountains of South Vietnam's Central Highlands. He had just beaten back, in a battle of a town called Kontum, an offensive by the South Vietnamese Army which had threatened to bring the Vietnam venture down in defeat.*
>
> *Those who had assembled to see John Vann to his grave reflected the divisions and the wounds that the war had inflicted on American society. At the same time, they had, almost every one, been touched by this man. Some had come because they had parted with him along the way, but still thought of him as a friend; some because they had been harmed by him, but cherished him for what he might have been. Although the war was to continue for nearly another three years with no dearth of dying in Vietnam, many at Arlington on that June morning in 1972 sensed that they were burying with John Vann the war and the decade of Vietnam. With Vann dead, the rest could be no more than a postscript* (Sheehan, 1988, pp. 3–5).

Analyze the Sheehan description, separating it into a recording of the events and facts from the reflections upon them. A number of your journal entries may fit this pattern.

Barriers to Journals and Jumping the Barrier

The main barrier to keeping a journal is our tendency to be run by our habits, which seem more powerful than our reasoned decision of how to live. Life is so daily that we often let the rhythm and momentum determine our actions. Consider writing a journal as daily an activity as eating, sleeping, or dressing. The only other barrier that most of us have to fight is lassitude. New knowledge gained in journal-keeping informs the rest of your life, so do not fight the journal, for it is about you. Rather welcome the opportunity to learn more about yourself, to learn how you relate to others, and to learn, when possible, the skills of interpersonal relationships and leadership.

Examples from Some Famous Journal Writers

In this part of the text, we invite you to learn about journals by examining some models of entries drawn from well-known public figures and writers, and then to practice some journal writing of your own.

Thomas Huxley and Charles Darwin

As Julian Huxley, editor of the Thomas H. Huxley journal, points out, it is "interesting that the publication of this Journal should follow so soon after that of Darwin's. The two greatest British biologists of the nineteenth century each began his career as naturalist on a long voyage of scientific exploration" (Huxley, 1935). One of T. H. Huxley's entries from 1847 follows:

> *"Feb. 25th.*
> *In the morning I made a drawing of the animal of the Ianthina. The figures in Mrs. Grey's book are very bad. I also endeavored to make a dissection of one, but what between the rolling of the ship and the small size and delicacy of the object, I did not succeed at all well. Another Physalia was caught and I carried out the examination further"* (Huxley, 1935).

In his journal, Charles Darwin recorded the following observation, similarly short, from two days in September, 1835 (later revised into his *Journal for Sciences*):

> *"Sept. 16th & 27th [1835].*
> *When I see these Islands [Chatham & Albermarle Isd] in sight of each other, & possessed of but a scanty stock of animals, tenanted by these birds, but slightly differing in structure & filling the same place in Nature, I must suspect that they are only varieties"* (Herbert, 1980, p. 299).

Darwin made fast, short, cryptic entries, such as the one above, in what became called *The Red Notebook,* which he kept during his voyages as an ongoing record of fact or speculation and later turned into the research articles published as *The Journal of Researches.* In this notebook, one can see that Darwin is learning through his records and continuing observations that he could, and should, separate entries on geologic observations from entries on species. At this stage, however, Darwin's dominant organizing theme is chronology. But within each entry would be observations and references to others whose works Darwin had on the *H. M. S. Beagle* with him, or whose works he knew to check later for verification of his memory. This stage of intellectual growth is what a notebook or record offers. Darwin simultaneously could record what seemed to him to be "new knowledge" (his daily observations) while he checked resources (or reminded himself to check later) to verify that his observations were, indeed, new, and that what he saw had not been seen, recorded, or interpreted in this manner before. Notebooks then allow one to see where one has been, and what one has learned, either intellectually or psychologically.

As an editor of *The Red Notebook* observed, the notebook provided Darwin a record from which he was able to begin to perceive the "complexity and interchangeability of names, and a place to record citations from the work of others, as well as a place to record his observations" (Herbert, 1980).

> *Of importance was that the diary Darwin kept during the voyage furnished the basic narrative for his* Journal. *[He] included two additional kinds of material in the published work. They included references to the work of previous travelers and brief summaries of his own scientific researches. Frequently,* The Red Notebook *was used in compiling citations of the first kind, as is evidenced by the transfer of citations from* The Red Notebook *to* The Journal of Researches. *Less often, but at several points most strikingly,* The Red Notebook *also served as an instrument of recording scientific speculations. These, too, passed to the* Journal [of Researches] *although, because of the organization of the work, rather unobtrusively. In any case, it is clear on inspection that* The Red Notebook *served Darwin in writing* The Journal of Researches" (Herbert, 1980, p. 13).

A sample entry from *The Red Notebook* follows:

> *"up to . . . July 1835, the excess of harbor = 180*
> *See Daubisson both Volumes, and Molina 1st Vol [& Lyell]*
> *Sailed . . ."* [December 27, 1835]
> *Friday*
> *Thursday, 29th, gale*
> [Lyell's Geology]" (Herbert, 1980, inside front cover).

Here the cryptic note reflects not only the weather at departure and in the first few days, but also refer to authors d'Aubuisson and Molina, two geographers, as well as to Sir Charles Lyell, a well known British geologist. Darwin's simple observation ("gale on Thursday, Dec. 29th") is amplified by his including resources to be looked at on return.

As journal writers, like Darwin, we have to learn what it is we wish to record, and, as observers, we have to learn to pay attention or to focus on something within the wide range of our total experience. Darwin was trained and was in training, for his experiences were aided by his knowledge and at the same time his knowledge grew from his experiences.

A second entry reinforces his desire to record that which he sees even when he may not be sure of its value:

> *". . . surface to where highest spray (there palegreen confervae) coated with living beings. In smooth seas (& even turbulent as at St. Helena) I have mentioned point of greatest action; now having seen Pernambuco believe much is owing to the protection of Organic productions."* (Darwin, in Herbert, 1980, p. 56).

Even though extremely cryptic, these notes permitted Darwin both to seek detailed citations from other sources and to note what the situation in July of 1835 was. He then was able to interpret and turn these facts into the logical research published later.

Charles Lindbergh

Charles Lindbergh is another famous person who found daily (or near daily) entries essential to his memory and to the truth. Reluctant to publish his wartime journals, Lindbergh was encouraged to do so by Robert Jovanovich. Correspondence about the value of journals as a resource for the journal-keeper and then for the public for whom the journals may not have been intended follows:

> *The historian will attempt to read the whole record of the past so far as he is able, but since he cannot write the whole record, he will select these events and circumstances that accommodate his thesis or his bias or his style or whatever. Those selected items of occurrence become, as Max Weber concluded, the facts of history.*
>
> *So, too, in writing of the moment, as in a diary or a journal, an act of selection takes place. One must decide what was significant in the course of a day before he can keep a reasonably short record of its passing. Yet the journal becomes, in the hands of a serious and candid person, an exceptional means by which events can be depicted literally, which is to say depicted with both accuracy of account and a consistency of view.* (Jovanovich, 1970, xi).

In a letter to his editor, dated December 19, 1969, Charles Lindbergh explains why he had not published his journals to date:

> *You ask why I waited twenty-five years before publishing my World War II journals. Various reasons come to mind. In the first place, when I wrote them, I had no intentions of publication.*
>
> *. . . Second, some of the data they contain were too sensitive to be published before the passage of time has exerted its buffering effect. A third factor relates to the objectivity that comes with years and the eyes of a new generation. Even now, the effect of World War II bitterness and propaganda have not entirely disappeared* (Lindbergh, in Jovanovich, 1970, xii).

Each of you, as journal-keepers, can begin to understand the power of the moment and the self-reflecting power of the mind as you read the following sequence in which Lindbergh clearly recognizes the significance of the moment he is writing, as well as the brevity of the moment and the value of the future when he would be able to take time to reevaluate his journal:

> *"Saturday, November 1, 1941*
> *I have started the second draft of an account of the flight from New York to Paris in the* Spirit of St. Louis. *This draft will be an expansion of the first draft. I want to write down all the details of the flight so they will not escape my memory. I will not try for the correct balance, shading, sequence, and accuracy until the third draft"* (Lindbergh, in Jovanovich, 1970, p. 552).

> *"Tuesday, January 27, 1942*
> *Finished second draft of* Spirit of St. Louis *manuscript. But I am not at all satisfied with it. The manuscript will have to go through at least two more drafts. If I only had six free months, I feel sure I could finish it as I want to"* (Lindbergh, in Jovanovich, 1970, p. 558).

"Sunday, May 20, 1945

I asked Messerschmitt when he first began to feel that Germany would be defeated. He said he had been much concerned in 1941 when he saw the American estimates for aircraft production, because he thought we could meet them, although most people in Germany did not. . . ." [Messerschmitt was an airplane designer whose knowledge Lindbergh respected quite highly.] (Lindbergh, in Jovanovich, 1970, p. 957).

Discussion Questions

1. What differences do you see between the styles and observations of Darwin and Lindbergh?
2. How can you differentiate among the terms *journal, diary, memoirs, daybook,* and *notebook*?
3. Why should you write in your journal on a regular basis?
4. What should you record in your journal?
5. What are the specifications for journal writing in this course?

Sample Journal Entries

Each chapter in the text contains suggestions for journal entries. The following examples demonstrate how you can translate class assignments and daily experiences into journal topics:

1. *Sample question:* Are you a good listener? Evaluate [in your journal] your listening skills in various situations (a class you like, with a friend, parent, or sibling, etc.).

What to do: This topic might be approached by recalling past events and experiences, by observing yourself over several days, or both. In your writing, first record events simply. Tell the story. Focus on one time, one person; don't generalize or be abstract. For example:

Yesterday I talked to my younger sister Ruth on the telephone. Although I wanted to tell her about my new job, I first asked her about her school work. After she finished telling me about her school work and the A she received in math, I said, "You must feel pretty good about that grade in math; that teacher has high standards." We chatted a little longer about Ruth's activities, and then only after she asked about how college was going, I told her about getting a job as a student worker in the Math Department (of all places!). She laughed when she heard that.

The next part of the entry, perhaps written after some reflection, may be an evaluation of how well you did listening to Ruth. You might also record conversations you have over several more days with others before you determine how skillful a listener you are and what areas you need to improve in.

2. *Other Journal Ideas*

a. Write about your own writing process—when you find it easy to write, and when you find it difficult. Consider the conditions, and determine what you can do to take responsibility for journal-keeping.

b. Analyze each chapter's journal assignments, and classify the kinds of knowledge each addresses and will permit you to develop (intellectual, emotional, interaction skills, or leadership behavior).

c. Do you find knowledge about yourself interesting? Why or why not? What do you like to learn about yourself most and least?

LEARNING POINTS

✓ Journals, diaries, and daybooks are virtually interchangeable terms.

✓ Journals contain written records of the day's events.

✓ The subjects of journals are selected by the writer who gives entries shape and focus.

✓ In this course, you write your observations about interpersonal communications, leadership, your perceptions of each, your reactions to certain assigned projects, as well as your own personal intellectual, perceptual, and emotional growth during the semester.

✓ Daily or frequent recording is necessary because we seldom remember experiences, scenes, and dialogue very accurately.

✓ Journals can be recorded in different formats.

✓ Journal writing both requires and contributes to self-discipline.

REFERENCES

Barth, J. (1995). *Further Fridays: Essays, lectures, and other nonfiction, 1984–1994.* Boston: Little, Brown.

Herbert, S. (Ed.). (1980). *The red notebook of Charles Darwin.* Ithaca, NY: Cornell University Press.

Huxley, J. (Ed.). (1935). *T. H. Huxley's diary of the voyage of the H. M. S. Rattlesnake.* London: Chatto and Windus.

Jovanovich, W. (Ed.). (1970). *The wartime journals of Charles A. Lindbergh.* New York: Harcourt.

Sheehan, N. (1988). *A bright and shining lie: John Paul Vann and America in Vietnam.* New York: Random House.

INDEX

Improvised Role Plays, 64
Interview, 65
Mirroring, 63
No Body Talking, 60
and perception, 76
proxemics, 55-56
using to advantage, 56-57
Note-taking, as device for remembering information, 25

Observable traits, and perception, 76
Observation Sheet (exercise), 258
On Being Different (exercise), 275
Openness, and trust, 194-95
Organization, and conscious mind process, 78
Organizational sources of per, 228
Orientation, 269-70
Outer physical world, 76-77
Ownership of problems, and servant leadership, 304

Paraphrasing:
  and empathy, 252
  as verbal response, 25
Party Body Behavior (exercise), 62
Passive behavior, and inappropriate uses of power, 230
Peak communication, 174
Perception, 69-86, 273
  accuracy of, case study in, 69-70
  attitude, 72
  attribution, 79
  belief systems, 77-78
  and conscious mind process, 78
  context, 73
  culture, 76
  defined, 71
  desire, 72
  elements of, 72
  emotions, 72
  errors in, 78-79
  expectations, 72, 74-75
  faulty, 79
  gender roles, 76-77
  halo effect, 78-79
  How I Lead, 80
  inner world, 72-75
  interest, 72
  metaperception, 72, 73-74
  Metaperception of Leadership, 82
  model of, 72
  nonverbal communication, 76
  observable traits, 76
  of others, 75
  outer physical world, 76-77
  readiness, 72
  self-perception, 72, 74
  Self-Perception of Leadership, 81
  stereotyping, 78
  tendencies, 72
  theories of, 71-79
  verbal behavior, 76

Perception checking, and empathy, 252
Personal appeal, as influence trait, 229
Personal reactions to words, as psychological barrier to active listening, 27-28
Personal sources of power, 228
Personal space, 55
Physiological barriers to active listening, 26
Politics, of gender, 285-86
Poor motivation, as psychological barrier to active listening, 28
Positive nonverbal behavior, and empathy, 252
Posture, as body language, 52-53
Power, sources of, 227-28
Power and influence, 222-44
  Analyzing Personal Responses to Power and Influence, 238
  Best Leader I Have Ever Known, The, 241
  case study in, 223-24
  influence attempts:
    outcomes of, 230
    resistance to, 230
  influence building, personal strategies for, 231-32
  influence tactics, 228-29
  influence traits, 229
  leadership, defined, 225-26
  My Responses to Influence Attempts, 239-40
  personal responses to inappropriate uses of, 230-31
  Practice Using Influence, Power, and Assertive Behavior, 233-36
  Some Ways to Diagnose and Talk about Our Uses of Power and Influence, 237
  sources of power, 227-28
  transformational leadership:
    four I's of, 226
    transactional vs., 226-27
Practice Using Influence, Power, and Assertive Behavior (exercise), 233-36
Practicing, and empathy, 250-55
Prisoner's Dilemma (exercise), 204-5
  tally sheet, 205
Private Papers of Henry Ryecroft, The (Gissing), 71
Proxemics, 55-56
Psychological barriers to active listening, 26-29
Public space, 55
Pygmalion effect, 74

Questioning, and empathy, 252
Questions, as verbal response, 25

Rational persuasion, as influence trait, 229
Readiness, and perception, 72
Reciprocity, and self-disclosure, 176
Referent power, 227-28
Regulators, body language as, 55
Relationship maintenance/enhancement, and self-disclosure, 176
Relationships, rhythm of, 178-79